ADVANCES IN RUGBY COACHING

Contemporary sport coaching studies have moved beyond simple biophysical approaches to more complex understandings of coaching as a set of social relationships and processes. This is the first book to examine what that means in the context of one major international sport: rugby union. Drawing on cutting-edge empirical research in the five most powerful rugby-playing nations, as well as developments in pedagogical and social theory, the book argues for an holistic approach to coaching, coach development and player and team performance, helping to close the gap between coaching theory and applied practice.

With player-centred approaches to coaching, such as Game Sense and Teaching Games for Understanding, at the heart of the book, *Advances in Rugby Coaching* covers key contemporary topics in coach education such as:

- Long-term coach development
- Experience and culture in coaching practice
- Positive coaching for youth rugby
- Improving decision-making ability
- Collaborative action research in rugby coaching.

Informed by work with elite-level rugby coaches, and examining coaching practice in both the full and sevens versions of the game, this book encourages the reader to think critically about their own coaching practice and to consider innovative new approaches to player and coach development. It is essential reading for all students of sport coaching with an interest in rugby, and for any coach, manager or administrator looking to develop better programmes in coach education.

Richard Light is Professor and Head of School: Sport and Physical Education, in the College of Education at The University of Canterbury, New Zealand. He played and coached rugby in Australia and Japan and has conducted research on coaching and learning in sport across a range of sports and cultures. His recent publications with Routledge include, *Game Sense: Pedagogy for Performance, Participation and Enjoyment* (Light, 2013), *Contemporary Developments in Games Teaching* (Light, Quay, Harvey and Mooney (eds), 2014) and *Ethics in Youth Sport: Policy and Pedagogical Applications* (Harvey and Light, 2013).

John R. Evans is Associate Professor in the Faculty of Education and Social Work at the University of Sydney. He has extensive experience as a rugby player and coach in Australia, Japan and France and is the first Indigenous Australian to be awarded a PhD in the Faculty of Education and Social Work at the University of Sydney. His research focuses on the use of Game Sense in team sports with a particular interest in rugby.

Stephen Harvey is an Associate Professor in Instructional Methods and a member of Physical Activity and Sport Sciences at West Virginia University, USA. Stephen has an extensive background in field hockey as player and coach and, before moving to the USA from the UK, was a National Governing Body coach educator and active field hockey coach, coaching with the England U16 Boys. His research is centred on improving teaching and coaching practice through the use of game-based approaches.

Rémy Hassanin is completing a PhD at Federation University Australia under the supervision of Richard Light. Rémy is a French citizen who played and coached rugby in South Africa and France. His PhD study looks at the role experience within particular social and cultural settings plays in shaping rugby coaches' practice. His study examines these processes in Australia, South Africa and New Zealand.

ADVANCES IN RUGBY COACHING

An holistic approach

Richard Light, John R. Evans,
Stephen Harvey and Rémy Hassanin

LONDON AND NEW YORK

First published 2015
by Routledge
2 Park Square, Milton Park, Abingdon, Oxon OX14 4RN

and by Routledge
711 Third Avenue, New York, NY 10017

Routledge is an imprint of the Taylor & Francis Group, an informa business

British Library Cataloguing-in-Publication Data
A catalogue record for this book is available from the British Library

Library of Congress Cataloging-in-Publication Data
Light, Richard, 1951–
Advances in rugby coaching: an holistic approach/Richard Light, John R. Evans, Stephen Harvey, Remy Hassanin.
pages cm
Includes bibliographical references and index.
1. Rugby football – Coaching. I. Title.
GV945.75.L54 2014
796.333 – dc23 2014013646

ISBN: 978-1-138-80572-9 (hbk)
ISBN: 978-1-138-80573-6 (pbk)
ISBN: 978-1-315-75203-7 (ebk)

Typeset in Bembo and Stone Sans
by Florence Production Ltd, Stoodleigh, Devon, UK

Printed and bound in Great Britain by
TJ International Ltd, Padstow, Cornwall

CONTENTS

ACKNOWLEDGEMENTS

We would like to acknowledge the contributions made to this volume by colleagues other than the four listed authors. We begin by thanking Alain Mouchet from the Université Paris-Est Créteil Val de Marne, France. Alain contributed to Chapter 3, co-written with Richard Light and Stephen Harvey, *Improving decision-making in sevens rugby*. His work with French colleagues, and with some of us, on subjectivity in decision-making in rugby provides an innovative way of thinking about decision-making that he outlines in English in *Contemporary Developments in Games Teaching*, published by Routledge in 2014. Alain was also the major contributor to Chapter 6, *An holistic approach to investigating French rugby coaches' in-match communications with players*, also co-written with Richard Light and Stephen Harvey.

We also wish to acknowledge the contribution made to Chapter 9 by Paul Reid from the University of Bedford in the UK . This chapter on the Rugby Football Union's implementation of Game Sense-informed coach education programmes draws on his PhD study, supervised by Associate Professor Stephen Harvey.

ABBREVIATIONS

AFL	Australian Football League
AR	action research
ARC	Australian Rugby Championship
ARU	Australian Rugby Union
CAR	collaborative action research
CBS-C	Coach Behaviour Scale for Coaches
CLT	complex learning theory
COMEREM	Communications des Entraîneurs de Rugby en Match
CoP	communities of practice
CPD	continuing professional development
FIFA	Fédération International de Football Association
GBA	game-based approaches
GCA	Games Concept Approach
GPS	Greater Public Schools
IRB	International Rugby Board
NGB	National Governing Body
NRL	National Rugby League
NSWRU	New South Wales Rugby Union
PETE	physical education teacher education
RFU	Rugby Football Union
RWC	Rugby World Cup
SoC	Sense of Coherence
TGfU	Teaching Games for Understanding
UKCC	United Kingdom Coaching Certificate

INTRODUCTION

A decade and a half ago Potrac *et al.* (2000) issued a call for a move towards a more holistic approach to coaching. This reflected growing recognition of coaching as a social practice with others since also adopting and promoting an holistic approach to coaching and to understanding coaching and coach development (see, for example, Cassidy *et al.* 2009; Light *et al.* 2014a; Poczwardowski *et al.* 2006). Since then the socio-cultural approach to coaching has generated a well-developed understanding of the social nature of coaching and the range of social and cultural influences that act upon it. This volume adopts an holistic approach to coaching and research on it that is similar to that suggested by Potrac and colleagues, but which takes the concept a little further through a specific focus on the sport of rugby union. It sees coaching as a social practice that takes place within, and is shaped by, particular social and cultural contexts, but expands the notion of an holistic approach by considering people (such as coaches and players) as whole beings that are inseparable from their social environment and of rugby matches as a whole, complex phenomena that cannot be reduced to discrete component parts.

The four authors who collaborated in writing this book have coaching backgrounds with two currently coaching. Three of us have backgrounds as rugby coaches with playing and coaching experience in Australia, France, South Africa and Japan. Stephen Harvey has a background in field hockey and was coaching at elite youth levels in the UK up until his move to the United States in August 2013, and is currently working with his PhD student, Paul Reid, on the use of Game Sense in Rugby Football Union (RFU) coaching programmes. We all conduct research on sport coaching from an holistic perspective and have previous collaboration in sport pedagogy.

We chose to focus on rugby due to the weight of research we have conducted on it and our familiarity with it. We felt that focusing on one sport would allow us to ground some recent developments in sport coaching in a specific example and that there was a need for a high-quality book that did this. There has been a number of publications that present a broad perspective on recent developments in coaching and coaching research (see, for example, Cassidy *et al.* 2009; Lyle and Cushion 2010; Potrac *et al.* 2013). Taking a slightly different approach, this book presents and explores a particular approach to coaching and researching by focusing on one particular sport. The approach we have chosen to take seeks to complement these publications and others like them by focusing on taking an holistic approach and illustrating some recent developments in coaching 'in action'. It also allows us to present cutting-edge empirical research on rugby coaching conducted in Australia, New Zealand, South Africa and England. In fact, seven of the ten chapters in this book present the findings of empirical studies on rugby coaching, making it 'research heavy'.

Learning, pedagogy and the socio-cultural perspective

Sport coaching is a relatively new field yet one that is expanding and developing at a rapid and exciting pace. Initially dominated by sport science and biophysical knowledge, it has expanded exponentially over the past two decades to draw on socio-cultural knowledge to better understand and develop coaching in a way that reflects recognition of it as an essentially social practice. Significant advances have been made in research on coaching as it develops into a sophisticated and multi-disciplinary profession that recognizes, and can account for, the complex, socially situated nature of coaching (Potrac *et al.* 2013). This is an ongoing process with the quest to understand and improve coaching, drawing on knowledge and research approaches from a range of disciplines and sub-disciplines, such as sociology, anthropology, psychology, philosophy, education and physical education as a field that has significant overlap with coaching.

For us, recognition of the central importance of *how* to coach is one of the more significant developments in sport coaching over the past two decades and particularly when tied into an appreciation of the social nature of coaching and the influence of context. This is because enquiring into *how* to coach and the influence of socio-cultural context has required moving beyond the use of objective, biophysical knowledge and the positivist research paradigm into the more 'fuzzy', human and less predictable world of socio-cultural knowledge and understanding. This interest in the socio-cultural aspects of coaching is underpinned by recognition of its essentially social nature, the importance of human interaction and the extent to which it is socially situated, identified in the 1990s (see, for example, Schempp 1998; Strean 1995). As Dewey notes, 'A being whose activities are associated with others has a social environment . . . A being connected with others cannot perform his (*sic*) own actvities without taking the activities of others into account' (cited in Potrac *et al.* 2000, p. 187). The essentially social nature of coaching and player learning suggests the need to consider the dynamics of relationships in coaching contexts and to focus on human interaction as a central mode of learning (see, for example, Gréhaigne *et al.* 2005; Light 2013b; Potrac and Jones 1999).

Over the post-Second World War period scientific advances made in the preparation of military personnel during the war were adapted and applied to the preparation of athletes with unquestionably positive results in their psychological and physiological preparation (Kirk *et al.* 1996; Potrac *et al.* 2000). This saw the rise and development of sport science, as the application of biophysical knowledge and research paradigms to sport, which has had a profound influence upon thinking about coaching. Within this context coaching developed as a 'science' along bioscientific lines that emphasized its physiological, psychological and biomechanical dimensions (Potrac *et al.* 2000; Woodman 1993). It focused on *what* and *when* to coach, paying little attention to *how* to coach (pedagogy) or *where* coaching was undertaken (socio-cultural context), with an emphasis on player/athlete preparation. This conception of coaching sees the coach's primary role as being the transfer of objective knowledge and information to players/athletes that Potrac *et al.* (2000) argue deskills players in terms of cognitive and human interaction.

There were concerns expressed with this linear, simplistic approach three decades ago that have since seen its limits increasingly scrutinized. Critical concern with the influence of culture on learning in the physical education field (see, for example, Sparkes *et al.* 1993) encouraged some to consider the same issues in coaching. For example, in 1982 Tinning argued for the need to take into account the complex, situated nature of coaching and player development by considering how culture, ethics and ideology influenced it. Martens (1996) also challenged a simplistic view of coaching as being merely the transfer of knowledge and information in which the coach only needed technical skills. He argues that coaches also needed the pedagogical skills of a teacher, but recognition of the importance of pedagogy in coaching was slow to develop. Kirk (2010) suggests that this neglect of pedagogy was mainly due to the desire of coach educators to distance themselves from school physical education teacher preparation and the underdeveloped study of pedagogy in sport coaching when compared to the sport sciences. This is supported by his contention that, when the importance of pedagogy *was* recognized, writers and researchers were forced to borrow heavily from the physical education teaching research literature because so little research on it had been done in coaching.

Pedagogy now receives much more attention (see, for example, Cassidy *et al.* 2009; Evans 2014; Jones 2006, 2007; Kirk 2010) but, while this is a move in the right direction, research suggests that it is still widely overlooked or given a low priority by coaches (see, for an example in rugby, Light and Evans 2010). While it is recognized that coaching and teaching have distinct differences, there is a significant overlap and there is much coaches can learn from teaching (see Light 2013b; Potrac *et al.* 2000). Recognition of player development and the enhancement of team and individual performance in competition as a process of learning have influenced thinking about coaching (see Kirk 2010). When player improvement is recognized as learning it highlights what coaches, coach educators and researchers can gain from applying knowledge generated from research on teaching and learning and how it can be adapted to different coaching contexts (Potrac *et al.* 2000).

Making sense of complexity

Socio-cultural perspectives on coaching and player learning informed by educational, learning and social theories and socio-cultural knowledge reject views of coaching and learning as linear processes. Instead, they seek to recognize, understand and account for the complexity of coaching, coach development and player learning as social processes (see, for example, Cassidy *et al.* 2004; Evans 2014; Potrac and Jones 1999; Potrac *et al.* 2000; Schempp 1998). Pedagogical assumptions and approaches sit upon particular views of human learning with growing interest in the physical education field, and more recently in the sport coaching field, in theorizing learning. This arises from increasing sophistication in both fields that involves growing appreciation of the complexity of learning whether in relation to players or coach learning.

Interest in theorizing learning in and through participation in sport has been particularly marked in games teaching because of the nature of games and team sports as complex, dynamic environments. Constructivism is a branch of epistemology that provides a particular perspective on what constitutes knowledge and how we acquire or develop it. It does not see knowledge as something that exists 'out there' and separate from the learner. Instead, it sees knowledge as something that is part of the learner because it is constructed by him/her and critically shaped by his/her existing knowledge, experience and dispositions. Constructivism includes a range of variations that are generally seen to cluster around one of two camps. One is psychological or personal constructivism developed from the work of Piaget, and the other is social or socio-cultural constructivism developed from the work of Vygotsky. Both have been used in physical education and sport coaching, with Vygotsky's social perspective more popular in the games literature (see, for example, Gréhaigne *et al.* 2005). Also sitting upon a constructivist epistemology, Lave and Wenger's (1991) concept of situated learning, proposed for use in understanding learning in physical education by Kirk and Macdonald (1998), has also been used in coaching (see, for an example, Cassidy and Rossi 2006).

In 2003 Davis and Sumara proposed the concept of complex learning theory (CLT) to circumnavigate some of the contradictions between the two camps of constructivism. The idea of CLT was informed by core features common to all constructivism and influenced by complexity theory. Davis and Sumara (2003) propose that what all constructivism has in common is that learning involves *adaptation*, is an *interpretive* process and is a social process (Light *et al.* 2014a). Davis and Sumara have since focused on developing and applying complexity theory to education (see, for example, Davis and Sumara 2008), but Light and colleagues have applied CLT to analyses of learning in and through physical education and sport (see, for example, Light 2009, 2013b; Light and Kentel 2013; Light *et al.* 2014a). CLT should not be confused with complexity thinking or complexity theory. Like constructivism, CLT is focused on understanding and explaining learning, while complexity theory focuses on the object of study.

Over the past few years there has been a sudden increase in interest in complexity theory in the physical education field and to a lesser extent in sport coaching. Increasing interest in complexity theory in education (see, for example, Davis and Sumara 2006, 2008) has been followed by interest in physical education (see, for example, Jess *et al.* 2011; Ovens *et al.* 2013). This has made a valuable contribution towards recognizing and accounting for the complexity of learning in and through sport and physical education. Other theorizations of learning, such as constraints-led theory, also strive to recognize and make sense of complexity but sit on different sets of assumptions from motor learning theory (see, for example, Renshaw *et al.* 2010, 2012).

An holistic approach to coaching

The holistic approach that this book adopts for coaching and research on coaching follows on from Potrac and colleagues' (2000) call for a move towards developing an holistic understanding of coaching over a decade ago, but takes it a little further. In addition to recognizing and striving to account for the socially situated nature of coaching and its complexity we argue for the wholeness of people and the complexity of rugby matches. We use the term 'holistic' in reference to people (players and coaches) as whole beings who cannot be reduced to component parts such as the mind, the body and spirit or emotion, thinking or acting. We see rugby matches as being complex entities or phenomena (as complexity thinking suggests) with people, learning and performance inseparable from the immediate, dynamic, physical and socio-cultural context and wider social and cultural contexts.

Poczwardowski and colleagues (2006) provide an example of work in sport coaching that attempts to illuminate and understand its holistic nature. To understand coaching from an holistic perspective they employed a phenomenological approach that suggested how both coaches and players live in an inherited 'world' that they rewrite on a day-to-day basis through their actions and interactions. This holistic view of coaching and the worlds in which coaches learn and practise emphasizes how coaching, coach development and player and team performances in matches cannot productively be broken down into discrete components such as dismantling a car engine. It is strongly influenced by a philosophical position that challenges the dualism that separates mind from body, learner from what is learnt and objective from subjective.

The focus on rugby

This book outlines and discusses contemporary developments in sport coaching that are holistic in nature through a specific focus on rugby union. This includes conducting research on rugby coaching (and thus player learning) and the development of coach expertise that emphasizes its complexity and socially situated nature. It focuses on one specific, major sport upon which a significant body of research has been conducted from an holistic perspective over the past few years, but the issues it raises have broader implications for sport coaching more generally (see, for example, Evans 2014; Light *et al.* 2014a; Mouchet 2014; Mouchet *et al.* 2013).

The Rugby World Cup (RWC) is the third biggest sporting event in the world behind the FIFA World Cup and the Olympics. Although participation in rugby is dwarfed by association football (soccer), it is played in over a hundred countries and boasts 5.5 million players, including children, women and men. 'Sevens' rugby is now an Olympic sport that is growing quickly and attracting more investment from national sporting bodies across the globe. Beyond the fact that rugby is a significant global sport, the issues covered in this book are those that are common to most other sports and particularly to team sports. There is also overlap with some issues in physical education, such as teacher development and innovations in pedagogy (see, for example, Light *et al.* 2014b). This overlap is largely the result of the extent to which this book draws on learning and educational theory and the way in which it sees player and coach development as a process of learning.

The contemporary developments that this book focuses on involve the application of theories from the social sciences, and particularly from the fields of sociology and education, to better understand and improve coaching, and athletes' experiences of it. It does so by drawing on socio-cultural knowledge in sport coaching (see, for example, Cassidy and Rossi 2006; Evans 2011; Jones 2006, 2007; Jones *et al.* 2011).

Aims of the book

This book promotes an holistic approach to coaching, coach development and conducting research on coaching. The four co-authors have prior collaboration, which assists in producing a cohesive volume but which also provides a range of perspectives on the central issues dealt with in the book and allows us to draw directly upon empirical research conducted by the authors, which is a feature of the book. Two authors are Australian, one is French (but played and coached rugby in South Africa), and one is British but living in the United States. This allows for the book to present, in detail, cutting edge, empirical research conducted in the four countries that have won a Rugby World Cup (New Zealand, Australia, South Africa and England) with France playing in three finals. Drawing on a wide range of experience in playing, coaching and conducting research on rugby, this volume presents innovative ideas on coaching, contemporary research on rugby coaching and coach development and new approaches to research methodology.

There have been two areas of research in and on coaching generally, and in rugby coaching more specifically, that this book focuses on. One is the recognition of the complexity of coaching and coach development and the influence of social and cultural context on them, and the responses to this in research (see, for example, Cassidy *et al.* 2009). This is an area in which this book presents cutting-edge empirical research conducted on rugby coaching and in the four nations to have won a Rugby World Cup (Australia, New Zealand, England and South Africa) and in France. The other area that this book pays attention to is the growing interest in player-centred approaches to coaching. These include Teaching Games for Understanding (TGfU), Play Practice (Launder 2001) and Game Sense (see Light 2013b). Game Sense in particular has had a significant influence upon coaching across the world as is evident in this book. One chapter presents an innovative approach called positive coaching for youth rugby that is based upon Game Sense and is influenced by Positive Psychology. There are also chapters on the use of Game Sense in coach education by the RFU in England and an examination of elite-level coaches' dispositions towards Game Sense in Australia and New Zealand. The chapter on CAR (collaborative action research) also deals with Game Sense by looking at a coach's collaboration with a 'sport pedagogue' to develop particular aspects of Game Sense in his coaching through this innovative approach to coach development.

More specifically, this book has been written with the following objectives:

- To present the most recent developments in holistic approaches to coaching, coach development and conducting research on these areas through a tight focus on the sport of rugby union.
- To present cutting-edge empirical research conducted on rugby from an holistic perspective. In particular, to address a lack of empirical studies on how and what coaches learn from experience.
- To stimulate coaches from youth levels to elite levels in team sports generally, and rugby specifically, to think critically about their practice and to consider the possibilities that holistic approaches to coaching and coach development offer.
- To encourage governing bodies of sport to consider the ways in which they educate coaches at all levels and the coaching approaches they promote.
- To encourage more research on coaching that is conducted from an holistic perspective rather than the dominant, rationalistic instrumental approach.

The book

The book is divided into two sections – Part 1: *Issues in coaching and coach development* and Part 2: *Research on coaches and coaching*. It closes with our concluding thoughts.

Part 1 begins with an overview of the literature in *Contemporary developments in coaching*, outlining developments over the past decade in thinking about coaching and research on it that highlight its complexity as a socially situated practice. It examines new perspectives on the notion of coaching effectiveness that suggest the idea of coaching quality might offer a more helpful focus for improving coaching and discusses the use of learning theory to inform developments in coaching pedagogy with a focus on holistic approaches. It finishes with a detailed discussion of Game Sense as an example of an holistic approach that is prominent in this volume. This is followed by *Positive coaching for youth rugby*, which introduces a new concept for coaching that, although focused on coaching youth rugby, can also be applied at elite levels. Developed from game-based approaches such as Game Sense (Light 2013b) it maximizes game performance while providing learning experiences that provide positive experiences of learning and foster learning how to learn while promoting positive experiences and positive social, moral and personal development.

Chapter 3, *Improving decision-making in sevens rugby*, draws on Game Sense pedagogy and CLT to make suggestions for improving decision-making in sevens rugby. It focuses on situating decision-making within an immediate physical context that replicates match conditions and within the larger social and cultural environments that indirectly influence it. This chapter is grounded in a practical suggestion for activities for coaching sevens rugby. Chapter 4 provides an overview of the literature on *Coach development*. It draws on some recent research to consider coach development as a long-term, situated process located in experiences within particular settings and influenced by interventions such as coach accreditation courses. In this context, formal coach education, coaching experience, playing experience and mentoring all influence coach development and the development of expertise but as a process of learning that is essentially interpretive and social. These influences are typically set against a background of individual biographies and life experiences, some directly related to the sport and others more general in nature but still significant.

Widely used in research on sport coaching, Bourdieu's concept of *habitus* offers a useful concept for understanding how experience comes to shape coaching practice, which forms the focus of Chapter 5. This chapter begins by outlining its use in the sport coaching literature and discussing its relationship with Bourdieu's other key concepts of practice and field. It then examines the use of *habitus* in research on rugby coach development by drawing on two studies that used it as a methodological tool.

Part 2 begins with Chapter 6, *An holistic approach to investigating French rugby coaches' in-match communications with players*. This chapter draws on a study that enquired into in-competition coach behaviour in French rugby (Mouchet *et al.* 2013) with a focus on its methodology to illustrate the significant contribution to knowledge in sport coaching that holistic approaches can make. The holistic nature of the research approach used in this study provides an example of what we have argued for in this book by exploring both the 'public' and 'private' aspects of coach decision-making and locating this within multiple levels of context. Drawing on contemporary developments in France in sport coaching it accounts for the inseparability of coach decision-making and behaviour from context(s) and the subjective dimensions of coaching that has been neglected in the coaching literature.

Chapters 7 and 8 also report on empirical research but are presented as extended chapters that are each divided into two studies. In Chapter 7, *The influence of experience and cultural context on rugby coaches' beliefs about coaching*, Study 1 provides an example of how *habitus* is used in research on rugby coach development and learning. *Making better people: coaches' beliefs in moral learning through rugby* reports on a case study that enquired into how coaches' beliefs about and dispositions towards coaching were developed through long-term experience. Conducted in Melbourne, Australia, it focused on three coaches working at high-performance levels who were from the three different countries of Australia, South Africa and New Zealand. The findings highlight the powerful influence of socio-cultural context on the construction of a coaching *habitus* and the ways in which it structured coaching. Study 2, *South African and Australian coaches' encultured beliefs about coaching* follows on from the Melbourne study (Study 1) to explore the influence of cultural context on the development of coaches' beliefs about coaching with both studies forming part of a larger PhD study being conducted by Rémy Hassanin. It specifically investigates the cultural contexts within which two coaches in the Melbourne study learnt to coach and developed their beliefs about coaching and dispositions towards it. One study was conducted in Pretoria, South Africa, and one in Sydney, Australia. The Pretoria study aimed to explore the impact of the socio-cultural context on Robert's development as a coach in South Africa, with the Sydney study aimed at gaining insight into the nature of the cultural setting within which Paul, the Australian coach in the Melbourne study, learnt to coach.

Chapter 8, *Elite-level rugby coaches' interpretation and use of Game Sense in Australia and New Zealand*, draws on a larger PhD study conducted by John Evans (Evans 2011). Study 1, *Dispositions of elite-level Australian and New Zealand coaches towards Game Sense*, identifies the characteristics of the individual coaching *habitus* of eight elite-level rugby coaches, four in Australia and four in New Zealand, to suggest how this shaped their dispositions towards Game Sense. Research on game-based approaches (GBA) in physical education teaching and sport coaching consistently identifies the ways in which the epistemology and assumptions about learning that underpin them can present problems for coaches (and teachers) interested in adopting them (see Butler 1996; Jarrett and Harvey 2014; Light 2004) and impede the wider uptake of Game Sense and other game-based approaches (see Curry and Light 2014; Light 2004; Roberts 2011). Study 2, *Elite-level coaches' views on learning and the implications for coaching pedagogy*, redresses this oversight by examining the views of four elite-level, Australian rugby coaches from Evans' larger study on how players learn and how this shapes their use of Game Sense.

Chapter 9 is also focused on Game Sense in rugby but as implemented by the Rugby Football Union (RFU) (England) and its interpretation by both RFU staff delivering it in coach education programmes and practitioners. *The interpretation and misinterpretation of Game Sense in its implementation by the RFU* uses data generated from coaching course observations, and interviews with course tutors and participants, the various facilitators and inhibitors of course participants' potential adoption of authentic Game Sense pedagogy and its integration into their coaching practice. Chapter 10, *Bridging the gap between theory and practice through collaborative action research (CAR)*, presents an innovation for coach education called CAR (collaborative action research). It does so by reporting on a study that enquired into the use of CAR to bridge the gap between coaching theory and practice, with an Australian rugby coach wanting to improve relationships and communication with his players and seeking the help of one of the authors who operates as the 'sport pedagogue'. The CAR process involves equal collaboration between the coach as the practitioner and the 'sport pedagogue', who brings pedagogical knowledge and a theoretical understanding to the partnership and conducts research on the intervention.

PART 1

Issues in coaching and coach development

1

CONTEMPORARY DEVELOPMENTS IN COACHING

This chapter focuses on contemporary developments in sport coaching that are relevant to the book's focus on holistic approaches to rugby coaching and research on it and that emphasize its complexity and socially situated nature. The developments it focuses on are characterized by the use of theories from the social sciences and particularly from sociology and education as the drive to understand and improve coaching and athletes' experiences of it looks beyond knowledge from the biophysical sciences (see, for example, Cassidy and Rossi 2006; Evans 2011; Jones 2006, 2007; Jones *et al.* 2011). There have been two particular areas of research interest that are significant for rugby coaching. One is recognition of the complexity of coaching and responses to this in research (see, for example, Cassidy *et al.* 2009). The other is the growing interest in athlete/player-centred approaches to coaching such as Game Sense, Teaching Games for Understanding (TGfU) and Play Practice (see, for example, Breed and Spittle 2011; Launder and Piltz 2013; Light 2013b; Slade 2010). Both these developments challenge embedded practices, beliefs and ideas about coaching. One of the most significant developments in coaching is the shift from a focus on what the coach does to what the players learn. This then requires a major reassessment of the coach's behaviour because s/he must pay attention to what and how the players are learning and make appropriate adjustments and modifications in his/her coaching that demand more sensitivity to learning.

There is, of course, no one distinct, traditional approach to coaching but there are some core features of it that have proven to be very durable. The term 'traditional' is used here in reference to coaching approaches that tend to be coach-centred and emphasize the mastery of technique or skills, referred to by Bunker and Thorpe (1982) as the technical approach. We do not, however, suggest that coaching is always either one or the other but, instead, that there is a spectrum of practices ranging from the very conservative, traditional approach we identify here to the holistic approaches we contrast it with and argue for in this book.

This chapter begins by outlining the 'traditional' end of the spectrum to identify the features of it that distinguish it from holistic approaches that have been developed more recently and upon which this book is focused. The traditional approach makes the coach the central figure responsible for deciding what is coached and how training is conducted, placing responsibility on him/her to transmit knowledge to his/her players. This is a coach-centred approach in which the focus is on what the coach does more than on what and how the players learn. This approach typically uses a directive or prescriptive coaching style, drawing heavily on biophysical knowledge from the sport sciences (Cassidy *et al.* 2004; Jones 2006; Kidman 2001, 2005). It is characterized by a strong emphasis on what to coach, when to coach and the physical preparation of athletes, tending to neglect the issue of *how* to coach and paying little attention to how to enhance player learning and what they are learning. It tends to see coaching as a non-problematic and linear process that is informed by knowledge from motor behaviour, skill acquisition theory and the information-processing model (see, for example, Magill 2004; Schmidt 1991).

From the post-Second World War period coaching has been primarily informed by biophysical knowledge, but the past two decades or so have seen growing recognition of the socio-cultural aspects and complexity of coaching (see, for example, Cassidy *et al.* 2004). This has been strongly influenced by increasing recognition of the relevance of educational theory for coaching (see, for example, Jones 2006, 2007; Kirk 2010), which encourages seeing improving performance in sport as a process of learning that can be enhanced by drawing on pedagogical and learning theory.

Traditional approaches to coaching tend to employ a directive, or command, style of teaching/coaching (Mosston and Ashworth 1990) in which the coach directs and attempts to determine learning. This is based upon an objective view of knowledge as something that exists separate to the learner and which the coach transmits to him/her. In this approach coaching is seen as a linear process of transmitting knowledge with a focus on the refinement of technique or skill. At this stage we want to make a distinction between technique and skill as used in this book. For this we use the distinction proposed by Bunker and Thorpe (see, for example, 1982) in the Teaching Games for Understanding (TGfU) approach in which technique is performed in complete isolation and skill is technique performed in the game or a game-like situation. This difference is also suggested in motor learning with the notion of closed and open skills. The technical approach reflects a positivistic influence of the sport sciences that seeks to reduce complexity to component parts that can be measured, manipulated and experimented upon to enable confident predictions. It sees technique and skill as being discrete components of the sport that the players must be able to execute to be able to successfully play the game. This invariably involves the coach engaging the players in repetition of the technique, providing feedback and having them refine performance as they move towards 'correct' execution of the technique. This is based upon the assumption that there is one most effective way to perform the technique and that extensive periods of repeated repetition are required for players to become expert performers.

From a traditional perspective the coach holds knowledge that s/he passes on to the players as passive receivers – as empty vessels – that are filled with knowledge by the coach (Kirk and MacPhail 2000). This linear conception of the learning process assumes that with adequate time devoted to practice the player can reproduce skill or technique in its ideal or correct form. Coaches who adopt a traditional approach take responsibility for player learning. They typically value being respected and feel that they need to provide a good example for the players to follow (see, for example, Light and Evans 2013). The coach is central to player learning because s/he is seen to hold the knowledge needed by the players and is responsible for transmitting it. Coaches using this approach can have good relationships with players and do not necessarily have to be authoritative but are explicitly in charge and directing learning.

From this perspective there are comparatively limited opportunities for player decision-making in or about the practice session (Kidman 2001) with the coach clearly in command and responsible for learning. There is also typically pressure on the coach to conform to popular conceptions of the coach's position and of behaviour that suggests confidence, strength, power and being in control (Cushion 2013; Light 2004). This can make coaches sensitive to the expectations of others and encourage them to demonstrate the widely accepted behaviours of a 'good' coach as suggested by Kidman (2001, p. 13): 'coaches believe that unless they are seen to be telling athletes what to do and how to do it they are not doing their job properly'.

According to Cassidy *et al.* (2004), the traditional coach is positioned as the 'boss' or 'expert'. The perception of coaches as being explicitly in charge and holding the power of superior knowledge can also be seen in Light's (2004) study of Australian coaches who noted the problem this causes when taking a Game Sense approach. The player-centred, enquiry-based, Game Sense approach, which requires the coach stepping off centre stage to engage in dialogue with players and use questioning to empower them, can create problems for many coaches with Light (2004, p. 129) suggesting that, 'Game Sense can be somewhat threatening to coaches who are used to the traditional role, where the coach is supposed to know it all.'

Socio-cultural views of coaching

The past fifteen years have seen the emergence of a socio-cultural perspective on coaching that challenges and questions reductionist conceptions of it as a simple process of knowledge transmission. Most of this work has been done by researchers who have drawn on developments in physical education pedagogy and the application of contemporary learning theory to teaching and coaching sport. This work suggests that learning to play sport involves far more than the refinement of de-contextualized technique and the internalization of knowledge as an object and that learning to play sport and learning to coach are culturally and socially located. These developments basically show how coaching and learning to play sport are far more complex processes than traditional approaches seem to assume. As Davis *et al.* (2000) suggest is the case with teaching, most coaching seems to be based upon a view of learning as a linear, binary (mind and body) process in which players learn by adding on knowledge or skills.

Conversely, contemporary learning theory sees learning as being a transformative process that actively engages the learner as a participant in the learning process (Prawat 1999). This is evident in some of the more recent coaching literature that promotes player-centred coaching (see, for example, Jones 2009; Kidman 2001, 2005; Light 2013b; Slade 2010). Traditional coaching can be viewed as training where the main aim is for the athlete or player to develop competence in a skill or range of skills, but this overly simple conception of coaching places limits on athlete and coach interaction as an important means of learning (Cassidy *et al.* 2004). Rather than limiting this interaction, coaching should stimulate it to enhance learning because the player is not a machine but instead is a thinking, feeling and physical being with needs in these areas.

The central role that interaction and language play in learning is a central concern of social constructivist learning theory (see Barker *et al.* 2013; Fosnot 1996; Vygotsky 1978). Indeed, social constructivism emerged from the work of Vygotsky, was further developed by others such as Bruner, and was influenced by similar approaches to learning such as that of Dewey (see, for example, 1916/97). Vygotsky was a Russian psychologist, cultural theorist and a deep thinker about education whose work focused on the relationship between thought and language. He placed great emphasis on the role of language in mental development as a tool for thought that shapes thinking with the use of language being central to learning and human development to the extent that it could create consciousness and free will (Bruner 1987).

A more holistic conception of coaching and learning is suitable not only for youth coaching but also for coaching rugby at the highest levels. The New Zealand All Blacks are the dominant team in world rugby, winning the 2011 Rugby World Cup, finishing 2013 undefeated for the year and being the IRB (International Rugby Board) team of the year for the fourth year in a row. Research suggests that they adopt an holistic approach that is influenced by Game Sense and which emphasizes caring for all players as people and not just objects (Evans 2012).

Drawing on work in physical education by Mosston and Ashworth (1990), Cassidy *et al.* (2004) suggest that the five teaching styles proposed by them can be successfully applied to coaching. Comprising a spectrum moving from teacher-centred to student-centred styles, these five styles are direct, task, reciprocal, guided discovery and problem solving, but were later expanded. This spectrum of teaching styles encourages coaches to think about different ways of coaching and matching a style of coaching to the particular nature of the situation, the experience, skills, knowledge and motivations of the players and the aims of the session or season. Although the notion of teaching styles cannot be seen as providing substantial, specific pedagogical detail, it is very useful in encouraging coaches to think about different ways of coaching to suit the situation and ways of coaching fitting into a spectrum ranging from coach-centred to player-centred coaching.

At the coach-centred end of the spectrum the command style is commonly used in traditional coaching. The other styles move towards a player/athlete-centred style with the problem-solving style being the most player-centred and enquiry-based style. The styles at the player-centred end of the spectrum are most suitable for developing players as problem solvers who are less reliant on the coach and independent learners and thinkers. These styles (guided discovery and problem solving) engage athletes' cognitive, affective and psychomotor abilities while encouraging them to take responsibility for their learning.

The player-centred approach to coaching has had a significant influence on coaching in New Zealand from the 2011 RWC champions, the All Blacks, to young children learning the game (see, for example, Evans 2012). For example, the Small Blacks junior development model for rugby players aged six to thirteen uses modified games to, 'help players develop their rugby skills as their physical ability develops, making the game as simple and safe as possible' (Small Blacks Model 2013). There has also been a realization of the situated nature of coaching, and the need to appreciate the lives of players outside rugby and to consider more than their performance on the field at elite levels in New Zealand (Evans 2012).

In 2005 the New Zealand All Blacks organization critically assessed a number of the foundations underpinning its operations (Kitson 2005). This began with a review of the 'haka', which is a distinctive ritual 'war dance' performed before all international matches and holds powerful cultural meaning by connecting the culture of rugby in New Zealand with Maori culture. The review recommended ensuring everyone in the All Blacks community understood and bought into the cultural meaning and importance of the haka. Second, the coaching staff made a decision to embrace athlete-centred activities in practice to improve the decision-making ability of players in the high-pressure environment of international rugby. The traditional skills approach previously used by All Blacks coaches was seen to inhibit player performance, the cohesion of the team as a unit and its ability to perform at the highest possible level.

Third, it was decided that players needed to have a balanced life and that their identity should not be determined solely by their rugby ability (see Evans 2012). Fourth, it was seen to be necessary for all players to take a leadership role in implementing decisions. This empowerment approach galvanizes players into a more cohesive unit as a team and is seen to enhance the ability of players to handle challenging situations both on and off the field (Kidman 2001). As Jones (2009) suggests, caring for athletes promotes empowerment and encourages them to explore situations and to find solutions to problems. The socio-cultural approach recognizes players as complex, feeling people who are members of communities and societies, and the culturally and socially situated nature of learning, rather than seeing them objectively as athletic talent.

Coaching effectiveness

The term 'coaching effectiveness' is commonly used in the coaching literature but its meaning is difficult to determine precisely. In a general sense, it refers to a coach's ability to observe, analyse, synthesize and be flexible (Brooker and Abbott 2001). Does effectiveness also mean winning as a measure of coaching effectiveness? In what appears to be an attempt to quantify and measure coaching the term 'effectiveness' has been used to describe a coach's performance in terms of results (Cassidy *et al.* 2004). This use of 'performance' refers not only to the win/loss record, but also to the key performance indicators of players such as fitness levels or game statistics such as metres run, time in possession and time in the opposition half. If this approach is accepted as a measure of effectiveness, how then would less tangible humanistic variables be judged in regard to effectiveness? Lyle (2002) argues that effective coaching may well be more about good practice related to delivery, with effectiveness not so much about winning or losing but about the attainment of agreed goals. According to Lyle (2002, p. 266), 'Effective coaching performance takes place within the acknowledged set of constraints and, perhaps more importantly, within a given time, place and organizational setting.'

The organizational setting takes into account the culture of the team and its participants, but players' opinions and feelings in the past have been largely ignored in the assessment of coaching performance (Rushall and Wiznuk 1985). Brooker and Abbott (2001) suggest the need to consider player perceptions about coaching and coaching practices as factors when evaluating coaching effectiveness, with Solomon (1999) adding that player satisfaction with the coach should be considered when attempting to evaluate coach effectiveness. In this move away from quantifiable objectivity towards more subjective evaluation of effectiveness, Kidman (2001) argues that an effective coaching style is one in which athletes have an opportunity to be involved in decision-making activities leading to player empowerment. This approach takes a more holistic view of effective coaching to the point where the athlete is a part of the relationship and is a reflection of the coach's inclusiveness of athlete aspirations (Lyle 2002). It implies that goals exist within a dynamic environment that may or may not be associated directly with winning. Taking this a little further, Cassidy and colleagues (2004) suggest that the concept of effectiveness is inherently problematic (as it has been in teaching) and should be replaced by consideration of the 'quality' of coaching, with Vallée and Bloom (2005, p. 190) claiming that, 'success may be attributed to the relationship these coaches formed with their athletes'.

This move towards a more holistic conception of players as people that goes beyond seeing their utility for achieving wins is evident in an Australian newspaper report on Wayne Bennett's approach to coaching rugby league, which makes the following observation: 'The recurring theme down the years has been that parents want Bennett to coach their sons. They know he will turn them into better footballers, sure, but more importantly, he will turn them into better people (Smith 2006, p. 31).

This more holistic conception of effectiveness or quality coaching implies empowering players as people beyond the sport (Brooker and Abbott 2001; Kidman 2001, 2005). In turn, this suggests the need for a range of coaching pedagogies that promote player welfare, personal relationships and the role of reflection. These aspects of effectiveness in coaching are not as readily quantifiable as instrumental or practical characteristics such as organization, technical knowledge or athlete management.

Coach reflection

Experience does not necessarily always produce an expert coach, but expert coaches are experienced (Abraham *et al.* 2006) and the ability and propensity to critically reflect upon practice has been identified as a characteristic of expert coaches (Cassidy *et al.* 2004). In the philosophy of education, Dewey (1916/97) suggests that there are three important characteristics necessary for a person to engage in effective reflection. These are that s/he has whole-heartedness, open mindedness and responsibility, with Dewey (1963) suggesting that those who question and reflect upon their assumptions take responsibility for their actions.

Schön (1983) sees reflection as being a practice that is central to professionals seeking to become better practitioners. This view is supported by a Canadian study of coaches working at varsity level that suggests coach reflection is common in expert coaches and is necessary for building a successful programme (Vallée and Bloom 2005). Reflection provides coaches with a way of learning from 'mistakes' or with an analytical and evaluative tool for coaching performance that determines what can be done better in the future (Abraham *et al.* 2006; Knowles *et al.* 2006). Chapter 2 outlines a positive coaching approach in which mistakes and errors are seen to be essential for player learning and this same concept can be applied to coach development when critical reflection forms a core concern.

Coaches who take the time to reflect on their actions are able to evaluate and rationalize their reasons for coaching (Abraham *et al.* 2006; Brooker and Abbott 2001). By reflecting on practice they can also challenge their own assumptions about what good coaching is and question their beliefs about coaching and cultural elements of coaching that they have previously taken for granted (Brooker and Abbott 2001; Butler 2005). Reflection can provide a conduit for coaches to develop an understanding of coaching as a complex activity in which players (learners) have different needs and are complex feeling, thinking and emotional beings. Some of the work being conducted by Mouchet and colleagues in France emphasizes this aspect of coaching by focusing on player subjectivity (see Mouchet 2014).

Without the ability to be reflective coaches are likely to struggle to develop an understanding of the influence that training sessions have on the team and the nature of the players' experiences of them. A coach who recognizes that learning is complex and that a team is more than the sum of its parts (players), and who can critically reflect, is more capable of knowing the differences between what the intended learning of a session was and what learning actually occurred. The literature suggests that 'effective' coaching may then well depend upon the ability and inclination of the coach to reflect upon his/her practice and to understand players' experiences of it as a process of interpretation based upon their previous experiences and beliefs and influenced by subjectivity. Reflection is an area of critical thinking that positions coaches in such a way that it allows for a fuller appreciation of what is possible and the degree to which innovative pedagogy can be introduced. It does, however, need to be informed by a humanistic approach to coaching through which the subjective aspects of players' experiences can be considered, both at practice and in the competitive match (see Mouchet 2014).

Quality coaching

Rather than considering whether or not a coach is efficient or effective, Cassidy *et al.* (2004) propose that we consider the question of the *quality* of his/her coaching. Coaching in recent times has transcended previous ideas about one person (the coach) transmitting knowledge to players as passive learners. Cassidy *et al.* (2004) suggest that quality coaching involves practitioners exploring ways in which their practice can be made more meaningful, purposeful, just and enjoyable. These are precisely the positive outcomes that are facilitated through the use of game-based coaching approaches such as Game Sense (see Light 2013b). Understanding the ways in which learning occurs through the use of a Game Sense approach (and other game-based approaches) and its development has usefully been informed by drawing on constructivist theories of learning and related, complex learning theory and situated learning (see Gréhaigne *et al.* 2005; Kirk and Macdonald 1998; Light 2004, 2013b).

Informing quality coaching with learning theory

Constructivist learning theory sees learning as a process in which the learner draws on existing knowledge to interpret and make sense of learning experiences to construct new knowledge. Instead of merely adding on new knowledge this involves change or transformation. This suggests that coaches need to understand or consider what experiences and knowledge the athlete or player brings with him/her and the social and physical environment in which they practise, in order to accommodate meaningful change and learning. Social constructivism emphasizes the central importance of dialogue and interaction in learning, which is also a feature of complex learning theory (CLT) as proposed by Davis and Sumara (2003) and later developed by Light and colleagues (see, for example, Light and Kentel 2013). CLT is aimed at circumventing some of the contradictions between different forms of constructivism and is influenced by complexity theory. It sets out the three core themes of learning as (1) a process of adaptation, (2) a social process and (3) a process of interpretation.

From this perspective, Davis *et al.*'s (2000) notion of structuring learning activities is useful for looking at how coaching can facilitate learning that is meaningful, relevant and transformational. In some ways this is similar to the non-linear, constraints-led approach in which the coach uses constraints to 'facilitate the emergence of functional movement patterns and decision-making behaviour' (Renshaw *et al.* 2010, p. 120). The dynamical systems theory of Bernstein (1967) that this draws on sees the learner as a complex system but it uses constraints to produce predetermined goal-directed movement and to have the learner reproduce specified movements. Davis *et al.* (2000) propose using structuring acts or tasks as 'enabling constraints' that, through placing certain constraints, generate other possibilities and, in doing so, promote creativity. For example, in rugby coaching, playing a practice game in a long narrow space restricts options for going around the defence and for finding space to penetrate, but opens up and encourages use of the space behind the defence through tactical kicking. If the defence then drops players back to fill this space in response to effective attacking kicks this will open up space elsewhere.

New approaches to coaching that are player-centred also tend to emphasize player learning through engagement with the environment rather than through direct instruction from the coach. This is typically achieved through the use of practice games as the physical learning environment within which players have to solve the problems that arise and are typically asked to reflect upon by the coach. This includes the appropriate socio-moral environment and team culture. As John Dewey, the most influential educational thinker of the twentieth century, suggests, transformational learning is achieved, not through direct teaching, but instead through structuring the learning environment and active learning (Dewey 1916/97).

Content knowledge is also more complex than has been assumed by directive, technical approaches to coaching. Content knowledge is multi-faceted and is more than good memory for drills, because it needs to display an understanding of pedagogical approaches that facilitate learning by the player(s) (Cassidy *et al.* 2004). Drawing on the work of Shulman (see 1986), Cassidy and colleagues suggest that this knowledge can be broken down into subject matter content knowledge, pedagogical content knowledge and curriculum content knowledge (Cassidy *et al.* 2004). These developments in coaching are beginning to redress the lack of attention in coaching paid to pedagogy, whereby the focus has been on *what* and *when* to coach and not *how* (Light 2013b). As Woodman (1993) noted in Australia two decades ago, coaching concentrates on athletic performance and achievement, but any consideration of the pedagogy of coaching has been largely absent in coach education programmes.

Game Sense in rugby coaching

There has been increasing interest in game-based approaches (GBA) to coaching across a range of cultural and institutional settings, as is evident in this volume, and in some of the ideas and the philosophy underpinning them. This interest is mostly focused on Game Sense, with significant attention paid to it in this volume and in Chapters 8 and 9 in particular with their enquiry into its interpretation at individual and institutional levels in England, Australia and New Zealand. With this in mind we complete this chapter with a brief overview of Game Sense.

Game Sense has had a significant influence on rugby coaching, which is probably most noticeable at the elite level with 2011 Rugby World Cup champions, the All Blacks' extensive use of it in their training (see, for example, Evans 2012; Kidman 2001, 2005). There now appears to be considerable interest in Game Sense from national and provincial rugby organizations across the globe, such as the RFU in England (see Chapter 9), and in New Zealand from junior levels to the All Blacks. Deeper investigation, however, suggests that the versions of Game Sense disseminated throughout many organizations do not always adopt the player-centred, enquiry-based pedagogy of Game Sense. Indeed, while rugby coaches (and coaches of other sports) commonly and effectively use practice games, the literature suggests that its distinctive pedagogy is not well understood (see, for example, Light and Evans 2010).

Game Sense offers a wide range of possibilities for coaching rugby (see Chapter 3), but there is also a range of significant problems that coaches in rugby and any other team sport have to face when taking up this approach (see, for example, Harvey *et al.* 2010a; Roberts 2011). Research conducted specifically on rugby suggests that this can lead to misinterpretation of the approach and the implementation of watered-down versions of it that lack authenticity (Light and Evans 2010). The literature on TGfU and similar approaches such as the Games Concept Approach (GCA) in Singapore, and more broadly with GBA in physical education across the world, suggests that there are similar problems with teachers' understanding and implementation of them in schools (see, for example, Curry and Light 2014; Fry and McNeill 2014; Jarrett and Harvey 2014).

Learning in and through Game Sense

The Game Sense approach sits upon constructivist epistemology (the nature of knowledge and how we acquire it) that sees knowledge as something that is constructed by the learner and as a process of change or transformation rather than one of transmitting knowledge as an object.

Game Sense pedagogy places learning within modified games or game-like situations that contextualize learning. In Game Sense learning adopts a problem-solving approach with players being challenged to solve the problems arising from playing games designed by the coach to achieve specific learning outcomes. This involves the design of practice games and their management to provide an appropriate physical learning environment that keeps players on task and maintains the right level of challenge to optimize learning (see Light 2013b). The embodied, non-conscious learning that arises from playing well-managed practice games is linked with conscious learning that involves reflection upon action and dialogue. The coach promotes thinking and dialogue between coach and players and between players through an emphasis on questioning (see Light 2013b). John Hattie's (2008) meta-analysis of academic achievement over fifteen years of research and involving 80 million students enquired into what factors contribute most towards 'visible' learning. It identifies a number of important factors among which one of the most important is the interaction and relationship between the teacher and the students. Although rugby coaching is a little different from teaching in schools, the implications for good coaching at any level are clear here.

Game Sense uses games or modified games as the basis of a training session that creates conditions for implicit learning and, in doing so, generates deeper learning and more transportable learning outcomes (Brooker and Abbott 2001; Hadfield 2005; Light *et al.* 2014c).

Challenges for coaches taking up Game Sense

As a player-centred approach Game Sense stands in contrast to coach-centred approaches. In coach-centred approaches the focus is on what the coach does (coach behaviour) to determine learning with her/him seen to hold knowledge that is transferred to the players. A player-centred approach focuses on how and what the players learn and sees the players as being active learners. Put simply, it shifts the focus from instruction to learning. The Game Sense coach shapes and guides learning through the management of learning environments that replicate, to different degrees, the conditions of the competitive match and through questioning and encouraging interaction between players and between players and the coach. In Game Sense, the modified games and 'game-like' activities (Light 2013b) provide challenges the players must meet and which involve the interrelated execution of skills, tactical knowledge, decision-making and awareness as they try to solve the problems arising from the games or activities. The use of questioning is a critically important feature of Game Sense coaching for promoting player understanding, independence from the coach and empowerment (Kidman 2001; Light 2013b). It also creates conditions that promote implicit learning and, in doing so, generates deeper learning that is more transportable to competitive matches (Brooker and Abbott 2001; Hadfield 2005; Kidman 2001, 2005).

The role of the coach

The role and behaviour of the coach in Game Sense is very different from that in the traditional 'technocratic' approach, where the coach decides on what is required and coaches via direct instruction (Tinning 1996). In Game Sense the coach is responsible for structuring the learning environment through the use of a game or game-like activities (Light 2013b). Even when a coach wants to focus on a particular skill it is not isolated from the other aspects of the game. In this case the coach tightens and narrows the focus of the activity and the options available to the player(s) but maintains the development of awareness and decision-making, even if at a low level (Light 2013b).

In Game Sense the coach is a facilitator, rather than a director of learning who focuses on how s/he can influence and enhance learning. Instead of the coach telling players what to do, s/he constructs a physical learning environment such as a modified practice game in which players have to make decisions and solve problems (den Duyn 1997) through reflection, collaboration and interaction (Light 2013b). In his program of research on student achievement in education Hattie (see 2008) identifies the central role that the teacher's explicit intervention makes to student achievement in education. This does not mean that the teacher or coach has to tell players what to do. Stopping play in a game to ask questions and clearly direct and enhance learning is completely in line with the Game Sense approach, and there are also times when the coach needs to step in and engage in a little direct instruction that does not necessarily detract from developing player empowerment and independence.

In Game Sense the coach steps off centre stage as the distributor of knowledge to become a facilitator of learning, but s/he can explicitly intervene when it is needed to interact with players and, at times, provide some direct instruction. However, stepping back is something that many coaches struggle with (Light 2004). They can also struggle with the different relationships that this requires between coach and players (see, for example, Evans 2014) and questioning (Roberts 2011). This is a radical change for coaches but it does not mean that the coach cannot intervene or that s/he has to abandon previous practice. There is no model in Game Sense but, instead, a framework for practice that allows flexibility and room for coaches to adapt Game Sense to their coaching (Light 2013b).

The impact of Game Sense on rugby coaching

Many rugby coaches working at high performance levels use games in their training and most have heard of the Game Sense approach but the extent to which game-based training in general, and Game Sense in particular, is used is yet to be established. While many coaches in Australia use games as part of their training few adopt the player-centred pedagogy of Game Sense (Light 2006a; Light and Evans 2010).

The pressure to coach winning teams or have superior win–loss ratios can discourage coaches from being innovative by forcing them to adhere to existing conventions about coaching (Evans 2006b; Light and Evans 2010). Another factor operating against the uptake of Game Sense is the pressure that coaches are under to produce immediate results and the way in which this can lead them to see the Game Sense approach as an ineffective use of training time (Light 2004). It can also be at odds with a common view by others of good coaching being well ordered when Game Sense sessions can often appear messy and even chaotic (Light 2004).

The impact of professionalism on rugby coaching

We live in a rapidly changing world to which professionals in any field constantly have to adapt. No longer can a set body of knowledge carry a professional through his/her career and rugby coaching is no different. This is probably more acute with rugby coaching due to the profound changes in its practice since professionalization in 1995 (see, for example, Ryan 2008) and its rapid commodification (a process through which it becomes a commercial commodity). The professionalization of rugby is one of the most significant changes in its long history (FitzSimons 2003), with the transition from amateurism to professionalism a defining moment in its history and one that has had a profound impact upon coaching.

Rugby has its origins in the nineteenth-century elite, middle-class secondary schools in England, where it was used as a vehicle for the education of young men in the officer classes with a clearly articulated emphasis on delivering a class-specific, moral education (Chandler and Nauright 1999; Mangan 1981; Nauright and Chandler 1996). The notion of rugby union as a vehicle for moral education has endured through significant social changes in the many countries within which it is played and particularly in the schools of the privileged in Australia, the United Kingdom, South Africa and New Zealand (Chandler and Nauright 1999). As the last major sport to accept professionalism it has also long been influenced by the ideals of amateurism, with Chapter 7 suggesting its ongoing influence on coaching practice and coaches' beliefs about what players should learn from a lifetime of participation in the practices of rugby.

The changes in the practice of rugby across the world that followed professionalization have been intensified by its transformation into a highly valuable commercial commodity. The first Rugby World Cup was staged in 1987 as an amateur event, compromised to some extent by 'grey area' payments to New Zealand players (Nauright and Chandler 1996). However, its future was enshrined by the significant profit of £2.3 million it generated and the 300 million television viewers it attracted. For the 2011 RWC staged in New Zealand the television audience grew to 4 billion with profits increasing to £90 million from gross commercial revenue of £142 million. The RWC is now the third biggest sporting event in the world behind the FIFA World Cup and the Olympics and has made a significant contribution to the growth of rugby with 5.5 million men, women and children now playing rugby across the globe.

Players at the elite levels, such as Super 15 rugby, the Heineken Cup, the Rugby Championships, the Six Nations and international rugby, are full-time, well-paid professionals. The professionalization and commodification of rugby have also seen the emergence of coaching as a full-time, professional career. Professional rugby is now a viable career option across the globe and for the better players can set them up for life. This alone has effected a huge change in the pathways players take to playing at the highest levels and the experiences, expectations and attitudes they bring with them when compared to the amateur era in most countries.

For coaches at these levels, success and winning are commercial imperatives, as noted by Mark Ella (2008, p. 53), a former Wallaby captain:

> In the modern era coaches, and players, are expendable. If you don't deliver the results, you can expect to be moved on. Winning is now more than ever connected with profit and a career coach needs to be a winning coach.

The enormous growth in the economic value of rugby in less than two decades has profoundly changed coaching from an amateur pastime to a fully professional career. Since 1995 the coaching and playing landscape has changed remarkably.

2

POSITIVE COACHING FOR YOUTH RUGBY

From its origins in the schools of nineteenth-century England the games ethic spread throughout the British colonies and beyond to encourage an enduring belief in the positive social, moral and personal learning that can arise from playing team sports (Mangan 1981). Despite profound social and economic change across the globe since then, and the diversity of cultural settings across which the notion of the games ethic was disseminated, this belief has proven to be remarkably resilient in continuing to influence thinking about the function and purpose of sport for young people (Nauright and Chandler 1996). It has sustained an assumption that playing team sports promotes positive social and moral development (Light and Harvey 2013).

This enduring belief in the ability of sport to impart valuable lessons for life has, however, been questioned in contemporary societies, with increasing concern over the negative influence young people's participation in sport can have on their moral, social and physical development (see, for example, Light and Harvey 2013; Martens 1982). Many of the problems identified in youth sport can be linked to the influence of elite, professional sport (sport as business) as a highly valuable form of entertainment and the different values driving it when compared to the idea of sport as a form of education. Indeed, the field of professional sport, rugby as business, has been produced by the intrusion of the field of business into the traditional field of 'sport for sport's sake' (Webb *et al.* 2002).

These developments have been accentuated in rugby due to the role it has played in promoting the ideal of sport as a vehicle for moral learning from its origins in the schools of the rising middle classes in nineteenth-century England, and the late but rapid embracing of professionalism across the globe from the mid-1990s (see, for example, Ryan 2008). The rise of rugby as a commercially valuable commodity since 1995 creates tensions with its traditional role as a vehicle for social and moral development, particularly in schools. Elite-level rugby competitions such as the Rugby Championships, the Six Nations and the Rugby World Cup have core values and beliefs (*doxa*) that are very different from those of rugby as a form of moral and social education.

The emphasis on winning at all costs in rugby and other professional media-sport and widely publicized ethical transgressions of sportsmen, sportswomen and coaches, such as cheating, drug use and the use of violence to gain advantage, create justifiable anxiety about its impact upon youth sport (see, for example, Cook and Cole 2001; Kerr and Stirling 2013). These problems are all too evident in accusations of widespread doping in Australia's National Rugby League (NRL) and Australian Football League (AFL) over 2013. Overtraining, specializing too early, overuse injuries, eating disorders, sexual and emotional abuse by coaches, and doping have all been identified as problems plaguing youth sport across a range of countries (see, for example, Bringer *et al.* 2006; Coakley 2001; Kidd and Donnelly 2000; Stirling 2009; Stirling and Kerr 2008).

Despite the negative impact that elite, professional sport can have on youth sport such as rugby, belief in the propensity of sport to teach valuable lessons for life is not completely unjustified (Light and Harvey 2013). A range of positive outcomes is still possible through participation in youth sport (De Martelaer *et al.* 2013), including, but not limited to, pro-social behaviour, psychological adjustment, lower dropout rates from school and lower delinquency rates (Fredricks and Eccles 2006; Larson 2000; Mahoney 2000; Marsh and Kleitman 2002). It is not, however, an automatic outcome of participation in sport. As several authors have emphasized, this learning must be 'taught' rather than automatically 'caught' as a result of just playing sport (Harvey *et al.* 2014; Theodoulides 2003). However, this does not mean that coaches have to choose between focusing on performance or on fostering positive personal contributions towards the moral and personal development of young people. This is because there are pedagogical approaches that can make coaching for performance and promoting positive social, moral and personal development complementary.

Even in highly competitive youth sport such as at the Youth Olympic Games (see Parry and Lucidarme 2013) or in high-stakes youth rugby matches such as in the Sydney GPS (Greater Public Schools) rugby competition, which can attract up to 15,000 spectators to a game, and high-school American football in the United States, improving performance does not have to preclude positive social, moral and personal development.

Positive Pedagogy

The notion of positive coaching used in this chapter is the specific application of Positive Pedagogy (Light 2013c, 2014) to rugby coaching. Positive Pedagogy is pedagogy that maximizes learning to play well while making learning a positive experience that promotes the learners' capacity, motivation and inclination to learn. In addition to this primary aim, it can also foster the development of social skills and moral and ethical values and build positive personal traits such as self-confidence, resilience and creativity as a secondary outcome. Positive Pedagogy is essentially devoid of the negative feedback used in traditional, technique-focused, directive coaching that focuses on reducing or correcting errors in technique. In reference to teaching piano, George (2006) suggests that Positive Pedagogy provides positive learning experiences that foster a love of learning, imagination and problem-solving skills, and that develop active, inquisitive learners instead of passive receivers of knowledge. She argues that taking an approach to teaching that focuses on 'fixing' mistakes deprives learners of the positive experience of the joy of self-discovery that can build self-confidence and autonomy. She also contends that basing learning on the teacher correcting mistakes leads to a lack of learner focus, engagement and motivation.

The positive coaching suggested here for rugby has some alignment with Positive Psychology and the theoretical concepts that it draws on. Positive Psychology was developed in response to concern with an exclusive focus on pathologies in psychology that neglects the positive aspects of life that can 'make life worth living' (Seligman and Csikszentmihalyi 2000, p. 5). At a subjective level it focuses on well-being and satisfaction in the past, happiness and *flow* in the present, and hope and optimism in the future. It aims at building 'thriving individuals, families and institutions', 'finding and nurturing genius' and making 'normal life more fulfilling' (Seligman and Csikszentmihalyi 2000, p. 5). It draws on the concepts of flow and *mindfulness* to redress a perceived preoccupation of psychology with repairing the worst aspects of life by promoting its positive qualities. At an individual level this involves building positive traits such as resilience, courage, confidence, compassion, empathy, creativity and interpersonal skills (Seligman and Csikszentmihalyi 2000).

Varela and colleagues (1991) also draw on the same Buddhist concept of mindfulness that Positive Psychology does to help understand learning from an enactivist perspective. The notion of flow has also been useful in helping to understand the experience of playing sport (see, for example, Jackson and Csikszentmihalyi 1999). Mindfulness refers to an intentionally focused awareness of immediate experience, thoughts, emotions and surroundings grounded in the present moment. In a somewhat similar vein, the concept of flow refers to being absorbed in the experience of action or activity through intense concentration and with a loss of self-awareness as the athlete is lost in the flow of experience. Light and Kentel (2013) suggest that this is very similar to *mushin* as a key cultural concept in the Japanese martial arts (*budo*). From this perspective expertise is expressed as the unity of mind and body in the purity of action informed by years of training but free from the interference of the conscious mind. Flow and mindfulness tend to be interpretations of Eastern concepts from a Western psychological perspective that, while recognizing the importance of the body and experience, tends to emphasize the mind. Cohen (2010, p. 10) argues that these Buddhist concepts have been appropriated, with the meaning of mindfulness being transformed from a gentle, 'attending to one's being and a wakeful awareness to one's doing' to a coping mechanism used for dealing with the stresses of modern living. Nonetheless, they draw attention to and suggest the inseparability of mind and body.

Positive coaching

Over the past few decades, a number of player-centred and enquiry-based approaches to coaching youth sport have emerged that offer alternatives to 'skill drill', technique-focused, directive approaches to coaching. For example, Positive Youth Development Through Sport, instead of seeing youth as a problem to be solved, sees the potential that is waiting to be developed in them (Holt 2008; Larson 2000). There have also been suggestions made for integrating some of these approaches with those more focused on improving performance such as integrating cooperative learning with Tactical Games (Dyson 2005) and Sport Education with TGfU (Alexander and Penney 2005), but these suggestions are more focused on physical education in schools than on club or community-based sport.

There are, however, approaches to coaching focused on improving performance that, although not developed with this in mind, provide consistently positive learning experiences and contribute towards positive social, personal and moral development. The oldest and most established of these approaches is Teaching Games for Understanding (TGfU), first outlined by Bunker and Thorpe in 1982. Later variations of this game-based approach were developed in Australia as Game Sense (den Duyn 1997), in the United States as Tactical Games (Griffin *et al.* 1997) and in Singapore as the Games Concept Approach (GCA) (see, for example, McNeill *et al.* 2004). Similar approaches have also been developed, such as the Tactical-Decision Learning Model (Gréhaigne *et al.* 2005) in France and Play Practice (Launder 2001) in Australia. Of these approaches Game Sense and Play Practice were specifically developed for sport coaching and not physical education.

Although Game Sense and Play Practice focus on performance (developing better games players), their use of learner-centred, enquiry-based pedagogy can foster positive attitudes towards, and confidence in, learning and social, moral and personal development (see, for example, Dyson 2005; Light 2013a). Research on these approaches has focused on performance (see, for example, Mitchell and Oslin 1999; Mitchell *et al.* 1995) and the affective aspects of participation such as fun and delight (Kretchmar 2005; Light 2002; Pope 2005). Less specific attention is being paid to the positive contribution they make towards learning how to learn and the personal, social, moral or ethical development of young learners (see, for an exception, Light 2013a). Light (2014) appropriates Antonovsky's (1979) Sense of Coherence (SoC) model to make coaching and teaching pedagogy positive through making learning *comprehensible*, *manageable* and *meaningful*.

Antonovsky was a medical sociologist who challenged the dichotomy of health and disease to identify the social and affective conditions that promote good health and well-being. The three elements necessary for good health in his model have been appropriated by Light (2013c, 2014) to identify conditions that promote positive experiences of learning. For learning to be *comprehensible* it must make sense for the learner. Learners must know why they are learning something and where it fits, thus leading to deep understanding. In Positive Pedagogy *manageability* refers to achieving the right level of challenge in games and activities. This means that the challenges set by the coach extend the players beyond their 'comfort zone', but that they have the skill and understanding to meet the challenge and can draw on the social resources of teammates and the coach to meet these challenges. *Meaningfulness* is strongly linked to comprehensibility and refers to seeing learning tasks clearly related to the sport and to the interests of the player(s). When something is meaningful it makes challenges in practice sessions interesting, relevant and worthy of emotional commitment while engaging the learner.

The Game Sense approach

As outlined in the previous chapter, Game Sense coaching involves designing a game or sequence of games to achieve particular learning outcomes, asking questions to stimulate thinking and reflection and ensuring that there are opportunities for group discussion, collaboration and the formulation of ideas/solutions that are tested and evaluated. The significant change in pedagogy and the role of the coach involved in Game Sense often proves to be problematic for coaches in rugby and other team sports (see Evans 2006a, 2011; Light and Evans 2010; Roberts 2011). The four core pedagogical features of a Game Sense approach to coaching (Light 2013b) are discussed here with a focus on how they can provide positive coaching while improving game performance. They are that coaching Game Sense involves (1) designing and managing a (physical) learning environment, (2) emphasizing questioning to generate dialogue, (3) providing opportunities for reflection, the collaborative formulation, testing and evaluation of ideas/solutions and (4) developing a supportive socio-moral environment.

Designing the learning environment

Game Sense focuses on the game itself, as a whole, rather than on discrete components of it such as technique (den Duyn 1997; Light 2013b). As complexity thinking suggests, the game is a complex phenomenon (Ovens *et al.* 2013) within which learning to play involves adapting to its dynamics with tactical knowledge, skill execution and decision-making all interconnected as knowledge-in-action. Game Sense helps make learning to play rugby *meaningful* and transferable to the competition match because it occurs within the context of modified games or game-like activities that resemble the real match (Light 2013b). Even when the focus of coaching is more on the development of skill in Game Sense, learning is contextualized with the modified practice games or game-like activities reproducing some conditions of a competition match. Even the simplest activity, focused on improving a skill, must involve (and develop) perception and decision-making (what is happening and what do I do?).

To illustrate this approach we provide a brief example of using it to develop skill in passing and catching. Players can work in groups of four or five in a large grid, passing and catching while running from one end to the other. Once warmed up (mentally and physically) each group turns and returns from the end of the grid/space, running at the next oncoming group. This contextualizes the practice by creating the need for the passer and receiver to find space and use it while passing and catching and making decisions such as when to pass and what type of pass to use, but is simple enough for them to concentrate on skill execution. This requires and develops perception/awareness and decision-making for the execution of skill. In this activity players are still practising passing and catching but, at the same time, developing perception and decision-making by performing skill, *in context*. More demanding passing skills and patterns could be introduced within this context and, as skills improve, the space could be reduced or the number of players increased to apply a little more pressure. This learning is more likely to be transferred to the competition match because the practice context reproduces some of its conditions. This type of activity is also more engaging than standing in lines with players waiting their turn to run and pass.

The physical learning environment is designed to achieve the learning outcomes of the practice session and match the knowledge, abilities and inclinations/interests of the learners. Indeed, 'getting the game right' is of pivotal importance for the coach (Thorpe and Bunker 2008). The Game Sense coach also needs to be able to identify when training activities or games need modifying and undertake appropriate modifications. The right balance between challenge and success that the practice games provide is critical in youth sport coaching. Once the team adjusts to this approach players can be asked for suggestions about what modifications are needed and when to make the game better in terms of enjoyment and improving learning. This typically involves changing the size or shape of the playing space, the number of players and/or the number or type of balls used. For example, let's look at playing a five versus three game of touch or holding-tackle rugby in which the attacking team of five has to score as many tries as possible in a given time and has to retreat to the start for transgressions such as going out, knocking on or a forward pass. Making the space wide and short makes it easier to use the advantage of having two extra players for the attacking team of five players to score. Making the space narrower and longer makes it more difficult to score by passing and running but would open up space for a kick that places the ball behind the defence. If the defence then drops a player back in response, it opens up space for breaching the defence by running and passing and so on. By manipulating the shape and size of the playing space the coach can enhance understanding of how to use an advantage in player numbers.

Over time, as the players adapt to the Game Sense approach they can take on more autonomy and responsibility for their learning while developing their understanding. The coach can encourage them to participate in game modification and to identify when a game needs changing. This approach can also foster creativity through the way in which it provides creative learning environments – physically and socio-morally. It provides opportunities for players to be creative instead of shutting them down by asking learners to conform by reproducing 'correct' technique and predetermined patterns or plays. Early investment in players in this way pays off over time as they become increasingly independent and are empowered through the development of conceptual understanding and learning how to learn.

In the beginning, taking up this approach to coaching rugby is typically very challenging and time consuming but pays off over time (Light 2004). Players who have adapted to the Game Sense approach and feel comfortable enough to speak up and take responsibility for their learning will often make suggestions for practice game modifications to the coach without being asked. For a coach who is used to being in charge and the 'font of all knowledge', this can be confronting. For a Game Sense coach it indicates development of the understanding, independence and confidence in the ability to learn and solve problems that Game Sense aims to promote. These are also qualities and dispositions needed for players to make decisions for themselves on the field during competition matches. Seeing a coach following his/her team up and down the touchline constantly shouting out detailed instructions at the players suggests s/he has not done her/his job.

Learning by playing practice games occurs at non-conscious and conscious levels. It occurs at a non-conscious level through participating in practice games over time as players respond to the dynamics of the game. This is a process of adaptation, as emphasized by Piaget, complexity theory and a core principle of complex learning theory (Davis and Sumara 2003). The coach structures learning instead of trying to determine it with learning within a game context, making it meaningful and transferable to the competition game. This non-conscious learning is enhanced by bringing it to consciousness through the use of language for reflection upon action and dialogue (Light and Fawns 2003). However, even if the questioning used by the coach is ineffective or neglected, valuable, embodied learning that can transfer to competition still arises from playing the right game(s).

Asking questions that generate dialogue and learning

In Game Sense, questioning is used to stimulate thinking and dialogue, reflection and 'the debate of ideas' (Gréhaigne *et al.* 2005). The questions asked thus need to stimulate thinking by being open and generating dialogue rather than shutting down interaction with yes/no answers. This promotes a sense of enquiry, encourages curiosity and leads to the construction of new knowledge and understanding. From a constructivist perspective on learning, the learners need to generate possibilities and a range of answers or solutions rather than leading to predetermined answers that are 'correct' or 'incorrect'. Questions should not limit the possible responses but, instead, expand them (Wright and Forrest 2007). Questioning should not only come from the coach; players who are empowered should also be expected to ask questions of each other and of the coach.

Asking questions that generate learning can be difficult for teachers who are accustomed to telling players what to do (see, for example, McNeill *et al.* 2008). This has also been highlighted in a study on the use of TGfU in youth cricket in the UK (Roberts 2011). Coaches taking on a Game Sense or similar approach often struggle to find the right balance between letting the players get on with learning by playing the game and stopping the action to ask questions. This is something learnt over time but is no different from any coach's need to maintain the right 'pace' of the session and enough action to keep players motivated and engaged. The coach stops the practice session for questioning when s/he wants to make a significant change and/or give teams the chance to formulate solutions that they can test and evaluate. When this is undertaken the coach typically walks around to the different groups/teams encouraging the development of productive dialogue. The coach must *listen to* and think about what the players have to say, show that s/he values their opinions and ideas, and be open to their solutions. To encourage creativity and the joy of discovery the coach should not criticize players or tell them they are 'wrong'. They will know when they are 'wrong' through experience and reflecting upon it and will then find a different solution. This is how we learn anything.

Players who are not accustomed to being asked questions can be uncomfortable with being asked instead of being told and need to understand why they are being asked. It might also be worthwhile taking time to introduce questioning incrementally to avoid the situation where a batter in Roberts' (2011) study on youth cricket threw his bat on the ground and said to his coach, 'please just tell me, it's like being on *Mastermind*' (p. 43). Some of this player frustration can come from the coach asking too many questions. Too little questioning is better than too much (Light 2013a). Most coaches are aware of the need for things to keep moving along and this should operate as a guide as to when to intervene in action to ask questions.

Providing opportunities for formulating, testing and evaluating solutions

When reasonably complex practice games are used the teams should be encouraged to have 'team talks' at appropriate times. This would be introduced after the players have developed a feel for the game and are beginning to engage in it. It would typically follow the pattern of (1) explain the game and ensure they understand, (2) let them play the game, (3) stop and ask a few questions to identify or confirm the problem(s) to be solved, (4) let them gather as a team to formulate strategies or action plans through group dialogue, (5) let them implement the strategy or plan in the game and (6) stop to let them critically reflect upon how it went. If it worked ask them to suggest improvements or modifications. If it didn't work ask them to identify why it didn't work and formulate a new strategy or plan and test it (Light 2013a). This sequence is not prescriptive and is open to change according to the situation at hand.

Once players adapt to the Game Sense approach they often develop an enthusiasm for meeting the challenges presented by the coach or arising from the practice game and look forward to being part of a collective effort that involves not only playing the game, but also rich social interaction focused on a common goal. While the more confident and experienced players may initially dominate proceedings, the less experienced players can often make very valuable contributions when encouraged by the coach through participation in dialogue and the 'debate of ideas' (Gréhaigne *et al.* 2005). Using this approach means that players learn to be better players, to be more independent on the field and to be able to really work together as a team and draw on what each member of the group has to offer to meet the challenges provided in practice and competition matches, making learning *manageable*.

Typically, players will initially need to be encouraged to express opinions within a supportive environment and to see that mistakes are part of learning and improving. The development of trust and dialogue between all team members will also make a significant contribution towards a sense of team. Teams coached in this way should not need the coach shouting instructions from the sideline. How can we really expect young rugby players to be independent on the field if they have not learnt to be independent at practice? This interaction also leads to players understanding and knowing each other, encouraging empathy, compassion, meaningful relationships and care for each other. In a study conducted on the capacity for Game Sense pedagogy to engender more positive attitudes towards cricket among year six primary school children in Australia (Light 2008b), the strongest theme to arise was the extent to which it promoted interpersonal relationships and understanding and consideration of other students within the class.

Developing a supportive environment

The feel of a Game Sense practice session is different from that of a traditional one due to the different sets of relationships it develops between players and between them and the coach. Instead of the master and his/her students the teacher/coach and students/players become more of what Davis and Sumara (1997) refer to as *co-participants* in learning. This means that the coach is learning, or is at least open to learning, along with the players. In a traditional youth sport practice session players can avoid taking responsibility for their learning and hide as passive learners who do not engage. In a Game Sense class we ask them to speak up, come up with ideas, be creative, experiment and take risks. For young players accustomed to being told what to do this can be a daunting expectation that requires an environment in which they are comfortable to 'put their hands up'.

To get players to be actively engaged, take risks and speak up freely coaches have to build a supportive environment where they feel secure enough to take these risks. The same supportive environment can also foster creativity and is a socio-moral environment that DeVries and Zan (1996) argue is required for constructivist-informed teaching. This environment needs to encourage an understanding that making mistakes is an essential part of learning in sport and in any other aspect of life. When tactics don't work in a practice game the reflection and analysis that follow lead to valuable learning that may not have occurred had the players not made a mistake. It is certainly better to make the mistake and learn from it in practice games rather than on the field in a competition match.

This socio-moral environment provides for positive learning experiences and makes them relevant and meaningful beyond sport. This is not an easy task and takes time, just as it takes time for a team to adapt to the Game Sense approach. Empowering players is a positive objective for a coach but those players who fear being embarrassed or humiliated if they make mistakes are likely to be happier to just do as they are told. These children and young players can avoid responsibility for their own learning and if anything goes wrong blame it on the coach. For players like this, coaches need to be aware of the profound change in attitude towards learning that they are seeking to accomplish by taking a Game Sense approach.

Features of Game Sense that provide positive learning experiences

Game Sense pedagogy that emphasizes taking a positive approach allows coaches to improve team and player performance while fostering positive approaches to learning and the development of positive personal traits and social and moral learning. There is no need to compromise one aspect of learning for the other as they are intertwined in the delivery of learning as a whole-person experience. The positive personal, moral and social development arising from learning through a Game Sense approach was not consciously considered when TGfU and Game Sense were first proposed. Bunker and Thorpe (1982) developed TGfU to redress problems they identified with traditional technical approaches producing technically proficient players who could not play the game well. In a later publication on TGfU, Thorpe *et al.* (1986) recognized the links with positive personal and social development but this was not their focus. Likewise, the publication of the Game Sense handbook (den Duyn 1997) makes little mention of positive psycho-social or moral development as an aim of these approaches.

Game Sense takes an holistic approach that focuses on the game as a whole entity rather than breaking it up into discrete components such as techniques or skills. It recognizes and accounts for learning as a complex, whole-person and social process of adaptation (Light 2008a). From this perspective, technique or skill (technique performed in context) is not separate from the game. Just as words are given meaning in language by the context, effective skill execution is dependent upon the specific context within which it is done and how it meets the demands of the situation. There is thus no ideal 'correct' form of a technique because it must be appropriate to the unique physical situation at the time. It is also shaped by the tactical situation at the time and the 'decisional background' as a reference to conditions such as the agreed strategy for the match and the significance of the match for the season (see Chapter 3). There is thus no point in pursuing 'mastery' of the technique through a process that requires providing negative feedback as the player attempts to reproduce it.

A coach can be on warm terms with his/her players and be very understanding but, essentially, the feedback used in a technical approach is negative. This is a particular problem with the players who are less skilful and less confident. Players can feel exposed and, in some cases, even humiliated (see, for example, Light and Georgakis 2005). No matter how technical practice is organized, there is also invariably some sense of being under the critical gaze of the coach and other players in the practice session. Although differences in skill level and understanding will be evident in game-based practice the players are far less visible. They are part of the game and tied in with other players in their team.

Locating learning within games avoids the constant correction of technique and provides for enjoyment, or even delight (Kretchmar 2005), when playing games and increased motivation at all levels (see Evans 2012). Games are essentially social activities that both require and develop social interaction at an articulated level and an unarticulated, corporeal level. Interaction during games occurs through what Light and Fawns (2003) describe as the conversation between teammates and between opposing teams achieved through the grammar of movement. In any game players communicate through this movement and through gestures and verbal communication during play.

Just as one needs to use language in context to communicate and not merely recite vocabulary, players develop as good players by using skills, tactical understanding and decision-making (and other aspects of play) in the competition match. This does not mean neglecting skills. Instead, it develops a deeper understanding of how skills fit into a game and how they are interrelated with other aspects of play. In Game Sense, practice games are not used to identify and develop predetermined skills as in the Tactical Games approach (Griffin *et al.* 1997). As long as the skill level is good enough to allow the practice game or activity to progress, it is adequate because skill is improved through playing practice games that increase in difficulty as the players improve. When skill performance is holding back the game the coach can modify the game. Alternatively s/he can stop the game and do a little skill-focused work by tightening the structuring of learning, which involves performing the skill within a context that, to some extent, represents some of the complexity of the 'real' match (Light 2013b).

There is also the deep, whole-person, engagement that players can experience and learn through while playing games with the right level of challenge that Jackson and Csikszentmihalyi (1999) refer to as *flow*. Flow refers to a single-minded immersion in an activity (in this case, a game), seen as a powerful means of engaging emotion in learning. While any player in a practice game might feel frustration, disappointment or a momentary sense of letting the team down at times, the overall experience of participating in training games is positive if the game has an appropriate balance between challenge and opportunities for success. It is here that the players are extended but can *manage* the challenge by drawing on their own capacities and the social resources of the group. When appropriately extended, players can be completely immersed in the flow of the game and achieve a state in which emotion, mind and body are united. When the game is seen as a complex phenomenon, as complexity thinking suggests it should (Ovens *et al.* 2013), this state of harmony can be seen as the experience of being immersed or even consumed in the game as a single, dynamic entity.

Recently it has been suggested that the Japanese cultural concept of *mushin* offers another means of conceptualizing learning as being a process of reducing the gap between mind and body (Light and Kentel 2013). *Mushin* is a key cultural concept in the Japanese martial arts with traditional training methods aimed at achieving mind–body unity in action and removing the interference of the conscious mind (see, for example, McFarlane 1990). Even at the highest levels of professional, elite sport, practice games motivate players who find them enjoyable and engaging as is evident in the use of Game Sense approach adopted by the New Zealand All Blacks (Evans 2006b, 2012).

When participating in practice games player inadequacies are not highlighted because they are part of the game and are developed within the game. When the games are more complex they can also contribute through discussions and 'team meetings' in which they collectively develop tactics that all players can contribute to. Negative experiences of being exposed during technical approaches in physical education were very evident in a number of studies conducted on pre-service, generalist primary school teachers (see, for example, Light 2002; Light and Georgakis 2005). In these studies the pre-service primary school teachers' responses to the Game Sense approach were overwhelmingly positive and, in some cases, very emotional. In particular, many females felt relief and described positive experiences such as feeling a sense of joy, being empowered by understanding the sport and being able to contribute to the team effort.

The emphasis on questioning is a key feature of Game Sense that is used to structure and shape thinking and understanding. The questions do not seek yes/no answers and in positive coaching there are no wrong answers. If the coach feels an answer or suggestion is 'wrong' s/he asks more probing questions instead of telling the player s/he is wrong. When teams in small-sided games arrive at tactical plans the coach may be convinced will fail, s/he should let them apply them and reflect on why they did not work (or did work) as a positive learning experience. This is an important part of Game Sense coaching where the coach builds a trusting and supportive environment in which players feel confident enough to offer ideas and possible solutions without fear of being humiliated. It is also central to developing a collective sense of team as something stronger and more meaningful than the mere sum of its parts (players) and can make a significant contribution towards building self-esteem and satisfaction among the less confident and less experienced players in a youth team.

Conclusion

Just playing team sports such as rugby does not necessarily teach young people teamwork and other positive social, moral and personal learning typically associated with team games (Long and Sanderson 2001). Nor will it necessarily help them learn how to learn, solve problems, find creative solutions and experience the joy of discovery. Having them actually learn teamwork and achieve the other positive learning outcomes that sport is assumed to promote requires effective interaction, developing respect for others, tolerance and an understanding of how each player can make a contribution towards getting the best team performance. The end aim may well be getting the best performance from the team (in small-sided practice games or in competition matches), but the process of achieving this through Game Sense pedagogy can also teach valuable social and moral lessons (Harvey *et al.* 2014; Light 2013b). It can also develop positive personal traits such as compassion, resilience, self-confidence, creativity and being prepared to compromise on personal desires for the benefit of the team. These are traits that are needed to get the best possible performance out of a youth sport team, but that also foster the learning of values, social skills, morals and psycho-social personal traits of great importance well beyond sport.

Of all the children and young people playing rugby around the globe only a select few will move up into professional or elite-level rugby as adults to make a career from it. For all the young people who grow up playing rugby (including those few who move into elite, professional sport) their experiences of youth sport should make a positive and lasting contribution towards their development into healthy, well-adjusted adults. The use of positive coaching can make a valuable contribution to this. Influenced by the many other complex factors shaping young people's experience of and learning in sport, it can make a significant contribution towards them developing a positive attachment to sport and also positive psycho-social skills, attributes and personal traits that are so important in helping people lead positive and rewarding lives.

3

IMPROVING DECISION-MAKING IN SEVENS RUGBY

(with Alain Mouchet)

The annual State of Origin series fiercely contested between the two states of New South Wales and Queensland is the pinnacle of Australian rugby league. With the series even at one game each in 2012 and scores tied at 20 points each and 6 minutes remaining in the third game, half back Cooper Cronk kicked a field goal to win the game 21–20 and clinch the series for Queensland. Reflecting upon what is now part of State of Origin folklore (Gould 2013) Cronk captures the coming together of mind, body, soul and the moment in what Gould describes as a fluid, almost Zen state by saying that, 'There was no noise in my head . . . every sinew in my body came together in one perfect whole' (Gould 2013, p. 58). Cronk's reflection upon his field goal illustrates the complex and holistic nature of decision-making in competition matches and the limitations of separating mind from body and player from environment. Gould also suggests how much more is involved in decision-making under pressure than the idea of the conscious mind controlling the body: 'When we are being completely free of our own expectations the body extends into its natural form without impediment. And things can happen' (2013, p. 58). This is one example of expertise in action – of mind and body coming together to enact years of experience and learning.

In this chapter we suggest how an holistic approach to coaching can foster the expert decision-making demonstrated by Cronk in sevens rugby. We argue that traditional approaches for improving decision-making in team sports are unable to recognize and account for its complexity and its physically, socially and culturally situated nature. In the fast-paced, open and highly dynamic context of play in sevens there is a particular need to develop players with vision, game sense and creativity who are consistently able to make the right decisions in matches. We first examine some of the current thinking on decision-making in team sports and move on to explore the complex and situated nature of decision-making in team sports to suggest how learning to make decisions in matches can be shaped and improved through holistic coaching.

The complexity of play in sevens rugby

Sevens matches comprise dynamic environments to which players must constantly adapt, and that they must make sense of and negotiate by making effective decisions and executing skills in appropriate ways. While this is also the case for fifteen-a-side rugby, the demands on players to make quick and appropriate decisions are greater in sevens due to its highly dynamic nature, the space available, the faster pace of matches and their shorter duration. The argument for adopting holistic, game-based coaching for rugby (see Light *et al.* 2014a) is even stronger in sevens where players must instantly adapt to changing conditions and have acute awareness and decision-making ability. Instead of trying to reduce the complexity of play to a number of distinct components, decision-making in sevens rugby is best improved by players practising making decisions in dynamic physical environments that replicate match conditions. Practice must replicate some of this sometimes 'chaotic' environment and the interaction between thinking and doing (Light 2005) involved in decision-making.

This chapter draws on Game Sense pedagogy and complex learning theory (CLT – Davis and Sumara 2003) to make suggestions for improving decision-making ability in sevens rugby by adopting an holistic approach to coaching. The term 'holistic' is used here in reference to the connections between the learner (player), the match (comprising of both teams) and the larger socio-cultural environments within which matches are played. Decisions are not made in a disembodied mind but, instead, by the whole person with their intellectual, emotional, affective and physical dimensions inseparable and intertwined as a complex organism. Rather than reduce sevens matches to the performance of discrete skills, we see matches as being complex phenomena, as is suggested by complexity thinking and informs complex learning theory (see Light and Kentel 2013; Ovens *et al.* 2013).

Research on the nature of decision-making in team sports

Most research on decision-making in sport has been conducted from a cognitivist perspective, which views it as an intrapersonal, linear process of inputting, processing and acting upon information (see Johnson 2006; Memmert and Furley 2007; Paques *et al.* 2005). This involves adopting 'a closed systems analysis, typical of the classical scientific method founded on a determinate world view' (Glimcher, cited in Araújo *et al.* 2006, p. 654).

The 'expertise approach' suggests the acquisition of knowledge as players progress along a continuum from 'novice' to 'expert' (Cushion 2011) to identify the types and amount of practice that seem to be needed to reach an expert level by comparing the practice histories of novice and expert performers. From an holistic perspective this does not adequately account for the complex range of factors that influence decision-making and of which many are very difficult to measure and/or control in ecologically valid situations. Laboratory testing is not able to account for the complexity of decision-making in team sports such as rugby, because it attempts to reduce the complexity of it as it occurs in matches to study aspects that are often not directly related to the processes involved in decision-making in real matches (Williams and Hodges 2005).

In response to dissatisfaction with the limitations of the information-processing perspective in both methodology and epistemology (Araújo *et al.* 2006; Araújo *et al.* 2009; Passos *et al.* 2008), the ecological view of decision-making is used to study how an individual reacts to changes in his/her environment. It seeks to identify how different action possibilities persist, emerge and dissolve as a consequence of laws of motion and time evolution of observable quantities (see, for example, Araújo *et al.* 2006). It sees decision-making as being a result of the interaction between the individual, his/her environment and the task at hand (Araújo *et al.* 2006). From an ecological perspective decision-making occurs through the management of the various degrees of freedom and internal and external properties that provide the system with information. It is based upon the assumption that, 'the capacity to be sensitive and attuned to ecological constraints . . . underpins successful decision-making in sport' (Araújo *et al.* 2006, p. 661).

Wicker (2002) argues that the ecological approach is limited in its ability to capture the complexity of everyday reality and, although it offers some ecologically valid explanations of decision-making behaviour in sport, research conducted from this perspective has been largely restricted to laboratory settings (see Araújo *et al.* 2006). From an holistic perspective this is a serious limitation because decision-making is situated in, and is specific to, the immediate game situation. It is also located within a socio-cultural context and shaped by previously existing knowledge as the 'decisional background' (Mouchet 2005).

Mouchet (2008) identified variations between rugby players' competence in being able to draw on 'decisional registers' (pre-agreed or decided strategies or tactics) during emergent decision-making in action and decision-making where deliberative (reflexive) cognitive activity prevails. He argues that this competence constitutes tactical adaptation to opportunities that the ball carrier can seize upon during the match. He also distinguishes between decision-making 'at-action' (at the point where attack meets defence) and rational decision-making made when there is more time, well before action by using the terms 'consciousness-in-action' (pre-reflective experience, implicit mode of reflection) and 'reflective consciousness' (conceptualized knowledge, judgements or explanations about a process).

Time-to-action and decision-making

According to Mouchet (2005, 2008), reflective, rational consciousness is dominant in situations where the player has more time, and when he/she is under 'temporal pressure' consciousness-in-action is dominant. Decisions made 'at-action' can also be influenced by the player's subjectivity because he/she reconstructs them in situations according to his/her perception and his/her own personal (subjective) logic. The relationship between conscious (reflective) cognition and embodied thinking (pre-reflective cognition) and the influence of the player's subjectivity depends upon the time available between making the decision and enacting it as 'time-to-action' (Gréhaigne *et al.* 1999).

Gréhaigne and colleagues use the notion of time-to-action to distinguish between strategy and tactics, divided into the three stages of micro, meso and macro. Strategy is formulated on a macro level with ample time available, tactical decisions used to achieve strategy are made closer to the action of the game at a meso level, with 'emergent' decision-making occurring at a micro level *at* the point of action. For example, this might be the point at which a player catches a high ball under pressure of a tackle and must instantly react.

Player learning

An holistic perspective suggests that just examining the 'intrapersonal' aspects of decision-making is limited because it cannot account for the 'interpersonal' aspects of decision-making and the match as a complex phenomenon. A team, and the match itself, are more than the sum of their component parts (players) and can be seen to be a whole entity – a complex phenomenon (Ovens *et al.* 2013). The application of social constructivist theories of learning in research and writing on games teaching and coaching over the past decade (see, for example, Rovegno and Dolly 2006; Wallian and Chang 2007) and, more recently, of complex learning theory (see Light 2008a; Light and Kentel 2013) and complexity thinking (see Ovens *et al.* 2013) further encourages views of decision-making as being a complex interpersonal process that involves distributed thinking and is highly context dependent. Organism and environment can also be seen to be inseparable (Dewey 1938) and this has been applied to the physical settings of team sports and games (see Quay and Stolz 2014). Player learning is socially constructed and deeply embedded within social and cultural contexts, including the relationship between the coach, the athlete and the environment (Cushion 2011).

Perception

The existential phenomenology of Merleau-Ponty (see 1962) challenges the notion of perception as a linear process of inputting and processing information by suggesting that what we actually perceive is shaped by our experiences as a process of interpretation. Others such as Clancey (cited in Lenzen *et al.* 2009) and Gibson (2002) also challenge the notion of perception as being merely the transfer of information, to suggest that perception and action occur simultaneously. From a philosophy of perception perspective, Gibson sees perception as being an animal's experience of the environment surrounding its body with perception and action being inseparable.

This notion of perception and action occurring simultaneously, and of embodied learning occurring through engagement with the environment, provides a key to understanding and enhancing decision-making in sevens. It suggests the importance of structuring or manipulating the physical environment for developing decision-making so that players can learn the appropriate 'habits-of-action' (Quennerstedt 2013) as a process of adaptation (Piaget 1974). Put simply, players improve their decision-making ability in team games by making decisions in contexts that replicate the conditions of competition matches.

Complex learning theory

Complex learning theory (CLT) draws on complexity theory and the core ideas underpinning different forms of constructivism to reject the idea that learning is an 'internal representation of an external reality' and to encapsulate the notions of the body's role in learning where action and cognition are intertwined. Davis and Sumara (2003) suggest that constructivist theories of learning share three broad and interrelated elements. These have recently been simplified by Light and Kentel (2013) as being assumptions that learning is:

- an ongoing process of *adaptation*;
- a *social* process;
- an *interpretive* process.

The interpersonal or 'social' aspects of learning, through which individuals embody the habits and culture of their environment in a spontaneous, non-conscious and embodied way, play a significant role in learning in and through sport (Light 2005). A CLT perspective, therefore, has implications for how we understand learning in team sports and the ways in which we can teach or coach decision-making. It suggests that a repositioning of the coach and his/her role in learning is required for players to be afforded the opportunity to make 'emergent' or 'at-action' decisions and be provided with opportunities to reflect on experience, make meaning of it and reconstruct knowledge while also reconstructing themselves through manipulation of the 'story of self' (Cushion 2011, p. 175).

Coaching to enhance decision-making

Playing in sevens matches involves an awareness of what is going on in a very dynamic environment, reading the conditions and constantly making decisions on and off the ball. The complex and dynamic nature of team sports such as rugby sevens makes game-based approaches (GBA) to coaching such as Game Sense highly suitable and able to make significant improvements because of the ways in which they emphasize context (Allison and Thorpe 1997; Gray and Sproule 2011; Harvey *et al.* 2010b). Decisions made in sevens are situated not only within the immediate match situation of games but also within the larger context of the game such as the pre-agreed strategy and the importance of the game in the competition, which we refer to in this chapter as the 'decisional background'. They are also situated within wider, social contexts that include the social-interactive and institutional-cultural aspects of the match (see, for example, MacPhail *et al.* 2008). Enhancing decision-making thus requires consideration of how wider social contexts influence it as well as managing the physical-perceptual aspects of games as learning environments.

Coaching for decision-making in rugby needs to focus on designing and managing an effective learning environment that replicates certain conditions in which decisions have to be made in competitive matches, while considering the wider game context and the wider social and cultural contexts influencing it. The coach needs to manipulate the physical game environment to suit the purpose of the practice activity and to find the right degree of challenge. Typically this would involve adjusting the ratio of defenders to attackers, the size and shape of the space they are working in, and the time available to make decisions. The activities provided in this chapter can be seen as being relatively simple but are only starting points for learning that the Game Sense coach would develop and modify in collaboration with his/her players to suit the purpose of the session and the skills and abilities of the players.

Learning to make effective decisions in a rugby match (fifteen-a-side or sevens) requires learning through engagement with the environment and not through being told what to do (Dewey 1916/97). This suggests that practice-game design is the key to improving decision-making (Almond and Launder 2010; Thorpe and Bunker 2008). The coach thus needs to be able to plan to provide opportunities for players to improve their decision-making by designing appropriate practice games.

Being placed in such (physical) learning environments can improve awareness/perceptual ability, tactical knowledge, decision-making and informed skill execution at a non-conscious level and as a process of adaptation. Good coaching pedagogy can accelerate this learning by bringing thinking up to a conscious level for discussion and reflection. This would involve players dealing with the challenges of the game long enough to get a feel for what is going on and to respond in embodied ways, which is the initial mode of learning. Typically, the coach would stop the game at an appropriate moment for questioning to stimulate critical reflection, interaction and collaborative problem solving, bringing learning to consciousness.

Improving decision-making involves providing players with the opportunity to formulate ideas that they test in the practice game and reflect upon to refine positive tactical responses and eliminate those that didn't work. Reflecting the social constructivist perspective on learning originating in the work of Vygotsky, this process highlights the central role of language in learning that requires conscious, rational processing, but on a collective basis. This creates a conversation in learning between non-conscious action and rational, conscious thinking through language (Light and Fawns 2003).

Drawing on motor learning theory, some research on TGfU and the Tactical Games approach identifies how the first stage of learning involves players (or students) being able to recognize and articulate what should happen in a game and what they should do, referred to as declarative knowledge (for example, see

McPherson and Kernodle 2003). This is developed through playing the practice game, reflecting upon experience and using language to discuss and 'debate' ideas (Gréhaigne *et al.* 2005). However, this is only a stage in learning because, as Light and Fawns (2003) remind us, 'knowing the game' means being able to demonstrate knowledge-in-action (Schön 1983). Effective coaching in decision-making must then be manifested in good player decision-making on the field in competitive matches. Effective coaching in decision-making must provide opportunities for players to engage in the 'ongoing conversation' of games that involves the interplay between action and language (Light and Fawns 2003).

A practical example of coaching to develop decision-making

We ground our discussion about developing decision-making in sevens rugby in a practical example, provided below, as a means of better connecting theory to practice and establishing a dialectic between them. While theory can inform practice, practice should inform the ongoing development of theories on coaching (Light and Wallian 2008).

The activities and practice games provided here may seem relatively simple but should act as the basis from which the coach and players develop and modify the activities and games to suit the skills, experience and dispositions of the players and the aims of the session. Playing any team sport always involves the manipulation of space and time as the 'big ideas' (Fosnot 1996) or fundamental concepts that the players need to understand. The coach's job in this approach is to manage a creative learning environment by manipulating a range of variables at hand to provide the right level of challenge. This is essential for quality learning and motivation (see Chapter 2) and for providing practice games in which players can experience a state of 'flow' (see Jackson and Csikszentmihalyi 1999). The variables that the coach manages to maximize learning include the size and shape of the playing space, the relative numbers of players in either or both teams, and the rules.

All training activities and practice games should involve some awareness and decision-making to allow them to transfer to the competition match. The session begins with a simple passing activity that acts as a mental and physical warm-up; this leads into a quick decision-making activity which is followed by a more complex practice game. These activities create a dynamic physical learning environment that demands and develops 'at-action' decision-making, awareness, communication, the appropriate execution of flexible skills, and adaptation to game conditions.

Activity 1. Triangle rugby

This game is a reasonably standard game of modified rugby with an uneven number of players favouring the attacking team to facilitate scoring, but adjusted as the players adapt to the game to attain the level of challenge desired by the coach.

The distinguishing feature of this game is that it is played in a triangle-shaped field providing a try line 5 metres wide at one end and 50 metres wide at the other end. This provides changing lateral space for the attacking team to use and take advantage of its extra players as conditions to which the players must adapt and under which they must make appropriate tactical decisions.

The aim of the game is to score a try with modified rules for tackling that could include two-handed touches or soft tackles in which the forward movement of the ball carrier after contact is limited. Rules for limiting competition for the ball at the tackle could also be introduced. This game is aimed at developing running and passing skills and related decision-making, meaning that kicking is initially not allowed but can be introduced later. The game might start with 7 v. 3 but be adjusted as the game develops, moving to a 6 v. 4 and then 5 v. 5. The space used is another tool that the coach can use to fine-tune the game. With ten players it could be played across a normal rugby field with the base of the triangle being between the normal goal line and the 22-metre line (22 metres) and the nipped apex of the triangle at the opposite sideline for a normal rugby field (5 metres).

The attacking team begins at the apex, 5 metres in front of its goal line, and attempts to progress towards the triangle's base and to score a try with the least number of phases. When there is an infringement such as a knock on, forward pass or going out, the attacking team must return to the start and restart its number of phases with a normal offside rule. If the defending side infringes the attacking team is awarded a 5 or 10-metre gain. If the attacking team scores at the base of the triangle they maintain possession and reverse direction to attack towards the apex of the triangle with space decreasing as they move downfield.

Players should be rotated through attacking and defending teams, and should be asked to identify challenges in attack and defence and to arrive at possible solutions that they test and evaluate. This should initially be done in 'team talks' by the attacking and defending teams but later pulled together as a whole group. Players will soon identify the need for conservative play in attack when space is tight to maintain possession for when they move towards open space where they can attack more freely. When moving from the base towards the apex they will typically try to make a break early. These broader ideas could be seen as strategy (Gréhaigne *et al.* 1999) that more specific tactics and skills might be employed to achieve.

Activity 2. Attacking the opposition line

This game initially has more players in the attacking team to provide gaps and possibilities for two-on-one situations (e.g. 7 v. 5), but this is adjusted to get the desired level of challenge as players adapt to it (as in the previous game). It is played between the halfway line and goal line using one sideline and cones set down the middle of a normal rugby field to play in a space one quarter the size of a normal field. Play begins with a scrum near the 22-metre line, towards the centre of the field, with the attacking team given a predetermined number of plays within which it has to score but having to restart where the game began if committing an infringement. The coach determines what type of tackling is to be used but he/she should allow the ball carrier to be brought to ground.

The coach structures opportunities and challenges for attack from the set piece (scrum) by directing the defensive team but without the attacking team knowing what the change will be. For example, this might involve one defender rushing up early and out of alignment. This puts pressure on one attacker but produces a gap that the attacking team should be able to recognize and respond to effectively. Another option is for the coach or another person to give the defending players numbers so that when a player's number is called he/she immediately drops to the ground. This eliminates a defender and creates an attacking opportunity that the attacking team should be able to see and take advantage of.

Prior to the beginning of each play the attacking team has a discussion to arrive at a quick plan of attack from the set play and options for their responses to the defence in the second and third plays. When the players have adapted to playing in this restricted space let them play using the full width of the field and ask questions in breaks about the different strategies needed to adapt to the increased space available. With both these practice games the coach constantly adjusts the level of challenge and the possible learning outcomes by adjusting the rules, numbers of players or size and shape of the space used, or can ask the players to suggest changes to make the games interesting, enjoyable and relevant. S/he also provides ample opportunity for dialogue and interaction within teams and within the group, and for both individual and collective reflection and evaluation of performance.

Enhancing learning

Learning in these practice games occurs through adapting to the conditions of the game, reflecting on decisions made as a group, formulating ideas and solutions to the problems identified, testing them and evaluating them. Punctuating play with tactical time-outs (Turner 2005), debate and discussion (Gréhaigne *et al.* 2005) and questioning will ensure that the coach can facilitate the development of decision-making. Questioning should be open-ended and generate thinking to encourage creativity and the emergence of possibilities (Wright and Forrest 2007).

Rather than telling a player that he/she should have passed to an unmarked support player, or criticizing players for making mistakes, the coach should take a more positive approach by asking questions. For example s/he might ask, *Do you think that was a good option? What other options did you have? Which one do you think might have been better? Why? Did anyone see other options? How does doubling the width of the field affect the tactics you used (in attack and defence)?* Accepting that making mistakes is a central part of learning the coach should encourage players to be creative and take risks. When they try ideas that don't work the coach might ask questions such as, *Why didn't that work? What could you do differently to make that work?* This allows for more positive experiences of practice for the players that can build confidence to learn and improve individually and as a team.

To add complexity the coach can construct a match scenario as the decisional background that will influence the risks taken. For example, if on the one hand the scenario is that the team is down by 5 points with 3 minutes remaining, the attacking team would be expected to adopt high-risk options that can offer high returns. On the other hand, if the scenario is that the team is 5 points in front of the opposition with 3 minutes remaining, the options and tactics adopted would likely be conservative and low risk. Decisions made in the first game of the season are likely to be different from decisions made in the same immediate situation in the grand final of the season.

This approach gets players thinking and engaging intellectually and can be built upon by encouraging small-team talks or whole-team discussions, giving the players ownership of tasks and empowering them to make their own decisions on the field (den Duyn 1997). However, learning this way takes time to be enacted in competition matches (Gréhaigne *et al.* 2005) and sometimes the pressure on coaches to get wins may outweigh their desire or ability to commit to developing team performance over time (Light 2004). This relatively simple practice game develops awareness as the players improve in picking up cues and responding to them with opportunities for decision-making under temporal pressure provided by the coach by adjusting the pressure to suit the players and his/her intentions; however, initially, players may have to be encouraged to look for, and see, opportunities as questions that stress external cues (Magill 1998).

The coach could directly determine what changes take place or provide a number of set changes that the defensive team can choose from themselves. Alternatively, and to increase player autonomy, they could have turns at running the activity. The players in attack should be given time to reflect upon the decisions they make 'at-action' as individuals but in relation to the team's tactics used to implement its agreed strategy. Depending upon the approach the coach wants to take, this could be directed by the coach or left up to the players to quickly discuss when they feel the need to. This reflection should lead to discussions about the options taken and how to improve both decision-making and skill execution in each case. The important point here is the need for the coach to ensure that learning is active and player-centred by facilitating it instead of attempting to determine it.

Coaches who want more control over decisions made in games could offer the players a limited number of options for a particular situation. This is a case of tightening the structuring of action and is along the lines of the non-linear, constraints-led approach in which the coach uses constraints to 'facilitate the emergence of functional movement patterns and decision-making behaviour' (Renshaw *et al.* 2010, p. 120). Although this approach sees the learner as being a complex system, it uses constraints to produce predetermined goal-directed movements. This could simply involve the coach asking players to choose one of two or three options, making the playing space long and narrow, or short and wide, increasing the number of defenders to apply more pressure or redistributing the defenders.

The decisions made in attack in a 'real' match are also shaped by predetermined strategy and larger contextual factors such as the score line, time remaining in the game and the team's position in the league as the decisional background (Mouchet 2005). To bring these into play in practice games the coach can decide on specific game scenarios in regard to such things as comparative scores, time remaining and the importance of the match in the season. This is what Launder (2001) considers with his 'action fantasy games', where players are presented with an 'action fantasy game' card that details the team's history, such as winning record, position in the league, titles won and so on, as well as setting the specific game scenario. These game scenarios should have a strong influence on the risk that players take in the practice game.

Coaching through practice games replicates aspects of competitive matches that the coach can easily manipulate to change the focus of the learning or the pressure under which the attacking team operates. It involves a degree of embodied responses 'at-action' (Mouchet 2005) due to the lack of time available to make decisions (micro), but the lead-in time before attack meets defence (meso) allows for more 'reflective consciousness' (Vermersch 2000). The structured reflection, discussion and formulation of ideas involves rational and conscious processing that can accelerate improvement in decision-making and is far enough away from the action that it could be seen to be macro-level decision-making (Gréhaigne *et al.* 1999). The key features of this activity are the central role that the physical environment plays in learning and the player-centred approach used that makes the players active learners who are responsible for their own learning. The coach designs and manipulates the environment to achieve learning outcomes, to adjust the balance of success and challenge and to suit the skills, attitudes and knowledge of the players. This management requires attention to be focused on the progress of learning and sensitivity as to how the team and the individuals in it are responding to the demands of the practice game. This management of the game is punctuated with periods of time for questioning, tactical time-outs and player debates about strategy and tactics with reference to the players' decisional background. This, and the ability to identify and understand how learning is progressing, are not only a significant challenge for any coach but are also the key to providing high-quality coaching.

Training games or activities need to match the skills, experience and capacities of the players and to be able to meet the objectives of the coach. This begins with the design of the game, which could be the responsibility of the coach, done through collaboration between coach and players or could even be a task set by the coach for players when they have had enough experience with this style of coaching. As training progresses coaches experienced in this approach should be alert to the progress of the players' decision-making and have modifications at hand to mould the basic game to the requirements of the situation (Light 2013b). Coaches working with players experienced in this approach might even ask them for suggestions about when modifications are needed and what they should be.

Discussion

In the suggested activities the central task facing the coach is the construction and management of an appropriate physical learning environment in the form of the practice game. S/he also needs to provide an appropriate social learning environment in which players feel free to experiment and to see making mistakes as an essential part of learning if reflected upon individually and collectively. It is informed by an holistic view of decision-making that accounts for its inherent complexity, its inseparability from its immediate physical environment and how it is shaped by larger socio-cultural contexts. The learning process involved through playing these practice games would occur primarily at a non-conscious or embodied level as a process of adaptation to a dynamic environment in which they draw on existing knowledge and skills. Through these experiences players would improve their decision-making ability, perception and the ability to pick up cues (Kirk and MacPhail 2002) and to respond to them as interrelated aspects of play and as a process of adaptation. From this perspective there is separation neither of skill execution from tactical understanding and decision-making nor of the learner(s) and from what is learnt.

The closer this training game is to the real game the more likely the skill(s) and capacities worked on are to transfer to the competition match (Launder 2001). The key here is to find the right level of challenge by managing the practice game and typically building the demands on players and pressure as the players adapt to the game. From another perspective, the knowledge and skills developed in this way are given meaning by the authenticity of the context within which they are learned. The extent to which the training game replicates 'real' game conditions (its authenticity) would depend on how the coach manipulates the environment, the complexity of the situation and the degree of pressure that he/she places players under when making decisions. The design and manipulation of the physical learning environment is a critical skill for coaches when taking an holistic approach such as that suggested in this chapter (Almond and Launder 2010; Thorpe and Bunker 2008) with Turner (2014) offering some ideas for designing these games. As the players adjust to being empowered they can and should have input into how the learning environment should be manipulated.

With elite-level players, coaches could provide a tighter structure that reduces options to those that the coach nominates and wants to work on, but with younger players s/he might encourage creativity by being open to any idea suggested by them because as much can be learnt from mistakes at training as successful responses (Light 2013a). Indeed, mistakes are essential for learning and to provide a supportive socio-moral environment in which players are prepared to take risks and experiment without being criticized or even ridiculed, and this is important for establishing a positive culture of learning as outlined in Chapter 2. This environment supports collaborative enquiry in which players identify and solve problems and where they can make *constructive* errors (DeVries and Zan 1996).

In the coaching that we suggest here language, social interaction and the capacity to critically reflect upon experience are central to learning/improving.

Conclusion

The ideas presented here for enhancing decision-making in sevens rugby emphasize player learning through engagement with the learning environment, reflection, dialogue and collaboration. The approach suggested in this chapter accounts for the complexity of decision-making 'at-action' while also facilitating players' learning in how to improve it. It reflects a view of learning as a complex process that can be enhanced or facilitated but not determined. Based upon an holistic view of players and of competitive matches as complex phenomena, the coaching we suggest enhances learning through engagement with the environment instead of direct instruction from the coach. Improvements in decision-making will emerge from playing well-designed training games but the pedagogy employed has a significant influence on the quality of learning that unfolds from playing these games. For some coaches this is likely to challenge their beliefs and practices. For others it may stimulate thinking about incorporating some of our ideas into their training regimes, while for some it may well seem to be common sense. There is no attempt here to tell rugby coaches what to do but, in presenting a particular perspective on coaching based upon recent research developments, we do hope to engage them in the debate that complex learning theory suggests is necessary for learning.

4

COACH DEVELOPMENT

A process of ongoing learning

Increasing government investment in improving the quality of coaching across a wide range of sports and levels of competition in developed countries reflects the importance placed upon coaching and coach development. This is particularly evident in the UK and Canada, where there has been substantial government investment in the revision of coach education programmes (Lyle 2007). For example, launched in 2008, the UK Coaching Framework aims to improve coaching in all areas of sport to make the country a world leader in sport coaching. It aims to make coaching a professionally regulated vocation through the establishment of a long-term coach development system that includes coach education and regular professional development.

Despite substantial government commitment to improving the quality of coaching in the UK, Canada and other countries there are significant challenges to be met in achieving this goal. Many of these challenges are related to the powerful influence of experience on coaches' practice and the relative ineffectiveness of formal coach education. Research and writing on coach development suggests that experience has a profound influence on how coaches coach and their dispositions towards innovation (see, for example, Côté 2006; Light and Evans 2013). Coach education courses are pitched at achieving change in practice through rational thinking at a conscious level over short durations, but experience influences coaches' practice and beliefs at a non-conscious level and is developed over long periods of time. This embodied, corporeal knowledge is particularly powerful because it operates at a level below consciousness as common sense. Research confirms the powerful influence that experience plays in the formation of coaches' beliefs about, and dispositions towards, coaching, while highlighting the apparent inability of formal coach education programmes to compete with it (see, for example, Cushion 2007; Cushion *et al.* 2003; Evans 2006b; Stephenson and Jowett 2009).

For the improvement of coaching in rugby, or any other sport, some of the more pressing questions seem to be (1) How do coaches develop expertise?, (2) What are the various elements that contribute to the development of that expertise? and (3) How can governing bodies influence and enhance this development? Playing and coaching experience plays a central role in developing expertise as a coach and is valued by most coaches over formal coach education programmes (Wright *et al.* 2007). Coaches recognize the role that experience plays in their development and develop deeply held beliefs about the value of learning to coach over time through ongoing participation in its practice (Culver and Trudel 2006; Lyle 2002).

Coach learning

Taking a view of coach development as an ongoing process of learning provides a useful way of accounting for the complexity and variability in experiences that lead to a person becoming a particular type of coach (Côté 2006; Lemyre *et al.* 2007). This perspective allows for the consideration of coach development as being a long-term, learning process situated in particular settings and influenced by formal education experiences such as coach accreditation courses. Accepting that learning involves semi-permanent change or transformation rather than just the memorization of information (see, for example, Bloomer 2001) is also helpful for thinking about how coaches develop expertise. Reporting on a four-year longitudinal study on fifty young people in a secondary school, Bloomer (2001) demonstrates the transformational nature of learning to argue that to understand its complexity we must recognize its situated, positional, relational and participatory nature. From this perspective, formal coach education interventions, coaching experience, playing experience and mentoring all influence coach development. From a constructivist perspective this means that we can see all these 'learning experiences' as being interpreted by the coach according to his/her prior knowledge, experience and dispositions. In this way s/he makes sense of them to construct his/her own understanding(s). Learning is thus not a process of adding on new knowledge but, instead, one of changing existing knowledge, occurring at embodied and conscious levels. From a constructivist perspective on learning we learn something from every experience whether we realize it or not. These influences are typically set against a background of individual biographies and life experiences with some directly related to the sport and others more general in nature.

Conceiving of coach development as learning is a relatively recent development that has arisen from the rapid growth of the sport coaching field and the influence of educational and learning research and theories (Cushion *et al.* 2010). The notion of *coach learning* expands conceptions of how coaches develop and can provide deeper and broader understanding about how coaches learn to become the coaches they do (Nelson and Cushion 2006). The use of the notion of coach learning enables and fosters a view of the development of coaches that 'extends far beyond any formal training program' (Côté 2006, p. 221). Despite recognition of the need for more research focused on how coaches learn (Cushion *et al.* 2010; Nelson and Cushion 2006), it remains under-researched, but three chapters in this book report on research conducted on how coaches learn through experience in South Africa, Australia and New Zealand.

Communities of practice

Lave and Wenger's (1991) concepts of situated learning and communities of practice have provided a useful means of examining the implicit learning that takes place through participation in practice within particular communities of practice such as sport clubs (see, for example, Cassidy and Rossi 2006; Kirk and MacPhail 2003; Light 2006b). Lave and Wenger's concepts of communities of practice, situated learning and legitimate peripheral participation have been used in these studies to understand how participation in practice involved the non-conscious learning of the culture and values of the community within which this occurs. For example, Light (2006b) demonstrated how, by participating in the practices of a surf club from the age of 6 years to late adolescence, young people learnt far more than the skills of surf lifesaving to include 'life lessons', identity and the culture of the surf lifesaving movement.

Implicit or informal learning is also a significant concern for research on adult learning and workplace learning. For example, a study on workplace learning (Fuller *et al.* 2005) used the concepts of situated learning in communities of practice (Lave and Wenger 1991) to identify individual and contextual factors that shaped learning. The notion of practice is central to Lave and Wenger's analytic concepts, with learning in a community of practice taking place through participation in the various practices of the community. This occurs over time as the individual moves from (legitimate) peripheral participation as a newcomer towards becoming an 'old timer' through increasing participation in the practices of the community. Lave and Wenger's view of learning offers, 'a means of better conceptualizing and understanding the range and depth of learning that takes place through sport, physical education and other physical practices' (Light 2006b, p. 155), with their concepts also used to identify and explain learning in coaching (see, for example, Cassidy and Rossi 2006; Cassidy *et al.* 2009; Cushion 2006).

Lave and Wenger's concept of a community of practice strives to capture the ways in which humans learn through participation in a range of practices in ways that are neither explicit, intended nor exclusively cognitive. Lave and Wenger's three core concepts of situated learning, communities of practice and legitimate peripheral participation reflect an holistic approach to learning that involves not just the mind, but also the body, its senses and experience. For Lave and Wenger, learning is not an individual, cognitive process but, instead, an aspect of engagement in social life that is social and which involves the whole person. Conceiving of learning as a complex, situated process requires a significant shift from a view of learning as an individual conscious process to learning through participation in the social world. Cushion *et al.* (2010) suggest that Lave and Wenger's perspective is supported by evidence from the workplace learning literature on how informal learning and knowledge evolve from practice. Participation in the practices of a community will always involve learning because participation in practice = learning. Su (2011) draws on Heidegger's phenomenological concept of *being* as the practical way of being in the world to suggest that the holistic notion of lifelong learning should be seen as *being* and not *having*.

The central role that practice plays in Lave and Wenger's work makes it highly suitable for research on, and thinking about, how implicit learning occurs through participation in sport – for players and for coaches (Light 2011). For example, in their study on Australian rugby coaches Light and Evans (2013) identified the role that rugby clubs played, as communities of practice, in the construction of a 'coaching *habitus*'. This suggested how their movement from peripheral members (newcomers) to old timers in their clubs not only involved learning the culture of the club and of rugby but also involved progressively moving into leadership positions as players and then into the beginnings of coaching in a transition from player to coach.

The development of coaches' beliefs, dispositions and practice

Coaches' practice is profoundly shaped by beliefs about coaching and how players learn, and by dispositions towards coaching that are typically unarticulated and unquestioned (see, for example, Cushion 2007; Evans 2011; Light and Evans 2013). This learning typically occurs at a non-conscious level to be embodied over time and operate at a non-conscious level, meaning that embodied beliefs exert a very powerful influence on practice. In regard to changing teachers' practice, Davis and Sumara (2003) suggest that this requires bringing these beliefs to consciousness by having teachers articulate them. This could be a useful idea for any attempts to significantly change coaching practice or implement innovations in coach education courses that might challenge the coaches' unarticulated beliefs, such as the RFU's attempt to implement a Game Sense approach in their coaching programmes (see Chapter 9).

Any coaching innovation is interpreted by the coach through sets of beliefs about coaching and dispositions towards it operating at a non-conscious level. This practical knowledge is embodied through experience as players, both of playing rugby and from their experience of being coached, and can form a significant influence upon the way in which they coach when their playing days are over (Cassidy and Rossi 2006; Cassidy *et al.* 2009; Lyle 2002). Tinning (1996, p. 14) suggests that one of the problems with this is the way in which it typically involves 'passing on' unquestioned information and practices, leading to reproduction by practitioners who 'accept without question the manner and mode of their mentors'.

Coaches' knowledge is also closely entwined with their identities and social history (Cassidy *et al.* 2009). The knowledge they use in their everyday activities is 'practical' and this practical knowledge is closely linked to 'social conventions' about how they are seen to coach in certain situations. As Cassidy *et al.* (2004, p. 128) suggest, 'the decisions that coaches make in taking up regimes that embrace drills and skill, taking an authoritarian style or wearing certain types of clothing are unconsciously made and follow a particular logic'. This line of thinking about coach development has encouraged interest in Bourdieu's key analytical concepts from his theory of social and cultural reproduction (see, for example, Bourdieu 1984).

In particular, Bourdieu's concept of *habitus* has been identified in the coaching literature as a useful means of understanding how coaches develop particular sets of dispositions towards, and beliefs about, coaching over time (see, for example, Cushion 2007; Harvey *et al.* 2010a; Jones *et al.* 2004; Light and Evans 2010). Bourdieu's key analytic concepts, and *habitus* in particular, have been used to explain the challenges associated with physical education teachers adopting innovations such as TGfU in their practice (Light and Tan 2004; Rossi 2000). More recently, the use of *habitus* in coaching research has moved beyond merely using it to explain results to being used in research on rugby coaches as a methodological tool to generate data (see Light and Evans 2013).

Jones *et al.* (2004) suggest that there is a strong link between experience, coach knowledge and the practice of coaching. This coaching knowledge and practice is typically difficult to articulate, is implicit and operates at an unconscious level on a day-to-day basis. Kirk (2010) identifies a link between *habitus*, learning and pedagogy in sport coaching by suggesting that highly trained individuals such as coaches have a *habitus* that relates directly to their immersion in, and socialization into, a sport. This involves developing sets of dispositions and beliefs about how things are done (Lyle 1999) that become 'second nature' as coaches negotiate their workspace. Coaches can also share a common, collective *habitus*, with Jones *et al.* (2004, p. 119) suggesting that, 'Coaching and the coaching process, while being original to one's self, at the same time, are common to a wider group'. This socialization may also impact on coaches and may mean they act often unconsciously to satisfy the expectations of a group.

The *habitus* comprises the socially constructed and embodied dispositions of coaches that manifest themselves in perceptions, appreciations, behaviours and competencies (Kirk 2010). These embodied dispositions occur over a lifetime and as a form of embodied social history, over experience and social contexts as well. Taylor and Garratt (2010, p. 131) suggest that, 'habitus serves to define and redefine the coaching terrain, producing rules and particularities of membership that are reciprocally constructed through social practice (e.g. social practice places limits on what is and what is not thinkable or intelligible)'. It can also comprise traditions of coaching generally or more specifically within a particular sport as Cushion (2001b, p. 188) suggests: 'the coach's practical mastery is developed and maintained by a deeply embodied habitus and . . . the traditions of coaching become embodied in the habitus'.

Harvey *et al.* (2010a) use *habitus* to explain the difficulties experienced by football (soccer) coaches in the United States in taking up Game Sense pedagogy. Their study provides an example of how the values, beliefs and dispositions of coaches can be challenged by the values and assumptions underpinning TGfU. For the two coaches in their study, '*habitus* and experiences reflect a practitioner's values, beliefs and dispositions about their practice' (2010a, p. 18). Several chapters in this book extend and develop this discussion about using *habitus* in research on coach development, with Chapter 5 focused on its use in research and Chapter 10 showing its application in exploring how experience structures elite-level rugby coaches' beliefs and dispositions.

Modes of coach learning: how coaches learn

Within the sport coaching literature suggestions have been made in regard to conceptualizing the different ways in which coaches learn to coach. For example, Trudel *et al.* (2013) draw on constructivist perspectives on learning to suggest that coaches learn through mediated, unmediated and internal learning situations. Nelson *et al.* (2006) draw on Coombs and Ahmed's (1974) work in education to propose three similar modes of coach learning as being formal, informal and non-formal, and this is what we draw on here to structure our discussion on coach learning. In sport coaching formal learning is similar to that which occurs in educational institutions such as schools and universities, with clearly identified learning objectives that are both explicit and intended. It includes learning through coach accreditation courses, professional development courses and programmes offered by national governing bodies. Informal learning is the learning that occurs in everyday life and could be described as implicit learning because it is typically unnoticed and unintended. Here we use the terms formal and informal learning to divide the width of learning involved in coach development.

Formal coach learning

The past two decades have seen growth in the delivery of formal coach education programmes in most developed Western countries (Cassidy *et al.* 2006; Nelson *et al.* 2013). Easy to standardize, formal coach education programmes can be used to educate large numbers of coaches but often involve merely retaining or remembering information. They often also work on the assumption that once the course is completed the participants have learnt what is required to coach at that level as an approach. Formal learning has been criticized in the coaching field (see, for example, Jones and Wallace 2005) but forms the foundation of many coach programmes and certification courses, which are typically necessary for progression through the coaching ranks (Cassidy and Rossi 2006). Although it has been heavily critiqued due to its inability to compete with long-term experience, formal learning for coaches does contribute to the development of coaching competence (Lyle 2002; Mallett and Dickens 2009).

Most developed countries have well-developed coach certification programmes that are progressively sequenced from entry level for coaching community-based or school sport to coaching at national and international levels. For many former players wishing to move into coaching, their first conscious experience of learning how to coach comes though formal coach certification or accreditation courses organized by regional, state or national governing bodies. These coach education programmes enable them to enter coaching and provide structured pathways through which they can progress towards paid, full-time, coaching positions (McCullick *et al.* 2005), but established professional coaches devote little time to formal coach education activities (Côté 2006). In developed countries such as Australia, New Zealand, the UK and Canada, large-scale, and often elaborate, formal coach education and accreditation programmes have been developed to improve the quality of coaching (Cassidy and Kidman 2010; Phillips 2000; Woodman 1993; Wright *et al.* 2007). Coach education is, 'central to the professionalism of sport coaching' (Lyle 2007, p. 19), but there has been only limited research conducted on the effectiveness of this education (Lyle 2007; Lyle and Cushion 2010; Trudel and Gilbert 2006). The research that has been conducted on the delivery and impact of formal coach education programmes strongly suggests that, although attendance can assist in coach development, most programmes are limited in their ability to prepare coaches for either professional or recreational coaching (Abraham *et al.* 2006; Cassidy and Rossi 2006; Nelson *et al.* 2013).

The majority of coach education programmes have traditionally been informed by the bio-sciences, typically drawing upon motor learning and skill acquisition theory to understand learning and guide coaching practice (Cassidy *et al.* 2004; Cushion 2001a; Cushion *et al.* 2006; Jones 2006, 2007; Kidman 2005). The complex and social nature of coaching is difficult to address in these short courses, a task made more difficult by what is commonly an approach that oversimplifies coaching with large-scale coach education programmes proving to be ineffective in modifying coaching behaviour once participants return to the real world of coaching (Abraham and Collins 1998).

A study of thirty-seven rugby coaches in Australia confirms the inability of formal coach education to influence coaching practice (O'Connor and Cotton 2009). In this study the formal education programme did not make any significant change to the practice of the coaches who attended it. More specifically, the course promoted the use of games in coaching but the coaches devoted very little time to games in their practice. There is growing recognition of the benefits to be derived from using practice games in coaching team games (see, for example, Gréhaigne *et al.* 2005; Launder and Piltz 2013; Light 2013b) and this is a constant theme throughout this book. Côté and Fraser-Thomas (2008) maintain that, at the elite level, game play should constitute 80 per cent of training time, but the research indicates that using games in coaching is not a priority for most coaches with training sessions continuing to be highly directed and technical in their focus (Ford *et al.* 2010; Harvey *et al.* 2010a; Jones *et al.* 2012).

A range of explanations for the apparent lack of influence that formal coach education courses and programmes have upon coaching practice have been offered, with one being that coach education has been under-theorized (see, for example,

Cushion *et al.* 2010). There have been a number of theoretically informed pedagogical approaches proposed (Nelson *et al.* 2013), including competency-based programmes (Demers *et al.* 2006), problem-based learning (Jones and Turner 2006) and coach mentoring (Cushion *et al.* 2003). It has also been suggested that the design of programmes that adopt a top-down approach (Côté 2006) and the lack of input from practising coaches (Nelson *et al.* 2013) contribute towards the inability of formal coach education to make significant changes in practice and beliefs about coaching. For us, the main challenge for formal coach education programmes lies in dealing with the powerful, deep and durable influence of long-term experience as players and coaches, which can make changing coaching practices and beliefs so difficult.

Informal coach learning

Informal learning exerts the most powerful influence in the way that coaches develop coaching knowledge (Cushion *et al.* 2003; Evans 2006b; Stephenson and Jowett 2009). One of the more prominent contributing factors coaches have recognised is the influence of playing and coaching experience as a central means of developing expertise in coaching (Wright *et al.* 2007). This is because learning is not just an ongoing process but also a social process that is not restricted to the ability to perform particular tasks (Cushion 2011).

In this section we discuss learning through experience by dividing it into playing experience and coaching experience. We begin by looking at learning through playing experience, which typically leads into coaching and further learning through coaching experience.

Playing experience

Coaches typically move from playing their sport for an extended period of time into coaching, drawing on their experiences as players for coaching (Galipeau and Trudel 2006; Wright *et al.* 2007). Much like physical education teachers, they want to extend positive experiences of sport as players. In rugby prior to 1995 there were limited opportunities for a career as a professional coach and most coaching was voluntary. The emergence of rugby as a professional sport has expanded opportunities to work as a professional coach, but most coaches still work as semi-professional or volunteer coaches, particularly in junior club rugby. For example, even though they were working in the Premier League in Melbourne, the three coaches who participated in one of the studies presented in Chapter 7 were not professional coaches.

Players intending to coach, or thinking about it, see playing experience as an important requirement for moving into coaching (Hutchinson 2008), with Evans' (2011) study on elite-level rugby coaches' use of Game Sense identifying how the transition from player to coach involved leadership experience in teams and/or clubs, but with the coaches in the study having entered coaching prior to the professional era. Most high-performance coaches played the sport they coach, with it being rare for non-players to coach at high-performance or elite levels (Erickson *et al.* 2007). The value attached to having playing experience at a high level of competition as a precursor to coaching and coach development is due to the importance placed on knowledge as an object that can be passed on to players by coaches.

Specific game knowledge that ex-players accumulated through their long-term immersion in the sport is valued above knowledge about how to coach by coaches (Dickson 2001; Rodgers *et al.* 2007), with many coaches' recruitment based upon their experience as players or athletes (Nash and Collins 2006) because their experience, sport-specific skills and technical knowledge are considered to be important pointers to future success as a coach (Gilbert *et al.* 2006; Jones *et al.* 2004). This appears to be underpinned by assumptions that sport-specific, technical and cultural knowledge of the game is more important for success as a coach than knowledge about how to coach (Evans 2011).

The recruitment of experienced players and the value placed on their playing experience occurs at the expense of education in the appointment of many coaches (Lyle 2002). In part, this is related to playing experience forming an aspect of an apprenticeship of coaching, where players observe the practices of coaches over the period of their participation in sport, gradually take on some responsibility for coaching or leadership and reproduce dominant practices (Cassidy and Rossi 2006; Cassidy *et al.* 2004). Coaching knowledge in this sense is 'passed on' without critical examination or analysis and accepted as *the* way to coach (see, for example, Tinning 1996). This lack of reflective development of coaching knowledge encourages an unquestioning reproduction of the status quo of coaching that Cassidy and Rossi (2006) argue leads to the development of 'robotic' practitioners. Cushion *et al.* (2006, p. 91) describe these experiences of athletes or players as being 'deeply integrated past experiences' that ultimately influence coaching practices and behaviours. The experience gained from extensive and diverse participation in sport also provides coaches with opportunities to access unmediated knowledge of coaching, teaching and interpersonal practices, where coaching skills, knowledge and values are learned (Erickson *et al.* 2007).

Coaching experience

The literature suggests the dominant role experience plays in the formation of coaches' beliefs and practice and the inability of formal coach education programmes to compete with it (see, for example, Cushion *et al.* 2003; Stephenson and Jowett 2009). Any attempt at changing coaching practice must, therefore, have an understanding of how experience shapes the knowledge that coaches develop, how they coach and their dispositions towards any alternative practices. The ways in which embodied beliefs and dispositions operate at a non-conscious level have a profound influence on how coaches act, speak and think. Experience is clearly important for the development of expertise, with Côté (2006) suggesting there may be a 'threshold of experience' for becoming a competent coach. Coaches rely heavily on craft knowledge developed through the experience of coaching that emphasizes teaching technique to improve sport performance (Brooker and Abbott 2001). To this end 'many coaches operate within a comfort zone of skills and drills replicating the same way that they were coached as athletes' (Cassidy *et al.* 2004, p. 3).

Abraham *et al.* (2006) argue that this reproductive approach leads to the development of 'tacit' knowledge, which is based on 'weak' problem-solving methods such as trial and error. Coaching experience has a far greater impact on the practice of coaches than formal coach education programmes (Nash and Collins 2006). This is a concern because, as Cassidy and Rossi (2006) argue, experience by itself is inadequate for the full development of a coach, with education required to 'accelerate' the development process and complement informal experience. This, we suggest, offers a key idea for the improvement of coaching quality that we discuss in more detail later in this chapter.

Coaches also gain knowledge and experience from being coached themselves, through observation of other coaches and through reading books and articles about coaching (Galipeau and Trudel 2006; Irwin *et al.* 2005; Lemyre and Trudel 2004). Empirical studies in the area of coaching knowledge indicate that coaches value the experience of observing other respected coaches for the development of coaching expertise (Côté *et al.* 1995; Jones *et al.* 2004; Saury and Durand 1998). This can be seen as an apprenticeship style of learning that, from a critical perspective, can be seen to be reproductive through the ways in which it replicates unquestioned principles of coaching (Cassidy *et al.* 2004). Certainly, apprenticeship learning tends to be reproductive, but we suggest that it could possibly offer one useful means of changing coaching practice by first working with what could be seen as 'master coaches' and having them take a leadership role in coach education courses and programmes.

Coach reflection

Bourdieu's key analytic concepts (or thinking tools) of *habitus*, field, practice and capital offer a valuable means of explaining and enquiring into how and what coaches learn through experience in ways that are implicit and non-conscious. Experience can, however, also be used to achieve intended learning outcomes for coaches with this approach having considerable potential for coach education. The notion of reflection is central to using coach experience in coach education or any intended improvement in coaching. As the most influential thinker in education over the twentieth century, Dewey's focus on the role of experience in learning makes his approach attractive for researchers working in physical education, outdoor education and sport coaching (see, for example, Dewey 1933). Dewey (1933, 1963) argues that education must be grounded in experience but emphasizes the central role of reflection in learning through experience.

Dewey (1916/97) sees learning through experience as involving two types of experience. First is the experience itself and the second is the experience of reflecting upon it. This has been used to theorize how learning occurs in games teaching when adopting a TGfU (Teaching Games for Understanding) approach (Light and Fawns 2003). Light and Fawns argue that, when using a TGfU approach, the teacher establishes and fosters a conversation between non-conscious learning through the experience of participating in modified games and the conscious, rational reflection upon action as a means of circumventing any suggestion of a dualist division between embodied and cognitive learning. They argue that this conversation develops comprehensive understanding and knowledge-in-action.

More specific to coaching, Gilbert and Trudel (2001, 2005) developed an experiential learning model that emphasizes how coaches learn through reflection and that Cushion *et al.* (2010) suggest provides a useful framework for explaining how coaches learn from practical coaching experience. Gilbert and Trudel demonstrated how six youth sport coaches learned by engaging in three forms of reflective practice that they identified as being (1) reflection in action (during action), (2) reflection on action (soon after action) and (3) retrospective reflection on action (Gilbert and Trudel 2004; Trudel *et al.* 2010). The idea of reflection *in* action has also been identified as a means of learning by Varela *et al.* (1991) in a challenge to the Western division of mind and body informed by Buddhist philosophical traditions. It has also been applied in research and writing on coaching and learning (see Light and Kentel 2013; Light *et al.* 2014a; Potrac *et al.* 2013).

To shape learning through experience practitioners such as coaches need to be able to identify problems, anomalies or puzzling situations and undertake a thoughtful process that seeks answers. This deliberate effort to look back is a way of improving a situation for future reference: 'Meaningful strategies are not isolated random actions, but carefully coordinated and independent tactics designed to achieve important and valued goals by the participants in the action' (Kruse 1997, p. 74).

Discussion and implications

It is clear that experience as a player and as a coach exerts a profound influence on coach development because it operates at a non-conscious, unquestioned and common-sense level and is developed over long periods of time. The problem here is that, because learning through experience occurs largely at a non-conscious level, it tends to be reproductive and can make coaches resistant to change in practice (Cassidy and Rossi 2006). As Tinning (1996) suggests, this typically involves 'passing on' unquestioned information and practices, leading to reproduction. Any systematic attempt to improve the quality and effectiveness of coaching, in any sport, requires initiating change and, therefore, challenging coaches' beliefs and practices but, as research suggests, formal coach education courses and programmes appear ineffective when compared to the influence of long-term experience (see, for example, Cassidy *et al.* 2004; Cushion 2007; Jones 2006). This then presents a challenge for improving or enhancing coaching practice because formal coach education is necessary because coaches cannot rely upon experience alone to develop expertise and take their careers forward (Lyle 2002).

Attempts to initiate significant change in coaching practice are often met with suspicion and resistance with the age-old phrase 'if it isn't broken why fix it?' tending to pervade coaching practices (Cassidy *et al.* 2004, p. 3). As Cassidy *et al.* (2004, p. 3) suggest: 'tried and trusted methods gleaned from experience have tended to override both the integration of academic knowledge into coaching practice, and the innovation that reflection upon such applied knowledge can produce'.

The answer to this problem seems to lie in using coach education courses to complement and draw on experience instead of challenging the learning derived from it. In this approach informed reflection is the key to success and the link between formal education and experience. That is to say, formal coach education must involve critical reflection upon existing practice and upon experiences of trying to implement different approaches, methods or techniques, but one of the problems with coach education is finding coach educators who can do this. Indeed, reflection is essential for the improvement of coaching practice at any level, and preferably consistent, critical reflection. This could extend to having coaches articulate beliefs about coaching and critically reflecting upon them when being faced with innovation that challenges their core beliefs, as Davis and Sumara (2003) suggest for teachers.

Coach education courses and programmes have proven to be relatively ineffective in modifying coaching behaviour once participants return to the real world of coaching (see, for example, Abraham and Collins 1998). We suggest that this is partly due to the separation of such interventions from the coaches' practice and could be improved by including some structured reflection on attempts to implement change in practice. Instead of offering a two- or three-day intensive course of study then releasing the coaches to go back to their normal environment, 'theory' should be integrated with experience through reflection. The importance of being able to reflect upon learner (player) responses to innovation in changing practice was evident in a two-year study conducted on teacher responses to the implementation of the TGfU approach to teaching games and team sports in a secondary school. It was not until the teachers had reflected upon what they saw as the students' positive affective responses to the beginnings of change in teaching that they began to change their beliefs and practice (Curry and Light 2014).

The importance of coach reflection has been widely recognized in the sport coaching literature, with suggestions offered for promoting it (see Gilbert and Trudel 2005). Chapter 10 on collaborative action research (CAR) offers another suggestion. It provides an example of how experience and coach reflection can be linked with academic literature, research and theory in coach development. Although it would be difficult to implement CAR on a large scale, it does suggest how reflection can be used to make 'theory' relevant and more meaningful for coaches by reducing the gap between theory and practice. The use of video in this study to assist in reflection by the coach has been suggested elsewhere to encourage coach reflection (Carson 2008), but keeping reflective diaries or recording thoughts about practice are other techniques that can assist in encouraging coach reflection (Harvey *et al.* 2010a).

5

USING *HABITUS* IN RESEARCH ON RUGBY COACH DEVELOPMENT

As we have noted in Chapter 4, research conducted for over a decade in sport coaching identifies the powerful influence that experience exerts on coaches' practice (see, for example, Cushion *et al.* 2003; Evans 2006b; Stephenson and Jowett 2009), but the number of studies that have enquired into how experience actually shapes practice is limited (see, for an example, Light and Evans 2013). The use of Bourdieu's analytic concept of *habitus* suggests that learning through experience, within particular contexts, can be seen as developing a practical mastery of 'the game' (an analogy for the larger social game), as *le sens pratique* (Bourdieu 1984). From this perspective, rugby coaches can be seen to develop beliefs about coaching and dispositions towards ways of coaching through long-term immersion in rugby and its culture at an embodied, non-conscious level (Light and Evans 2010). Coaching thus involves the use of 'structured improvisation' that is crucially shaped by experience and processes of socialization into the culture of coaching (Jones *et al.* 2003). Any intervention aimed at changing coaching practice must then have an understanding of how experience shapes the knowledge and dispositions that rugby coaches bring to any professional development or coach education programme or course (see, for example, Evans 2006b and Chapter 9 on the RFU's development of its coach education programmes). This is important because of the ways in which the corporeal knowledge developed through experience, and sets of dispositions towards coaching and learning, structure coaches' interpretation of formal education.

Bourdieu's attention to sport has proven to be attractive to researchers working in the sport coaching field, with his concept of *habitus* proffered as a means of understanding how coaches develop their practice over time and why it is so difficult to change (see, for example, Christensen 2009; Cushion and Jones 2006; Cushion *et al.* 2003; Jones and Wallace 2005; Light and Evans 2013; Piggott 2012; Taylor and Garratt 2010). *Habitus* allows research to locate coaches' current practices in their histories of past experiences, located in particular contexts. Bourdieu sees these contexts as being social fields or sub-fields, such as the field of sport, business or education, or the sub-field of rugby, or of rugby in a particular country. Tightening the focus to consider how the construction of the *habitus* is influenced within communities of practice (CoP – Lave and Wenger 1991), yet locating them within larger sub-fields or fields, can provide more detailed enquiry into context and into the agency of the individual (Light 2011; Mutch 2003). Using *habitus* to generate data and/or analyse it in research on coach development can provide insight into how non-conscious knowledge is acquired through experience and how it shapes practice (see, for example, Christensen 2009; Cushion *et al.* 2003). Chapters 7 and 8 in this volume provide good examples of the use of *habitus* as a methodological tool in research on coach development. These studies were conducted on rugby coaches operating at high performance levels and above. They identified the characteristics of a coaching *habitus* and the ways in which they were constructed through experience over time in particular social and cultural contexts.

Habitus is the embodiment and expression of an individual's social and cultural history (Light and Evans 2013), with individuals' growth and development influenced by these socially and culturally situated experiences that structure their understandings and their actions. The *habitus* is constructed through the individual's participation in the practices of a specific social field or sub-field with practice mediating between *habitus* and field. It operates at a non-conscious level to *structure* action but does not determine it. Beliefs and sets of dispositions are formed about a particular activity, which, in turn, predisposes the individual to view this activity from 'a filter through which all future experiences will pass' (Cushion *et al.* 2003, p. 218).

As suggested in Chapter 1, growing awareness of the complexity of coaching and learning to coach and the influence of social and cultural conditions on coaching and coaches has stimulated interest in social theory (Light 2011; Jones *et al.* 2011). The use of *habitus* in research specifically focused on rugby coaches by Light and Evans (2013) demonstrates how experiences over time and within particular settings or contexts come to form powerful influences on beliefs about coaching and dispositions towards particular ways of coaching. In their study it was used to gain an understanding of how coaches were disposed towards Game Sense and how their *habitus* influenced the extent to which they did or didn't use this approach as a coaching innovation. *Habitus* is particularly powerful because of the ways in which it is constructed and operates at a level below the scrutiny of the conscious mind (Bourdieu 1990).

Bourdieu's key concepts

This section begins with a brief outline of three of Bourdieu's key concepts, *practice*, *field* and *capital*, which are inseparable from *habitus* in any analysis (Light 2011). It is followed by a more detailed discussion of *habitus*.

Practice

Practice is a philosophical term referring to, 'human action on the natural and social world', emphasizing the transformative nature of action and the 'priority of action over thought' (Marshall 1994, p. 414). According to Marx it refers to the idea of the unity of theory and practice with thought/theory and practice being inseparable (Trombley and Bullock 2000). Marx sees thought arising from and developed by practice, arguing that the split between an irrational and a rational world can only be overcome by the development of a theoretical consciousness among social groups engaged in the *practice* of changing the real world (Trombley and Bullock 2000). Reflecting a challenge to mind–body dualism, he argues that life is activity; that knowing the world and achieving self-realization involves action (Henricks 2006). Rather than the freedom to think, what matters most to Marx is the freedom to act, to 'shape the public contours of the world' (as cited in Henricks 2006, p. 16).

For Bourdieu, the logic of the field is embodied and reproduced through people's participation in the range of practices that constitute the field or sub-field. The dispositions that come to constitute the *habitus* and the logic of the field are embodied through participation in day-to-day social practice. These practices are produced by the interaction of the social context (field) and the social action of agency. Participation in day-to-day social and cultural life is central to the construction of the *habitus* and the shaping of our social action and identity. Practice mediates between field and *habitus* so that not only is the *habitus* shaped by the field as structure, but it can also influence the field. Despite criticism of it as being deterministic, such as King's (2000) claim that it assumes individuals to be 'puppets' of structure, the *habitus* and the *field* are mutually constituting with *habitus* being a 'generative structure of practical action' (Lizardo 2004, p. 8). *Habitus* is a '*generative dynamic structure* that adapts and accommodates itself to *another* dynamic meso level structure composed primarily of other actors, situated practices and durable institutions (fields)' (Lizardo 2004, p. 4; original emphasis). In Bourdieu's intellectual project practice emphasizes action over thought and non-conscious learning as '*le sens pratique*' in reference to the knowledge-in-action that actors have of their social environment and that they cannot articulate because it operates at a non-conscious level (Light 2011).

Field

A social *field* is a semi-autonomous social arena with its own discourse and *doxa* (sets of beliefs), but fields are dynamic and not fixed. The relative power that determines positions of dominance and subordination is determined by the distribution and accumulation of capital. The value of various forms of capital is dependent upon its type, its volume and the nature of the field. *Fields* overlap to make up the larger society, with tensions between them leading to change, and over the span of an individual's life he/she passes through different *fields* (Light 2011). Fields are structures but are not fixed. Instead, they are open to change, overlap and can create tension with another field to influence each other. A relevant example is provided by the intrusion of the field of business into the field of sport for sport's sake and sport as education, with very different *doxa*. This has seen the creation of the field of professional sport or sport as business, and significant tensions between the *doxa* of sport as business and the ideals of sport as a form of education derived from the nineteenth-century schools of the rising middle classes.

Capital

Capital exists in social, cultural or economic forms that can be accumulated and converted from symbolic forms to more powerful, material, economic forms. Cultural goods such as books, instruments or artworks are objective forms of capital, but embodied cultural capital is more relevant to coaching and playing rugby, existing as durable dispositions of the mind and body. Social capital is basically the value of social networks and is described by Bourdieu (1983, p. 249) as being, 'the aggregate of the actual or potential resources which are linked to possession of a durable network of more or less institutionalized relationships of mutual acquaintance and recognition'. His treatment of the concept is instrumental and focuses on the advantages provided for those who possess social capital and its deliberate construction. *Physical capital* refers to physical attributes, such as athletic skill, deportment and physical strength, that can be converted into other forms of capital such as economic or social capital. The shape, size and use of the body are saturated with, and convey, social and cultural meaning. *Physical capital* can constitute a valuable form of capital that can be converted into more powerful forms such as the economic capital of wages, such as is the case for professional rugby players. *Capital* and *habitus* each generate and predispose one another, and thus create a durable set of dispositions.

Habitus

As the key concept in Bourdieu's intellectual project *habitus*, 'follows a practical logic, that of the fuzzy, or of the more or less, which defines the ordinary relation to the world' (Bourdieu, cited in Bourdieu and Wacquant 1992, p. 22). It is a very complex concept that Lizardo (2004, p. 5) argues saves Bourdieu's theory from becoming 'rationalist formalism with disembodied agents embedded in fields and engaging in strategies to accumulate different kinds of capital'. At a very basic level it refers to the embodiment of the individual's history of participation in social and cultural practices, shaped by the socio-cultural contexts within which they take place and how this operates to structure individual and collective actions and behaviour. It has a very strong focus on the body and practice in a challenge to the cognitive bias in the social sciences, but it does not ignore the influence of reflective cognition. In its challenge to dualism the concept of *habitus* strives to avoid or circumnavigate demarcations between body and mind, speech and action, subjective and objective.

Widely used in studies of embodiment, *habitus* emphasizes the range of non-conscious learning that occurs through participation in practice in particular *fields* to form a central part of Bourdieu's challenge to dualism and the cognitive bias in the social sciences. *Habitus* avoids making distinctions between the unconscious and the conscious and between the body and the discursive. Adopting an holistic view in line with the direction of this book, he emphasizes the inseparability of the individual from his/her social environment, arguing that the individual and his/her social world are in a state of mutual possession.

Habitus operates in relation to Bourdieu's other key concepts with the *practice*, *field* and *capital* being of particular relevance for enquiry into rugby coach development. *Practices* and *fields* are intertwined and contain socio-cultural appropriations with *practice* mediating between *habitus* and *field* (Bourdieu 1984). *Practice* is an important philosophical concept that is of particular relevance for enquiry into rugby coaching. It is a philosophical term referring to human action on the natural and social world that emphasizes the transformative nature of action over thought (Marshall 1994). As a philosophical term, *practice* refers to the idea of the unity of theory and practice, with Marx arguing that the two cannot be separated (see, for example, Marx 1999). This is important in sport coaching due to the separation of theory from the practice of coaching and practitioners' distrust of theory. Reflecting a challenge to mind–body dualism, Marx argues that life is activity and that knowing the world involves action (Henricks 2006). From a coaching perspective, this is not to say that action is more important than thinking but, instead, to emphasize the inseparability of mind from body and thought from action.

As a sub-field of sport, coaching is value laden because it is rooted in the culture of its practice (Saury and Durand 1998) to create a form of social conditioning (Light 2011). As Langer (1992, p. 72) argues, any system, 'while composed of individual members, has a structure, a history, a way of understanding the world and an institutional culture'. Sport coaching is a dynamic, socially complex and context specific practice (Cushion and Lyle 2010) that is structured and transformed by the very discourse of its dynamic, social complexity and contextualization. Coaches do demonstrate having knowledge of coaching that is needed to support and assist the design of coach education, but it is not 'out there' knowledge that can be seen as an object. It is knowledge that is in many ways unique to each coach because it has been constructed through a unique pathway of participation in the practices of a particular field, and which requires situating as its situated nature shapes its nature and development.

This means that understanding how knowledge is developed is important for understanding how and why rugby coaches coach as they do. However, an understanding of how such knowledge is developed from a socio-cultural viewpoint is scarce and it is in need of more attention in the coaching literature (Cushion and Lyle 2010). Furthermore, such a stance allows for a better integration of the complexity of coaching due to the non-reductionist assumptions required for this paradigm shift (Cushion and Lyle 2010), as opposed to the 'culture' of sport coaching requiring positivist principles as a guide for understanding and enhancing the coaching process. It is the recognition that such a complex activity requires tacit knowledge (Saury and Durand 1998) that situates our argument for the use of *habitus* within knowledge being developed as a social construction.

Habitus and the social construction of knowledge

The unconscious knowledge acquired from experience has featured in the sport coaching literature, with coaching sometimes referred to as 'the art of coaching' (Woodman 1993) or 'craft coaching' (Day 2011) and knowledge referred to as 'tacit knowledge' (Nash and Collins 2006). These views acknowledge sport coaching as being a complex practice that is socially and culturally situated, with informal day-to-day experiences exerting strong influences on the development of durable sets of dispositions (perceptions and appreciations) (Bourdieu 1977). These experiences structure rugby coaches' actions as they learn the 'culture' of coaching and of rugby through participation in its practices. This is not only a central idea for Bourdieu but also for Lave and Wenger (1991) with their key concepts of situated learning, communities of practice and legitimate peripheral participation. As Light (2011) suggests, the central role that practice plays in Lave and Wenger's and Bourdieu's work provides common ground for them in his suggestion for integrating learning theory and the social theory of Bourdieu through a focus on *practice*. It is over extended participation in the practices of a particular field (and the constant interaction involved) that the *habitus* is constructed, with our perceptions and appreciations of the field and its practices embedded in it. This complex interaction between field and practice is fundamental to the construction of a rugby coaching *habitus* and can be seen to be the key to Bourdieu's intellectual project. This has been suggested as a way of transcending structuralist thought, as it accounts for and engenders the infinite array of practices developed by the conflicts at interplay between each of these concepts: *habitus*, field and practice (Brubaker 1993).

This interweaving process embodies itself within the person with the body in society and society in the body (Bourdieu 1990). *Habitus* generates action through which corporeal knowledge (the social enacted through the body) is expressed and offers a powerful tool for understanding how rugby coaches' approaches towards coaching and the practices they adopt are the products of experience within particular contexts. As Light (2011) suggests, the influence of context can be considered from a macro or micro perspective. A macro perspective would look at context as a field such as sport that can overlap with, or be affected by, other fields such as business or education, or as a sub-field such as rugby or rugby in New Zealand. For a tighter focus on agency, research can focus on the construction of a coaching *habitus* within communities of practice (Lave and Wenger 1991), as has been done in research on Australian and New Zealand rugby coaches (see, for example, Evans 2012; Light and Evans 2013; and Chapter 8 in this volume). These approaches all allow for understanding how experience figures over a lifetime of participation in rugby in structuring coaching skills, attitudes, beliefs and inclinations that have been acquired to guide coaching practices.

Developing a feel for coaching

Through *habitus* Bourdieu illustrates how day-to-day practices become embodied in 'systems of actions' to structure the individual's practices and beliefs; Light and Evans (2013) argue that it exists exclusively as a corporeal manifestation of experience that is formed and operates non-consciously. This means that many of the functions performed by a coach seemingly occur without conscious awareness or rational consideration because the dispositions and knowledge that they draw on have been acquired over time and function as this 'feel' or 'sense' for coaching.

For rugby coaches this embodied knowledge and sets of dispositions have come to constitute the *habitus* over years of participation in practice within particular social settings (within particular *fields*), to act as what Bourdieu (1980) terms *le sens pratique*. In both English and French, 'sense/sens' suggests both conscious and embodied understanding or awareness. A lifetime of engagement in the practices and culture of rugby not only imparts the skills and game knowledge needed to play rugby but also embeds the logic of the sub-field of rugby and its culture. Read in French, *le sens pratique* has a peculiar significance that is not captured when translated into English as 'the practical sense'. Its meaning in French is better conveyed as a sense of what is practical, a *feel* for the field. Having a feel for something aptly conveys an embodied and non-conscious understanding perhaps captured in the notion of having a 'sixth sense'. This sense/feel lies at the centre of the interplay between *habitus* and *field* and generates dispositions required for a given practice (Coles 2009).

Habitus provides a useful concept for understanding how the durable effects of past experiences shape coaches' current practice and how the 'unconsciously acquired dispositions . . . profoundly affect subsequent performance' (Mutch 2003, p. 393). This then suggests that to understand why rugby coaches coach as they do, and to develop effective coach education or development programmes, there is a need to understand the social origins of their beliefs and dispositions. Thus, Atkin (2000) provides an account of 'lifelong learning' that Lemyre *et al.* (2007) pick up to argue for the importance of researching the effects of different learning situations within different settings as a confirmation of the importance of the socio-cultural context. However, it would seem that coach education programmes do not account for such interpretivist understandings and remain focused on objectified knowledge. This effect of isolating forms of learning and regarding certain types of 'knowledge' as certifiable while others are simply disregarded does not provide an understanding of the cultural and social subtleties that affect learning and thus knowledge. This is despite recognition of the fact that experience plays a crucial role in the development of coaching knowledge and exerts a far more powerful influence than any formal coach education interventions can (Abraham *et al.* 2006; Lyle 2002). It is thus no surprise that coaches see a 'feel' for coaching to be the mark of expertise (Nash and Sproule 2011) and particularly since the constant ambiguities coaches are faced with require practical knowledge; they are renowned for their 'on-the-field' know-how (Jones and Wallace 2005).

The situated nature of learning to coach

Saury and Durand (1998) identified how social conditions affect the attainment of goals. In this regard social theories have been used in sport coaching to promote a deeper theoretical understanding of this social and dynamic activity (Jones *et al.* 2011). However, research on, and thinking about, coach development is often critiqued for not utilizing social theories to improving coach education (Jones 2007). As such, social theory illuminates a dissonance between formal coach education and the reality of the coaching process as a practice that is complex. Furthermore, it has been suggested that coach education should mirror the dynamic real-life situations coaches are constantly confronted with (Jones *et al.* 2004), with growing attention being paid to the implicit aspects of coaches' practices in order to provide a more 'complete' understanding.

Saury and Durand (1998, p. 265) suggest that coaches use past experiences that are deeply embedded in a 'cognitive alchemy', to cope with the ambiguous nature of coaching, and it is these past experiences that generate particular dispositions that structure practice. These dispositions developed from such past experiences are what constitute perceptions and beliefs that assimilate our beliefs between 'good' practice and 'bad' practice. Cushion and Jones (2006) argue that it is linked to broader social structures. This is the reason why a unique *habitus* is socio-culturally constructed, as individuals never have exactly the same experiences and thus have not developed perceptions and appreciations of them in the same manner. However, people who have similar social positions, for example head sport coaches, would share similar *habitus* as the culture and sense of the practice of coaching becomes embodied (Light and Evans in press). These concepts are proving to be beneficial tools in recognizing particular patterns of coaching practices and thus have potential benefits for coach development.

Habitus and coach development

Recognition of the significance of implicitly established beliefs about coaching practices and dispositions towards them (Becker 2009; Nash and Sproule 2011) is reflected in the importance placed on developing a coaching 'philosophy' (Jones *et al.* 2004; Lyle 2002), in reference to the more common-sense notion of a philosophy as 'a set of principles that guide an individual's practice' (Cassidy *et al.* 2009, p. 57). Recognition of the ways in which coaches' beliefs operate at conscious and non-conscious levels marks a break from traditional views of coaching as objective, asocial, linear, rationalistic and unproblematic (Cassidy *et al.* 2009; Cushion and Lyle 2010; Jones *et al.* 2004) and has encouraged researchers to adopt diverse perspectives on coaching and situate it as a complex and socio-cultural practice (Cassidy *et al.* 2009; Jones 2006, 2007; Jones *et al.* 2011). Light and Evans' (2013) findings illustrate how social and cultural contexts shape certain dispositions towards coaching, as it is from these experiences within such social and cultural contexts that coaching knowledge is developed over time.

Habitus creates a durable attitude or sets of dispositions operating beyond the scrutiny of the conscious mind (Bourdieu 1990), to profoundly shape coaches' attitudes towards coaching and shape their practice, and this is how *habitus* operates to reproduce existing practice and social relationships (Bourdieu and Passeron 1990). It is this relationship between practice and field from which a *habitus* of 'incorporated schemes of dispositions, perceptions and appreciation . . . [that] orients our practice and gives meaning to them' is constructed (Kay and Laberge 2002, pp. 17–18). Although *habitus* is rarely used as an empirical tool for research on sport coaching, it is commonly recognized as an important concept for grasping the complex nature of coaching knowledge due to the powerful influence experience plays on forming coaches' practices (see, for example, Christensen 2009; Cushion *et al.* 2003).

The construction of coaching *habitus* in communities of practice

Lave and Wenger's (1991) view of learning as a social practice is complementary to Bourdieu's ideas on practice and largely due to the emphasis on non-conscious learning through practice (Light 2011). From this perspective learning can be seen to be an interactive process (constructivist), wherein it is predisposed to social influences. Furthermore, Mutch (2003) argues that a more precise way of depicting *habitus* is to examine the impact of previous experience on identity and meaning, which forms a core concern of Lave and Wenger within communities of practice (CoP). Following Mutch's suggestions, Light and Evans (2013) focused on the construction of the *habitus* of rugby coaches within CoP to provide a tighter focus and to enable the influence of agency to emerge more easily than working with the larger space of field. Their examination of the construction of the coaching *habitus* of elite-level Australian rugby coaches identified the profound role that long-term membership in CoP such as rugby clubs played in the construction of the *habitus*.

Agents participate in numerous overlapping CoP but with one typically being dominant (Lave and Wenger 1991). This is illustrated in Light and Nash's (2006) study on young people in an Australian surf club who were also members of the CoP of sport clubs and schools and how membership in these CoP shaped their identities. Multiple CoP that people participate in can be seen to constitute larger sub-fields such as rugby and allow the researcher to have a tight focus on agency yet locate the CoP within larger social arenas such as sub-fields and fields such as sport. In their study on elite-level coaches' interpretation and use of Game Sense, Light and Evans (2013) tightened the focus on context to CoP. This involved focusing on CoP such as schools, but more so on rugby clubs within which the coaches had developed as players and who had leadership experience as senior players as part of a transition from player to coach.

Using *habitus* as a methodological tool

In the sport coaching literature, as in the education literature, *habitus* has been used primarily as 'an explanation of data rather than as a way of working with it' (Reay 2004, p. 440). One exception is a study on elite rugby coaches in Australia and New Zealand (see Evans 2012; Light and Evans 2013) that uses *habitus* as a methodological tool to generate data. Several studies reported on in this book take the same approach. For example, Chapter 7 enquires into the origins of rugby coaches' beliefs and dispositions in Melbourne, Australia. Involving three coaches, originally from New Zealand, South Africa and Australia, it highlights the significant influence of the socio-cultural environment in which they grew up on the construction of their coaching *habitus* and the powerful effect this has on their coaching. In doing so it emphasizes the important influence of durable sets of dispositions formed by coaches through experience in particular cultural settings on their practice.

The looseness and vagueness of *habitus*, which can present a challenge for using it as a methodological tool, is, at the same time, its strength because it 'goes hand in hand with vagueness and indeterminacy' (Bourdieu 1990, p. 77). *Habitus* is difficult to identify or empirically specify (Jenkins 2002; Swartz 1997) because it 'follows a practical logic, that of the fuzzy, or of the more or less, which defines the ordinary relation to the world' (Bourdieu, cited in Bourdieu and Wacquant 1992, p. 22). As Reay (1995, p. 357) suggests, 'paradoxically the conceptual looseness of *habitus* also constitutes a potential strength. It makes possible adaptation rather than the more constricting straightforward adoption of the concept within empirical work'.

Light and Evans (2013) adopted Lau's (2004) suggestions for operationalizing *habitus* in a study on rugby coaches. Lau suggests that *habitus* can be illustrated in the three interconnected categories of (1) fundamental beliefs, un-thought premises or taken-for-granted assumptions, (2) perception and appreciation or understanding and (3) a descriptive and prescriptive practical sense of objective possibilities. Light and Evans sought to unearth some of the coaches' fundamental beliefs, un-thought premises and taken-for-granted assumptions by asking the participants what they thought the characteristics of a good coach were. To generate data on category 2, perception and appreciation or understanding, they asked questions about what the participants thought made good players and what the characteristics of good players were. For category 3, descriptive and prescriptive practical sense of objective possibilities and the forthcoming, they explored the participants' attitudes towards innovations. This was of particular relevance for them because the study was focused on coaches' interpretation and use of the Game Sense approach. The interviews were semi-structured and aimed at stimulating dialogue from which data might emerge that would suggest features of a coaching *habitus*.

Habitus is produced through the interaction of structure and agency and within the sub-fields of rugby, or even of rugby in Australia, the influence of structure on individual *habitus* was far more evident than agency. However, Light and Evans' (2013) use of CoP enabled the identification of some individual variation between the coaches and tensions within their *habitus* arising from the interaction of agency and structure. Their exploration of the 'descriptive and prescriptive practical sense of objective possibilities' of the participants illuminated some of the participants' dispositions towards Game Sense as a coaching innovation and variations between them.

Discussion

Following on from others in the sport coaching field we argue in this chapter that *habitus* offers a useful way of conceptualizing how experience comes to form such a powerful influence upon a coach's development (see Cushion and Jones 2006; Harvey *et al.* 2010a). *Habitus* can make valuable contributions in understanding how experiences shape coaching practices (see Christensen 2009; Cushion and Jones 2006; Cushion *et al.* 2003) and the profound influence of socio-cultural context on the formation of deeply held beliefs and durable sets of dispositions that shape coaches' practice and are difficult to change. This is, of course, an important consideration for governing bodies attempting to implement innovation in coaching at any level, such as the RFU in Chapter 9.

By opening up to and recognizing the overlap with other constructionist approaches such as Lave and Wenger's (1991) and Wenger's (1998) concepts of situated learning and communities of practice, which focus on social practice, *habitus* offers multiple lenses through which we can see and understand the complexities of rugby coaches' development in a complex, dynamic, social world (Jones *et al.* 2011).

The complexity of habitus

The discussion in this chapter is not an attempt to simplify the concept of *habitus*, or to bring closure to it by providing definite answers or detailed 'how to' instructions for its application in research. Any attempt to reduce the complexity of coaching, of how coaches develop, and of player learning to measurable quantities that can be manipulated and compared to make confident predictions is misplaced. Bourdieu's key concept of *habitus* offers a means of identifying the complexity of rugby coaching and accounting for it in enquiry into how coaches learn to coach in particular ways and how these are shaped by experience and context. The strength of *habitus* lies in its 'fuzziness' and vagueness. This 'conceptual looseness' can make it difficult to work with but is paradoxically also one of its strengths (Reay 1995). It is, therefore, imperative that the use of *habitus* as a methodological tool retains its vagueness and 'fuzziness' so that the use of it may help achieve a particular *sens pratique* of *habitus* itself.

PART 2

Research on coaches and coaching

6

AN HOLISTIC APPROACH TO INVESTIGATING FRENCH RUGBY COACHES' IN-MATCH COMMUNICATIONS WITH PLAYERS

(with Alain Mouchet)

As is evident in this volume, there is growing interest in game-based approaches (GBA) to coaching in team sports that can develop the player decision-making required for success in the dynamic context of competition matches (see Breed and Spittle 2011; Evans 2014; Kidman 2005; Light *et al.* 2014a; Slade 2010). At the same time, there is growing recognition of coaching as a complex, dynamic and context-dependent process (see Jones and Turner 2006; Lyle 2002; Nash and Collins 2006) that involves adapting to and making effective decisions in dynamic contexts (Abraham *et al.* 2006; Jones 2006; Saury and Durand 1998). However, research in sport coaching does not seem to have adequately explored the influence of context on coach decision-making and we suggest that this is largely due to the dominance of behaviourist research approaches that tend to employ a descriptive-analytic system of episodes (Abraham and Collins 1998; De Marco *et al.* 1996; Smith and Cushion 2006).

In response to this gap in the literature, this chapter draws on a study that enquired into in-competition coach behaviour (Mouchet *et al.* 2013), with a focus on the methodology to illustrate the significant contribution to knowledge in sport coaching that holistic approaches can make. The holistic nature of the research approach used in this study provides an example of what we have argued for in this book. It can account more effectively for the inseparability of coach decision-making and behaviour from context(s) and the subjective dimensions of coaching, which has been neglected in the coaching literature. The study draws on a body of work coming out of France that emphasizes the subjective dimensions of coaching and of player decision-making as an approach that can access both the 'public' and the 'private' aspects of in-competition coaching behaviour (see Mouchet 2014).

The notion of public aspects refers to behaviour that can be observed from an external and objective point of view, such as verbal behaviour and gestures. The private aspects refer to those that are not directly observable as behaviour, such as attention dynamics, thoughts, decision-making processes and the aim of communications. This follows on from suggestions for research that not only observes coach behaviour from an external point of view, but also explores the more private aspects of coaching (such as thought) through qualitative methods (Côté and Sedgwick 2003; Nash and Collins 2006; Smith and Cushion 2006). However, we take this a little further to argue for an holistic approach to research on coach decision-making. The study we draw on was conducted in France on in-competition rugby coaches' behaviour to provide an example of an 'in situ' model of in-competition coaching behaviour (Cushion *et al.* 2006) that accounts for the whole person and includes enquiring into the subjective dimensions of decision-making and action. The enquiry into what rugby coaches do within competition contexts also provides insight into coaches' embodied 'knowledge in action' (Barbier 2000) and how it shapes their practice. The study used a systemic approach (Le Moigne 1990) for studying coaches' communications in their naturalistic context (i.e. the flow of the match) and a multi-method approach for investigating coaches' interventions during some match events.

Theoretical framework

The theoretical approach used in this study draws upon the French tradition of the psychology of work (Leplat 2000) and the Russian school of psychology (Bakhtine 1984). In-competition coaching is a 'situated activity' because it is inseparable from, and interacts with, the context within which it takes place (Suchman 1987). Coaching is acutely shaped by the physical and socio-cultural environment in which it is practised and learnt. The dynamic nature of competition matches modifies and shapes 'the story of self' (Stroot and Ko 2006, cited in Cushion 2011) through an ongoing process of reconstructing knowledge of both the coaching context and the coach. This knowledge is then mobilized depending upon certain situations that occur within the match. This perspective on coaching leads us to propose a conceptual framework for studying coaches' intervention behaviour in competition that adequately considers the complexity of coaching.

Bouthier and Durey (1995) identified the three linked levels of analysis of 'macro, meso and micro', which frame and influence coach behaviour, moving from the broad context of the macro to the specific focus on the micro issues of the match. Mouchet and Bouthier (2008) have further developed this to distinguish between the general context, local context and particular events within the match. The larger, general context forms the coaches' decisional background that shapes his/her decision-making about interventions during the match. It is typically comprised of elements such as competition coaching rules, the predetermined match strategy, objectives for the season, personal conceptions and embodied experiences of coaching. This broad, general context influences the coaches' perceptions about in-competition intervention behaviour (i.e. what they think they do or should do).

Local context is the 'time of the match', beginning from arrival in the changing room and finishing with the completion of the post-match debriefing. This includes the examination of particular conditions on the day such as the weather and the state of the pitch, the strengths and weaknesses a priori and the particular expectations of the coaches. General and local contexts can influence in-competition communications through organization among the technical staff, positioning of the coaches in the technical zone or up in the stands, specific issues of the match such as the primary aim being to win the match or perhaps to test players in different positions and so on. Finally, the micro level considers the actual coaching intervention behaviour and/or communications with players, involving the coaches' 'public' and 'private' activity. Communications with players are specific to the local circumstances of the match while being located in a socio-cultural context and shaped by the 'decisional background' (Mouchet 2005; Mouchet and Le Guellec 2012).

There is also a need to explore the coaches' experience of communication in past situations, with a focus on the specific interactions between the context and the coaches' subjectivity that shape his/her actions at that particular moment. To understand the influence of the coaches' subjectivity we draw on the psycho-phenomenological theoretical framework of Vermersch (2008), who distinguishes between 'consciousness in action' (embodied, pre-reflective experience, implicit mode of reflection), and 'reflexive consciousness' (conceptualized knowledge, judgements or explanations about a process).

This approach strives to understand the subject's point of view and how it influences his/her actions through an in-depth analysis of the subjective experience as 'lived' by the actors.

The concept of a lived body derives from the work of Husserl's phenomenology as a challenge to positivism underscored by a belief that experience is the source of all knowledge (see Husserl 1962). In the study we report on here this framework distinguished between these two levels of consciousness (Vermersch 2000) to create the possibility of accessing the coaches' embodied consciousness, developed through experience that shaped their in-competition behaviours. This more holistic conception of coaching behaviour is able to pursue a more in-depth exploration of how the thinking processes (conscious and non-conscious) interacted with context to shape the coaches' decisions and action than the behaviourist approach can. For example, the 'silent' observation and analysis of the match has been identified as a deliberate coaching strategy (Cushion and Jones 2001; Horton *et al.* 2005; Smith and Cushion 2006; Trudel *et al.* 1996). But systematic observation instruments underestimate the cognitive processes associated with this activity. Further elucidation of the thoughts and/or cognitive processes of coaches' in-competition behaviour is thus required.

Methods

This study employed a multiple case study approach to systematically gain information (Berg 2007) on coaches' in-match interventions in rugby matches at either a World Championship or a European tournament. To document the complexity and subjectivity of coach activity during a match it employed a multi-dimensional approach to data collection. The triangulation of data obtained with various methods provided a more holistic understanding of the coaching process within the competition environment (Gilbert and Trudel 2004; Lyle 2002; Nash and Collins 2006; Potrac *et al.* 2000; Smith and Cushion 2006).

Participants

Six high-performance/elite-level rugby coaches participated in this study (five male, one female), two from each of the following national teams: (a) U/21, (b) France A Women and (c) France amateurs. All coaches possessed the required coaching diplomas for coaching at this level. Three are members of the 'Direction Technique Nationale' group, which is responsible for educational programmes, elite performance and development within the French Federation of Rugby. The others coach in semi-professional club settings with all names used being pseudonyms to protect anonymity.

Data collection

Semi-structured interviews

In the first stage, semi-structured interviews of approximately 30 minutes were conducted with each coach one week prior to the competition match. Interviews were recorded using a digital voice recorder and transcribed verbatim. The questions were focused on coaches' perceptions of their in-competition behaviour revolving around the three areas of (1) observation of the game, (2) player substitution and (3) communications with players. This chapter focuses on messages and how they were delivered to the players. Prior to the match the coaches were also spoken to for 5 minutes to ascertain the strategy for the match to explore any adaptations made on the day of the match before its commencement. The interviews were useful for identifying coach conceptions about the general and local context to help understand how the decisional background shaped their in-competition communications.

Coaches' behaviour and communications

In the second phase of the study coaches' behaviour and communications during the match were recorded. The recording was conducted by placing a video camera with a proficient zoom on the opposite sideline in a position advantageous to viewing the coach in his/her 'coaching zone' as well as being able to monitor interactions with players. The video was set up just before kick-off and removed at the end of the match. Microphones with digital voice recorders were attached to the coaches one hour before kick-off and removed after the debriefing of the match with their players. The temporal synchronization of the video and audio recordings was made on a computer post-match.

Match video

During the same phase, matches were filmed from the stands with a digital video camera. This enabled contextualization of the coaches' communications during the match and examination of how these communications affected match play and performance.

Explication interviews

Enquiry into the subjective experience of the coaches during the match used an explication interview (Vermersch 2008) of approximately 45 minutes. It was conducted the day after the match with the intention of investigating in detail important moments of the coaches' in-competition interventions, with coaches selecting these important moments. This interview technique facilitates retrospective verbalization of the pre-reflective part of personal/private experience by reliving past experience. It is not, therefore, a post-hoc reflection or rationalization of what happened at that moment. The aim of the explication is to access the coaches' lived experience by taking them back to their 'in the moment' recollections of the incident. The examination of the 'in the moment' decision-making prompts the coach to use various kinaesthetic elements such as sights, sounds, smells and feelings that may have been relevant at that specific time, in order that they trigger thoughts and actions that are embodied and previously private only to that individual coach. Thus, it enables the researcher to access the previously hidden or implicit meaning behind the coach's actions and decisions, and meaning that would remain unarticulated with other more traditional interview techniques.

Data analysis

Interviews

Interviews were subjected to a thematic analysis based on an interpretation of responses (Bardin 1993). Categories and subcategories were defined a priori with categories corresponding to the different parts of the interview and subcategories corresponding to questions inside each part. Categories and subcategories were classified according to meaning units composed by words or groups of words (Mucchielli 1996).

Coach behaviour and communications

Coach behaviour and communication were analysed using Mouchet and Le Guellec's (2012) observation tool, 'Communications des Entraîneurs de Rugby en Match' (COMEREM) [Coaches' rugby in-match communications]. Verbal and non-verbal interventions were sorted into categories inspired by previous studies (Bloom *et al.* 1999; Brewer and Jones 2002; Roy *et al.* 2007) and include: intervention number, transmitter, circumstances, people addressed, modes, contents, intention, intervention summary and effect, all of which were organized in a Microsoft Excel spreadsheet prior to analysis, an example of which can be seen in Table 6.1. A ticked box in each category was used to characterize the type intervention by each of the coaches. To provide two examples of this we focus on communication no. 8 and communication no. 14 (see Table 6.1):

> *Communication no. 8*: 5′20 E (calling number 9 during ball stoppage in front of him, for French player's injury): Titi, titi, relieve him with kicking, during the scrums and other game play! Take charge of kicks when we are in our 22m area! Relieve him (his partner no. 10) yourself, take the ball and kick it!
>
> *Communication no. 14*: 7′15 E: Patience, patience, patience! Come on, here we go, here we go, here we go! Laurent, Laurent, go in support Laurent! (player no. 1).

The Microsoft Excel spreadsheet included a calculation formula to automatically establish percentages in each category. Inter-observer reliability testing was conducted ahead of time with two people coding samples selected from different rugby matches until an 80 per cent agreement level was achieved (van der Mars 1989).

Match video

The 'evolution' of the match was represented in the 'scenario of the match' (match situation) (Mouchet *et al.* 2005) (Figure 6.1), which is a graphic representing the evolving opposition between the two teams. Utilization of this graphic enabled the contextualization of the coaches' behaviours and communications within the flow of events and focuses on the effect of coach intervention behaviours on resulting match production and player(s)' behaviour. As an example, in Figure 6.1 we can identify the 'boxes' (solid line) in which the French team lost possession twice after mauls. The first was at the 24-minute mark after a quick ruck with a turnover in favour of the South African (SA) team and the second 2 minutes later, after a long maul that was ended by a scrum for SA. This recurrent problem, which we can focus on using the video and 'scenario of the match', was also taken into account by the coaches in the coaching zone. In fact, one coach sent a message to his players in the next minute, which was relayed by the water carrier (water boy) who ran on to the pitch due to a French player's injury:

> 27′10 D (one coach speaking to himself): Oooh we keep losing the ball! But we come and take our positions anyway.

TABLE 6.1 Communications des Entraîneurs de Rugby en Match (COMEREM)

Intervention number	*5*	*8*	*11*	*14*
Transmitter (people who give the message)	*E*	*E*	*E*	*E*
Circumstances				
Event	Defence F after kick	Injury 14F and 1F		
Score	0/0	0/0	0/0	0/0
Moment of intervention	3'39	5'20	6'20	7'15
Ball stoppage		x	x	
In course of game	x			x
People addressed				
1 player	9	9	17	1
Group				
Team				
Manager (M)				
Other coach (E)				
Assistant coach (AT)				
Other people: 4th referee (IRB), water carrier (PE), doctor (D), physiotherapist (P)				
To himself				
Modes				
Gesture				
Shout or call out	x	x	x	x
Ask to come near the zone				
Talk				
Via intermediary: assistant coach (AC), other coach (C), water carrier (PE), doctor (D), physiotherapist (P), player (number)				
Enter and talk				
Via microphone				
Unilateral communication	x	x	x	x
Exchange				
Content				
Positive feedback				
Negative feedback				
Strategy and tactics	x	x		
Technics				x
Mental	x			x
Physical				
Substitution			x	
Other				
Intention				
To ask or guide (motor or mental actions)	x	x	x	
To induce an internal state modification (motivation, emotion, body state)				x
To convince (to modify a conception or belief)				
Game or player analysis				
Intervention summary	Pressing from no. 9	9 To use kick play	Tell 17 to warm up	1 to go in support
Effects	9 is running as defender	no	OK	OK

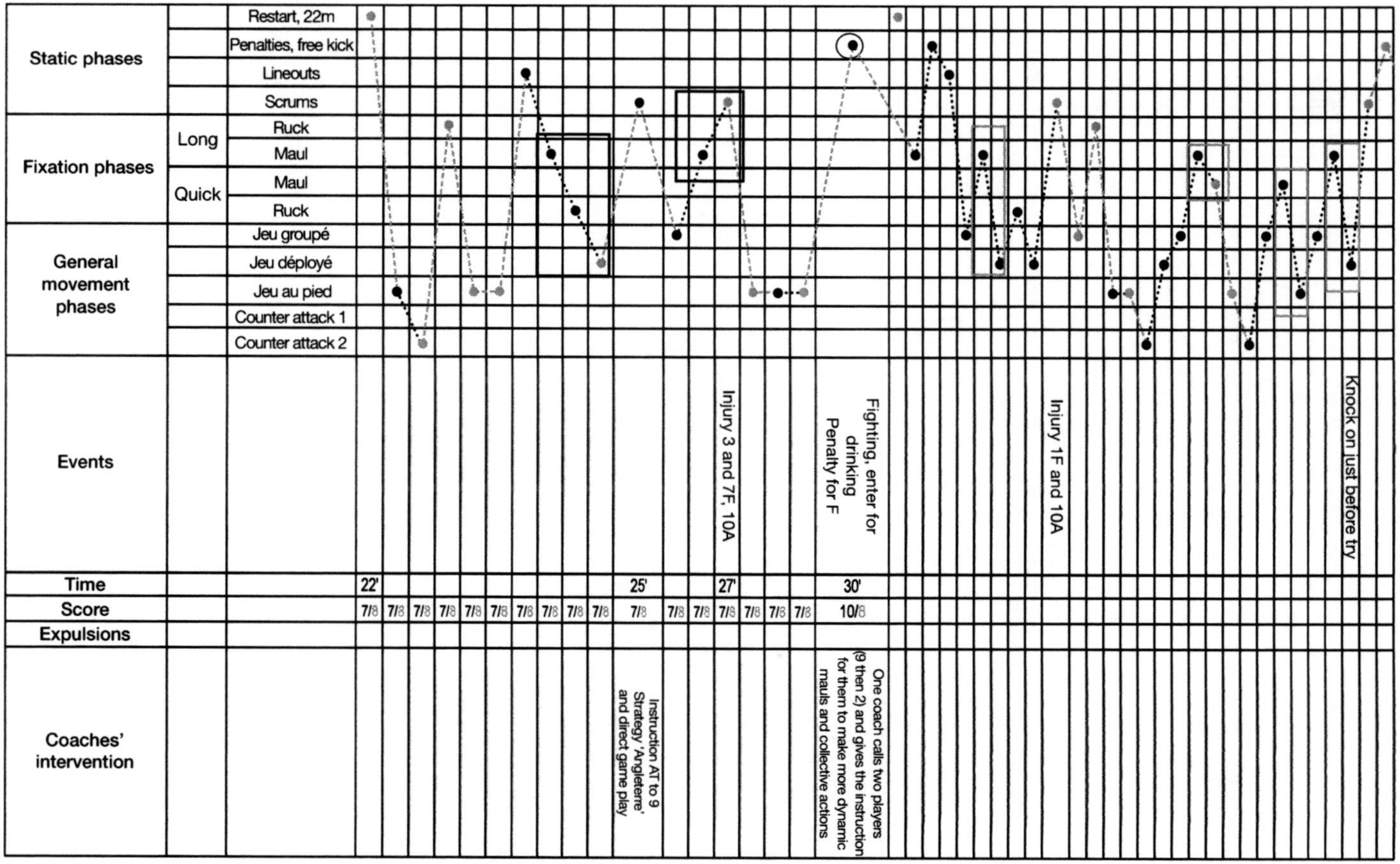

Static phases: Restart, 22m; Penalties, free kick; Lineouts; Scrums

Fixation phases: Long – Ruck, Maul; Quick – Maul, Ruck

General movement phases: Jeu groupé; Jeu déployé; Jeu au pied; Counter attack 1; Counter attack 2

Events: Injury 3 and 7F, 10A; Fighting, enter for drinking Penalty for F; Injury 1F and 10A; Knock on just before try

Time: 22'; 25'; 27'; 30'

Score: 7/8 7/8 7/8 7/8 7/8 7/8 7/8 7/8 7/8 7/8 7/8 7/8 7/8 7/8 7/8 7/8 7/8 10/8

Expulsions

Coaches' intervention: Instruction AT to 9 Strategy 'Angleterre' and direct game play; One coach calls two players (9 then 2) and gives the instruction for them to make more dynamic mauls and collective actions

FIGURE 6.1 Scenario of the match (adapted from Mouchet *et al.* 2005).

28′ D: But it's not possible! *Mais putain, on s'y file comme des merdes putain*! [Whore! we are playing like shit!] There is nobody. Hey! (to the water carrier). Tell them that it is useless playing mauls at two kilometres per hour (without any speed). We must clear the ball . . . With only one defender, they stop our maul. So tell them that they have to stop playing like that!

PE (water carrier): OK!

Explication interviews

Explication interviews were transcribed and analysed according to a method devised by Mouchet (2005, 2008). We reconstituted the subjective experience in each important moment selected by the coaches during the explication interview, distributing responses in categories such as aim, acts, attentional content, decision-making background and internal state. This allowed for a diachronic and synchronic description of the subjective experience based on the coach's point of view. In order to enhance reliability, two different researchers coded samples selected from the interviews (Culver *et al.* 2003). Moreover, participants received their verbatim transcript allowing them to verify the transcription and also comment on its interpretation by the researchers.

Results

Using COMEREM allowed for the identification of common coaching routines but with differences that were linked to context and/or dependent upon the personal profile of the coach. At the same time, the methodology enabled in-depth exploration of the coaches' subjective experiences during the match while highlighting their capability to adapt to particular in-match events.

This section presents some general findings in relation to each of the aspects of the COMEREM that illustrate the ways in which the research approach accounted for complexity and enabled a more holistic understanding than has typically been the case in the sport coaching literature. It then moves on to provide two in-depth examples of how accessing the coaches' subjective experience can be beneficial for developing an in-depth understanding and awareness of their ongoing coaching practice.

Quantitative data with COMEREM: common tendencies and differences

In this section we focus on the public behaviours of the coach, albeit, given our theoretical framework, we were also able to locate this public 'in the moment' communication behaviour in the general context or 'decisional background' as well as in the local context of the match using the pre-match interview records and the video of the actual match situation in which it occurred in order to provide a contextual description of the individual behaviours. In this section we overview each aspect of the behaviour.

Number and moment of interventions

Table 6.1 shows two different coaching profiles depending on the circumstances of the match action. For example, we first recognised a very reactive coach in the course of action when the ball is in play, where the coach would shout or call out to individual players with tactical, technical and/or motivational information as play ensued. Second, we found a more moderate coach who is proactive during stoppages of play, where s/he would provide strategic/tactical information to players or use the breaks in play to instigate changes in tactics via substitutions. Linking the quantitative data to the video and the 'scenario of the match' identified peaks of communications for all coaches during significant changes in the *rapport de force* ('flow' of the game) and resulting changes to the score line. These changes corresponded with 'strong or weak' periods of play for the team (i.e. territory/possession), which were identified through numerous encouragements by the coaches and/or interactions during a pause in the match after a try or during a penalty. This finding underlined the extent to which the coaches' behaviour was influenced by the local context, particularly the momentary *rapport de force* and also the coaches' adaptation to local circumstances such as breaks in play, where coaches seized opportunities to deliver messages.

Modes of communication

Table 6.1 further shows the major way that coaches communicated with players during the match was by shouting and calling. In conjunction with this finding the videos and 'scenarios of the match' demonstrated that the mode of communication remained somewhat constant whatever the score line and this pattern of behaviour was the same for almost all coaches independent of this element of local context.

On the one hand, this result is not surprising due to the constraints influencing coaching activity in rugby, which are part of the general context, because most of the time players are far away from the technical zone meaning that coaches have to shout. On the other hand, it was surprising to note the infrequent use of alternate forms of communication such as gestures, asking a player to come closer to the coach so as to be near the technical zone. Coaches of the France A Women's team were the exceptions, as they spoke in closer proximity to the players.

Evaluative feedback

We observed how coaches gave large amounts of positive feedback. This tendency is particularly pronounced with the France A Women's team coaches. In contrast, a lot of negative feedback was noted in the first half in the U/21 team coaches.

This made sense within the local context of the match: the outcome was important for both teams in this pool, and the video showed that the score line was very tight in the first half (i.e. 6/3 for France at half-time) and that there were many technical errors in the French team. Moreover, there was some tension on the pitch. However, this was reversed in the second half as France dominated and convincingly won the contest 32 to 3 with the possibility that this negative feedback may have motivated the players. In this match this strategy worked quite well, but this might not have worked as well in another situation.

The content of instructions

The majority of the coaches' in-match communications were focused on strategic and tactical aspects of play (see Figure 6.1). Linking this quantitative data to the semi-structured interviews gives it meaning in relation to the capabilities of the players and the priorities defined in the team project as elements of the general context and the local context considering coaches' expectations for those matches. However, Figure 6.1 also shows some peculiarities with the emphasis placed upon the mental aspects of play in communications to players by Noémie in the second half with the France A Women's team and by Denis with the U/21 team in the first half. These occasions illustrate how an understanding of these peculiarities is enhanced by data triangulation, using the multi-method approach.

In-depth analysis of coaches' communications

Example 1: understanding one coach's focus on the mental aspects of the game

With Denis, triangulation was useful for explaining his atypical behaviour in the local context of the first half. The video and 'scenario of the match' helped contextualize the importance of the 'mental' aspects of play emphasized in Denis' communications because several incidents of aggression occurred in the first 20 minutes. These included a fight, and three penalties for France because of rough play by Wales with French medical staff attending to players on the pitch three times and Welsh medical staff twice.

In the explication interview Denis was able to relive his preoccupation with this aggression from the opposition in the first half, saying, 'Oh yes! Yes, yes, there is something . . . The signs of the opposition aggression, who are beginning to provoke.' This brought to a conscious level the lack of emotional control that was a significant cue for Denis to respond to, stating that his preoccupation was 'a sign of powerlessness'. This verbalization of experience is confirmed by his intervention behaviour as viewed from an external, objective point of view with video and the 'scenario of the match'. During the first half, 38 per cent of Denis' communications focused on mental issues with him attempting to calm the players down to allow them to keep their concentration during this period of the match. For example, during the water break at the twentieth minute he gave the general message to his players to keep control via the physiotherapist then the number 8:

> 22 '55 (to the physiotherapist who is going on the pitch and taking water) 'You tell them not to react to the provocation, to remain focused on the game.'
>
> 23'08 (shout to call the physiotherapist during the break) 'Carlos, Carlos, Carlos! Tell them not to react to the provocation, to remain focused on the game, to recover possession, it is great!'
>
> 23'26 (to number 8) 'Nico, Nico, remain focused on defence, don't be provoked, stay in the contest!'

The impact of this intervention seems to have been effective because 3 minutes and 30 seconds later, during a collision that led to a penalty against Wales, the French players controlled their emotions. They ignored the quite explicit verbal and physical provocations of their opponents and moved away from them as observed on the video.

Example 2: Making sense of a particular intention

Figure 6.1 shows how asking or guiding the players is the principal intention of the coaches in their intervention with the exception of Noémie who, during the first half, was principally 'analysing the game or players'. Nevertheless, it is useful to build on this quantitative data by attempting to access the cognitive processes and subjective experience that shaped the coaches' decision-making and actions. For example, with the U/21 team during the first half, Eric intervened several times to guide the decision-making of the players (63 per cent). This contradicts the planned behaviour he articulated during the semi-structured interview, in which he said that, 'our role as coach is limited [during the match]'. This suggests a difference between what Eric planned to do and what he actually does in this match. The following paragraph focuses on one event during this period in an attempt to understand this apparent contradiction and to further illustrate the ways in which the holistic approach adopted in this study facilitated consideration and understanding of the complexity of in-match coaching.

In the explication interview Eric relived seizing an opportunity to develop a strategy for shaping his players' decision-making in response to a Welsh forward being sent to the sin bin for 10 minutes. Reliving the moment, Eric said, 'I don't want them to do that. I want them to put pressure on the Welsh and tire their forwards so that they leave some energy behind.' He mobilized a reflexive act (describing his observation of Michel (a forward): 'I think that he is going to say something . . . I see Michel who is discussing something with the backs . . .' This discussion was held just before the lineout held and was very significant for Eric who concluded that the French backs wanted to initiate a strategy.

The recording of Eric's communication during the match provided further evidence of his desire to direct this adaptation of the team's strategy towards a specific situation. Standing behind the barrier around the pitch, he asked the other coach (Denis), who was located in the technical zone, to relay a message about placing more pressure on the Welsh forwards. Denis immediately used the physiotherapist to give the message to the players during a stoppage. At the same moment, Eric also communicated with the number 9 (scrum half) who was coming for a drink near the 'coaching zone'. He repeated his communication with the same player before the lineout, which took place on the centre line, in favour of France and in the forty-second minute. The following is an extract of communications at this moment:

> 39′01 Eric: 'Denis! Denis! We need to put pressure on their forwards, this will tire them.' Denis: 'Yes. Carlos (the physiotherapist enters during a stoppage time), you tell them to put pressure on their forwards by using "Blacks" (i.e. that is the name of a strategy), this will work if there is support. OK, Carlos, give them the message, use "Blacks".'
> 40′ Eric: 'They are one down in the forward pack, so we need to play in the forwards. They are one down. Lineout! One forward fewer, lineout!'
> 42′39 Eric: 'Titi, Titi (no. 9)! Again, again, they are always one down, again, again, one down, they are going to leave feathers there!'

In the four minutes following the sending off of the Welsh forward, video data suggested the efficiency of Eric's request for the team to pressure the Welsh forwards. On two occasions, there was a lineout for France, followed by a maul, one of which advanced 30 metres and the other 15 metres, followed by dynamic attacking match play. This adaptation to circumstances demonstrates how the general context and local context influenced Eric's behaviour in one part of the match. He used both his decision-making background (knowledge about *rapport de force* in rugby and experience as an ex-backs player) and significant cues at one precise moment, to communicate effectively in the present match situation.

Discussion

Coaching 'genre and styles'

Clot's (2008) notion of '*clinique de l'activité*' and particularly the dynamic relationship between the '*genre et styles*' (Clot and Faïta 2000) is useful for conceptualizing the findings of this study and for situating them. 'Genre' is a shared part of the activity of people who are members of the same social and professional milieu and are classified as being social or technical. The 'social genre' of work is related to obligations that are shared by people who are working in the same context. 'Technical genre' is defined as the technical modes employed in a specific professional environment such as rugby coaching. The common tendencies in coaches' communications, with shared modalities of functioning, the nature of evaluative feedback, instructional content and main intentions, are indicative of a 'technical genre' that has a strong social focus, rooted in the broad playing and coaching culture of French rugby.

This study suggests that the coaches' in-competition communications are influenced by the broad social and cultural context of French rugby as a macro-system (Bouthier and Durey 1995) and the 'Direction Technique Nationale'. Light and Evans' (2013) use of *habitus* (see Bourdieu 1980) to enquire into the beliefs of Australian and New Zealand rugby coaches suggests that it may offer a way of further explaining or understanding what shapes the behaviour of rugby coaches in France (or any other country) due to the powerful yet implicit influence of a collective and individual *habitus*, operating at a non-conscious level. The use of *habitus* to conceptualize how coaches develop their practice from extended periods of time within particular social and cultural contexts is also evident in Chapters 7 and 8 in this volume.

Although the study identified shared 'coaching genre', there were differences between coaching 'styles' as individual adaptations or preferences in the application of techniques (Clot and Faïta 2000). This suggests that there is no specific 'one size fits all' coaching style at high performance-level coaching in French rugby. The differences in coaching styles displayed by coaches in this study are reflected in the reactive or proactive profiles as well as in specific modalities of functioning and instructional contents with the women's team. These 'styles' are based on personal characteristics, past experiences, objectives for the team, expectations for the game and characteristics of the players.

The in-depth analysis of match episodes illuminates individual adaptations to the local context and opportunities that are seized upon by coaches in particular situations. This seems to suggest the dynamic and complex nature of the individual coaches' interpretative actions (Saury and Durand 1998), situated within their general, local and micro-level contexts. When considering these results we should not forget that individual coaches' behaviour varies not only from one coach to another, but also from one context to another (Trudel 1997).

Implications

As we suggested in Chapter 1, good coaches constantly engage in reflection, not only on what they do but also why they do it (see Gilbert and Trudel 2001; Vallée and Bloom 2005). Recognition of the importance of reflection in coaching is also evident in suggestions for coach education and continuing professional development to utilize mentoring and critical reflection to situate learning in the practical experience of coaching (see Cassidy *et al.* 2009; Cushion *et al.* 2003). The study we report on in this chapter also supports Christensen's (2011) suggestion that utilizing actual practices and lived experiences could significantly improve coach education programmes.

Mouchet (2014) suggests using the reliving of specific moments in rugby matches through psycho-phenomenological explication interviews as a resource for improving player and team performance and it seems to us that it could also be used to improve coaching. This could be done by organizing an explication interview with the coach to access his/her in-competition behaviour such as game observation, communications with players, player substitution management or team talks before the match and/or at half-time. In line with the holistic research approach outlined in this chapter we suggest employing a mixed method approach using 'composite interview' and video (Mouchet *et al.* 2011) to access coaches' subjective experience during matches. Indeed, this study exemplifies how *in situ* analysis of practice could be an effective way of progressing the learning of coaches who are involved with young elite teams or sub-elite senior teams (Cushion *et al.* 2006).

Conclusion

The study discussed in this chapter employed methodology aimed at developing a comprehensive understanding of in-match coaching in rugby by taking an holistic approach. The use of case studies and a multi-method approach allowed for enquiry into the complexity and subjectivity of coaches' behaviour in the ecologically valid competition context. COMEREM allowed for the identification of coaching routines and communication profiles using quantitative data. Using data triangulation enabled the exploration of both the public and private facets of coaches' activity. We would argue that enquiring into coach behaviour both from an external, objective perspective and the internal, subjective dimensions of decision-making and locating of this within three, interrelated levels of context constitutes an holistic approach capable of accounting for the complex and situated nature of in-match coaching. We also provide a methodology that can address concerns with professional coaching knowledge being tacit, instinctive, intuitive and difficult for the practitioner to consider at a conscious level (Abraham *et al.* 2006; Gilbert and Trudel 2001; Nash and Collins 2006) and that can provide a means of dealing with the difficulty that Lyle (2002) suggests researchers have in capturing or accessing this embodied knowledge.

We also argue for the necessity to develop within coaching technical staff:

- functional modalities of communication utilized throughout the course of a match (i.e. use of gestures, summoning of players near the coaching zone . . .);
- responsibility and autonomy of players in the management of the match, notably with 'sector of game' leaders within the match (e.g. lineouts, defence . . .);
- adaptation to the circumstances of the match through the use of relevant contents and modes of intervention.

The approach reported on in this chapter offers a structured approach to using experiential learning to optimize coaches' ongoing professional learning and development. This requires advancement in the relationship between practice and operational knowledge, which can be achieved by reliving and sharing the subjective experience of coaching 'moments' to improve conscious understanding of their behaviour and the likely impact that it has on their players' and team's performance.

7

THE INFLUENCE OF EXPERIENCE AND CULTURAL CONTEXT ON RUGBY COACHES' BELIEFS ABOUT COACHING

Despite recognition of the powerful influence that experience exerts upon coaching (see Abraham *et al.* 2006; Lyle 2002; Nash and Collins 2006; Stephenson and Jowett 2009; and Chapter 4 of this volume) and of the development of coach knowledge as a long-term, situated, social process (Côté 2006; Jones *et al.* 2011), more empirical research conducted on how this occurs and/or what is learnt is needed. This extended chapter makes a contribution towards redressing this oversight by reporting on a study that enquired into how experience within culturally specific settings shaped the development of coaches' beliefs about coaching and their dispositions towards it.

The chapter is divided into two parts: Study 1 and Study 2. Following a brief chapter introduction, Study 1 focuses on three Melbourne rugby coaches who had learnt to play rugby and to coach in Australia, New Zealand and South Africa. It identified significant differences between them, highlighting the influence of early experience and culture on the development of their beliefs about coaching and dispositions towards it. Study 2 then explores in more detail the context of Afrikaans rugby in South Africa and professionalized rugby in Australia, which seemed to have shaped the coaching of two coaches in the Melbourne study. The larger study that this chapter draws on had not been completed at the time of writing, which is why there is no detailed investigation of New Zealand. However, the studies in South Africa and Australia provides valuable insight into how and what rugby coaches learn through experience.

Coach development

Chapter 4 discusses in detail how coaching beliefs and practices are developed through experience over time, with it being suggested that tacit knowledge forms the most powerful influence structuring coaching practices (Christensen 2009;

Nash and Collins 2006; Saury and Durand 1998). There is, however, limited understanding of how this occurs due to inadequate empirical research conducted on it to date. In one study that did specifically focus on this issue Light and Evans (2013) drew on Bourdieu to argue that, through participation in particular socio-cultural contexts, a socialization process occurs through which knowledge is developed according to the logic of the particular social field (such as sport, education or business) or sub-field (for example, rugby or rugby in a particular country). In this study, participation in practices within fields, sub-fields and the smaller social arenas of communities of practice (CoP – Lave and Wenger 1991) was seen to mediate between the setting and the individual to embody knowledge and inclinations towards coaching that operate at a non-conscious level to structure coaches' actions and dispositions.

The study

Constructivist grounded theory

The grounded theory approach adopted in both studies follows Charmaz's (2006) suggestions for a constructivist view of grounded theory that rejects the notion of the researcher as a detached observer in favour of seeing research as an interpretive process. In response to criticism of grounded theory, particularly from Glaser (1978), she highlights how the researcher's interpretations are made 'transparent' through the analysis being well articulated and grounded in the data.

The three main elements used in the three studies presented in this chapter are an integration of data generation (Charmaz 2006) and analysis, theoretical sampling (Glaser 1978) and memoing (Bryant and Charmaz 2010) as features of grounded theory (Birks and Mills 2011). The three participating coaches in Study 1 learnt to play and coach rugby in three different countries. This provided the opportunity for theoretical sampling strategies because highlighting the importance of the specific socio-cultural context in the initial analyses of the data generated led to detailed investigation of the socio-cultural contexts within which the coaches had developed. Memos were also used in all three studies as another core component of grounded theory that provides the impetus from which raw data are abstracted for analytical congruency (Glaser 1978).

Data generation and analysis

The term data generation is used as a way of conceptualizing the grounded theory approach as one in which the data, as part of the collection process, are simultaneously analysed. Data were generated through three semi-structured interviews with each participant that were transcribed verbatim and field notes with a research diary used to prompt analysis (Ezzy 2002). Data were reduced by using Auerbach and Silverstein's (2003) strategy of picking out relevant text. These sections of text were labelled (coded), and were either merged to form categories, or memo writing helped to induce abstractions of the raw data (Glaser 1978). It was at this point that literature was used to provide more depth and to develop themes and potential substantive theories. It was a combination of these strategies that prompted directed questions to be integrated into the conversational interviews with the participants (Rubin and Rubin 2005).

Study 1. Making better people: coaches' beliefs in moral learning through rugby

The three coaches in this study came from very different backgrounds and had quite different beliefs in coaching. The one common theme across the three coaches was the underpinning influence of the 'amateur ideal' and notions of rugby operating as a vehicle for moral education that has been embedded in the culture and practice of rugby for well over one 150 years.

Rugby and the 'amateur ideal'

Rugby formed a central mechanism in the development of the games ethic and the notion that team sports could be used to embody a class-specific morality in the English, nineteenth-century schools of the rising middle classes and its global dissemination over the nineteenth century (see, for example, Chandler and Naurigh 1999; Mangan 1981). For a century leading up to 1995 the class-specific ideal of amateurism was to rugby what the catechism is to the Catholic Church and the Talmud to Judaism:

> a badge that signalled the moral superiority of rugby union. It was a symbol of the sport's purity in the face of commercialism and professionalism. And it was a code by which the elect could live and the damned could be excluded.
> (Collins 2008, p. 1)

The idea of using team sport to embody preferred moral and social learning has proven to be remarkably resilient and particularly in rugby (see, for example, Ryan 2008). Despite increasing justification of physical education and sport in and out of schools as tools in the 'war against obesity' (see Gard and Wright 2005), moral and social learning continues to be seen as a rationale for the practice of sport in schools and youth sport settings (see, for example, Light and Harvey 2013). In particular, it has long been used to justify the dominant position of rugby in the schools of the privileged in Australia, England, South Africa and other former colonial nations as a means of developing morality and 'character' (see Light and Kirk 2000).

Site and participants

Study 1 was the first of four separate studies conducted in Australia, South Africa and New Zealand. A selective/purposive sampling strategy (Crotty 1998) was adopted, with participants recruited from the highest club level of club rugby in Melbourne in the state of Victoria, Australia. They were all head coaches of club teams competing at the premier level, but had played and begun coaching in the three different countries of Australia, New Zealand and South Africa. This set of circumstances highlighted the powerful influence of socio-cultural contexts on coach development that forms the focus of this chapter and that is further explored in Study 2. The names used in this chapter for clubs and people are pseudonyms used to protect the participants' anonymity.

'*Paul*' was born in the late 1950s and raised in Australia but only started playing rugby union at the age of seventeen. In a country where rugby league is one of the major team sports, he initially began playing rugby league as a child because it was the dominant sport in his hometown. However, he took up playing rugby union and went on to represent Australia as a Wallaby. '*Mike*' had an extensive playing career and early contact with rugby from the early age of five or six. He was born in the early 1970s in New Zealand and played all his rugby there in a country where rugby dominates the sporting landscape, forms a major cultural practice and is central to national identity (Crawford 1999; Jackson 2004). After coaching for five seasons he moved to Australia seven years prior to the study. '*Robert*' was born in South Africa during the mid-1960s and played all of his rugby in South Africa. He retired in his early thirties and coached for two seasons in South Africa before moving to Australia a decade prior to this study.

Results

Making better people: the influence of the 'amateur ideal'

The three coaches' experiences of growing up in rugby in three very different settings produced distinct differences in beliefs and dispositions. Despite these differences the study identified the common influence of the discourse of the 'amateur ideal', rooted in the games ethic of the nineteenth-century schools of the English middle classes (Mangan 1981) and manifested in common sets of beliefs clustered around the values of the 'amateur ideal' (see Collins 2008). They believed in the propensity of rugby to impart valuable moral learning and felt that a central aspect of a good rugby coach was his/her ability to contribute towards making 'better people'.

Fair play, moral learning and character

The three coaches believed that rugby should be played hard but should also promote fair play and other moral and ethical behaviour. They believed in the capacity of rugby to teach valuable life lessons and the need for coaches to develop players as good people and not just good players. They wanted to be successful coaches in terms of winning matches and championships but experienced some conflict between taking a pragmatic approach to winning required in a competitive environment and the value they attached to the *way* in which their teams won.

They did not see coaching only as a means of winning games, but also as a means of developing 'good' people with the 'right character' and integrity. They identified pressure placed on them for results from their clubs and their own desire to win, but there was tension between a 'win at all cost attitude' typically associated with professionalism and a belief in the need for moral learning. Each of them emphasized different aspects of what can be seen as the 'amateur ideal' in rugby (see Collins 2008) and the important moral and ethical learning that they felt should be developed through participation in rugby. Such values featured very strongly when asked for their views on good coaching, such as with Mike:

> I think what makes great coaching is a team feeling like they're in a different place and a better place than they were at the start of the year compared to the end of the year . . . so the best compliment I can have is not a player coming up and saying thanks coach we won. The best compliment I can get is a player that comes up and says thanks coach I look at things a lot differently than what I did before, and I have this complete new sense of belief in what I'm capable of, I think that's great coaching because you know you're not making a great rugby player you're making a great person, and great people make great rugby players.
>
> (Int.2, 13 September 2012)

Mike feels that rugby should make better people and that better people make better players. This was also a feature of Evans' (2011) study (and Chapter 8, which draws on this study), with the four elite-level New Zealand coaches believing that developing good players required moving beyond the confines of the playing fields to care about their lives outside rugby, in what could be described as an holistic approach to coaching.

Players should enjoy the game

The bifurcation of rugby into rugby union and rugby league occurred in England in 1895 when the newly formed Northern Rugby Football Union broke away from the Rugby Football Union. This was driven by class-based differences in the meanings attached to rugby that came to a head over different attitudes towards player payments. A decade later, in 1908, the same, class-based bifurcation occurred in Australia. The privileged classes who could afford to play rugby for 'the sake of the game' promoted the idea of playing to develop character, while the working classes were more competitive, and wanted to be compensated for injuries and the time off work needed to travel to games. While rugby league has been professional in both countries since its inception, rugby union remained amateur until 1995. During this time ideals connected to rugby operating as a vehicle for moral education were strongly promoted. Despite rugby having been professional for almost two decades by the time of the study, and the three coaches coming from very different backgrounds, all three of them espoused a belief in the need for players to enjoy rugby and not merely see it as a job, but something more associated with the amateur, pre-professional era as is evident in the following quote from Robert:

> I don't think coaching is rocket science I just think if you've got good people skills and if you have the interest of the players at heart that you'll go a long way. Bad coaches are driven for the wrong reasons and the right reasons are that; one, you want to develop the players, two, you want to make sure that when they get to the end of the season they can look back and say 'wow we had a good time'. If you win some silverware that's even better but you don't want to win silverware at the expense of people saying f**k I didn't enjoy that.
>
> (Robert, Int.1, 21 August 2012)

Focused on the three coaches as individuals the following section identifies distinctive features of their coaching *habitus* and how it was constructed over time.

Mike

Mike saw rugby as being far more than just a game. He valued the ethical and moral learning that he felt it should develop in young men. His belief in this was so strong that it seemed to operate as a quasi-religion for him. In some ways, the value he placed on player attitude and behaviour was similar to the emphasis Robert placed upon respect, commitment and discipline. The difference was that, for Mike, it was more focused on educating young men through rugby. He was also clear in suggesting that this approach to rugby was a way of life in New Zealand rooted in Maori culture. This very significant influence on his coaching shaped the construction of his coaching *habitus* through his participation in rugby in New Zealand as a player and then a coach:

> I'm a Kiwi and in New Zealand the influence of the Maori culture on all of us and in particular on rugby – rugby is spiritual in New Zealand – you know more than anything else it's spiritual. And when I played first XV we got our own haka and I knew what that meant to me personally – that we literally challenged the opposition. And that ritual galvanized us you know as a group and we were at one and our hearts beating simultaneously, you know during the ritual of the haka.
>
> (Int. 2, 13 September 2012)

The haka holds powerful cultural meaning by connecting the culture of rugby in New Zealand with Maori culture (Evans 2011) and in 2005 a review of the haka recommended ensuring everyone in the All Blacks community understood and bought into the cultural meaning and importance of it (Kitson 2005). This lends support to Mike's view on the influence of Maori culture on New Zealand rugby.

Following on from Light and Evans (2013), the focus on how context shapes the construction of a coaching *habitus* was tightened to consider rugby clubs as communities of practice (CoP). This allowed for the identification of more localized influences on Mike's beliefs and dispositions:

> My heart, if you like, is still very much a part of clubs like College Gunners and North Island University (pseudonyms) and the (New Zealand Super XV rugby team) more so than it is, to be honest, with Melbourne or the Rebels because this is a surrogate home for me.
>
> (Int. 2, 13 September 2012)

However, his career as a businessman created some tension between his quasi-religious beliefs about rugby and his business values and inclinations shaped by the *doxa* of the field of business.

While Paul and Robert enjoyed friendly relationships with their players, exchanged jokes from time to time, and valued being able to connect with them, Mike maintained a professional distance between him and his players. In Mike's case two quite distinct influences seem to have operated to shape his beliefs about coaching rugby and his practice. The beliefs he espoused suggested some tension between his business values and beliefs and his quasi-religious or almost spiritual disposition towards rugby as a way of life with deep meaning and significance. The construction of his coaching *habitus* had been strongly influenced by the culture of rugby in New Zealand, but it had also been influenced by his experiences in business as is evident here:

> Because business has been professional since it started, whereas like I've got a group of people that work for me at the moment and I can put my hand on my heart and say I care about all of them and when something happens at home or they get sick I want to make sure they are alright and just for very humanistic reasons. But at the same time I manage a professional distance with them because I need to perform at a certain level so that we get an output you know that is required.
>
> (Int. 3, 22 November 2012)

As with the other two coaches, Mike felt that playing rugby must be enjoyable and that if players did not enjoy their rugby the coach was not doing a good job:

> At the end of the day sport is about a bunch of grown-ups running around after a ball and you can never lose sight of that. It's called playing rugby it's not called working rugby, and so we go out and we play and if you don't feel the exhilaration of just being involved well then you know we are sort of failing.
>
> (Int. 2, 13 September 2012)

Although Mike promoted the spiritual nature of rugby and the importance of players learning life lessons through it he consistently emphasized the strong influence of his business values. Indeed, he suggested that his experience in business may have had a stronger influence on the way in which he coaches. However, it seems that the influence of growing up in a country where rugby forms a dominant cultural practice was deeply embodied. For Mike, rugby was a natural part of day-to-day life, inseparable from his memories of growing up in his family where rugby was always present:

> When I think about the friends that I have now you know I'm sort of 40 and when I go back, I grew up in a small country town, bump into the guys that I grew up with. Well our conversations and our earliest memories are all related to sport, you know so, can you remember when we went and played those guys, remember that time your dad spilled that pie down his shirt driving us to the game and nearly drove us into oncoming traffic you know . . . I suppose the earliest memories of it are, if I was to sum it up, feelings of friendship and fun, sort of day out type feeling.
>
> (Int. 3, 22 November 2012)

Paul

Paul grew up in rugby in Australia during an era that he felt was distinctive and which he refers to as the 'decision-making era'. He felt that this was an era in which Australian rugby emphasized creativity, flair and taking risks, which he contrasted with the style of rugby played by the Wallabies (Australia's national team) under the coaching of Robbie Deans, who was coach at the time of the interviews. He was very critical of play in the professional era and of the Wallabies in particular, whom he felt were too coach dominated, too structured, tentative and lacking in creativity and purpose. He contrasted this with his approach, which emphasized players learning through physical environments in which they felt free to experiment, take risks and learn to be creative, thinking players.

Paul enjoyed and valued a warm and friendly relationship with his players, who even called him by a nickname. Whether or not this is a feature of his easy-going coaching style (Lyle 2002) is uncertain, but what is certain is that he placed great emphasis on empowering players, giving them autonomy and finding ways of developing them into better thinkers. He described himself as a 'player-oriented' coach who wanted his players to be creative, take risks and be able to read the game:

> I give the players the skills to be able to go onto the field and show them within the skills I do what decisions they need to make to become better rugby players. I'm putting the emphasis back on the players they're on the field I'm not, they're the ones on the field who can read the plays and call them.
>
> (Int.2, 13 September 2012)

When asked what he felt his responsibilities were as a coach, his response reflected an emphasis on developing decision-making, player empowerment and getting players to think for themselves. He said that he's trying to get players 'to start thinking about what [they're] doing. I don't want [them] to take it as gospel from me' (Int. 2, 13 September 2012). He saw his role as providing learning environments in which his players found out for themselves and could be independent from the coach during matches:

> I think the creation of environment where players can succeed, strive for success, strive to be better, more skilled, all that sort of stuff, all that to create a really, really good environment to want, to want to do it that's what I think a good coach can do . . . That's what you've got to do as a coach.
>
> (Int. 2, 13 September 2012)

Paul said that his coaching aims to develop players with an exceptional 'sense' of the game. For him good or great players have the sense of the game that makes outstanding players (see Light *et al.* 2014a). In response to being asked what makes a good player he said that, 'Ah simple, the bloke who looks like he's got time and space to do everything, he's never cramped for room he has time to do things' (Int. 2, 13 September 2012). His criticism of what he saw as being over-structured coaching in Australian rugby over the past fifteen years reflects how much he values players having game sense:

> I find the issue with Australian rugby over the last – it has to be the last, at least 10 – it could be 15 – years, the emphasis has gone off the players with a high degree of skill, making the correct decisions at the right time and doing it under pressure, that's gone away from that to pre-packaged sort of stuff.
>
> (Int. 2, 13 September 2012)

Paul learnt and played rugby before the professional era and associated his approach with 'the amateur era', which he saw as being more creative, expressive and fun. He felt it expressed the 'real' Australian approach to playing rugby. Despite some influence on his beliefs, the meaning he attached to the term 'amateur' is not so laced with the historical emphasis on the values of the ruling classes discussed earlier. Instead, his references to the amateur era were more directed at a free, creative and expressive style of play evident before professionalization, which he contrasted with what he saw as being the highly structured and coach-controlled rugby of the professional era.

Robert

In all three interviews Robert emphasized strong belief in the value of *respect*, *discipline*, *hard work* and *commitment* that he identified as coming from his background in South Africa. He was proud of his South African origins and was critical of the lack of commitment and dedication of players in Melbourne when compared to players in South Africa. He prioritized a good work ethic and a respectful environment, while also expecting consistently appropriate behaviour from all his players. When asked what he felt his role as a coach was he responded by saying:

> I think the biggest, if you had to ask them, any of those players it would be that hard work bears fruit. That would probably be the single most important thing that I try and instil in them, you keep working hard you'll get the benefit and also just to keep your feet on the ground and you know when you start achieving things don't become arrogant because it's a big fall from arrogancy.
>
> (Int. 3, 22 November 2012)

These are the same values that he said characterize rugby culture in South Africa and were evident across all interviews with him during the study. The links to work ethic also featured when asked what he believes makes a good player, to which he responded:

> For me, it's about commitment and hard work. I would much rather play with someone who's committed and hardworking than with someone who's talented. Because the talented ones quite often sit back and depend on their talents, where the hard working guys they know they need to work hard, they're a lot fitter, you know their skills will probably never be the same as the very talented boys but they're a better player to have on your team.
>
> (Int.1, 21 August 2012)

As was the case with Mike and Paul, Robert thought that it was important that players enjoyed themselves and said that he developed a 'friendly' relationship with his players. However, his interactions with his players suggested more distance than Mike. This was because Robert believed that it was extremely important for players to know he was boss and he was 'running the show' as a clear indication of a coach-centred approach. He valued respect, commitment, dedication, playing as a team and courage in his players as traits he felt he exhibited and learnt over years of playing rugby in South Africa. He made it very clear that being liked by his players or being popular with them was not important to him, but that being respected was:

> Even at first grade we still try and make it fun for them because nobody wants to do stuff when you're not enjoying it and that's my commitment to them to make sure that all those boxes are ticked and that they enjoy, one playing rugby and that they enjoy being part of the club. But I don't try to be popular, I don't have to be popular because if you try and play the popularity game a lot of it goes out the window and that quite often

> prevents you from making tough decision if you try and be popular it just doesn't work. You should be respected but you don't have to be popular. Big difference!
>
> (Int.1, 21 August 2012)

He felt that coaches had to earn respect from players by displaying the ability to make hard decisions and this seemed to be linked to how he was coached as a player. He also consistently emphasized how his values and the traits he wants to see in his players come from his experiences of growing up playing rugby in South Africa:

> Look I think we do things a lot differently in South Africa. I for one – look I'm a straight shooter all the players know where they stand with me. If they stuff up I'll tell them but I never pick on people. I never take someone on in front of the rest if I've got a problem I'll pull them aside and I'll have a chat to them. I mean that for me is a given that's just respect. I mean you don't belittle someone in front of his teammates. But I think the biggest thing; I think – is we're straight shooters mate. I mean, if you come to SA we've grown up like that you know, coaching has been like that for many, many years in SA and it will probably always be like that.
>
> (Int.1, 21 August 2012)

Discussion

The importance placed upon developing 'character' by the three coaches suggests the influence of the 'amateur ideal' as a global discourse shaping the socio-cultural contexts within which they developed their beliefs and dispositions. It seemed to interplay with individual pathways through distinctly different socio-cultural settings and in tension with the values of professional rugby. Even at youth sport levels where we would expect that moral, ethical and personal development through sport might be emphasized, there is tension between rugby coaches' desire to achieve results and their feelings about fostering moral development in their players (see Romand and Pantaléon 2007). Each of the players' beliefs about coaching and dispositions towards coaching were different in detail and influenced by factors such as Afrikaans culture, Maori culture, the values of the business world and a particular era in Australian rugby particular to the lives of the three coaches.

The differences between the coaches originated from the different contexts within which they had learnt to play and coach rugby because of the unique nature of their journeys. Locating these differences in experience from an early age within three different countries and rugby cultures highlights the powerful influence of socio-cultural context on the construction of coaches' beliefs about and inclinations towards coaching that, in turn, shape their practice. Values and beliefs that can be linked to the values clustered around the amateur ideal were common across all three participants. The other features of the participants' coaching *habitus* that were identified can be located in far more specific socio-cultural contexts including the cultures of rugby in each country. More specifically, the influence of Maori culture on New Zealand rugby and of the Afrikaans culture on the rugby played in that region of South Africa played a significant role in shaping the construction of Mike's and Robert's beliefs about coaching and inclinations towards it.

The construction of Paul's coaching *habitus* seems to have been shaped by a particular era in Australian rugby that he refers to as 'the decision-making era'. This is the era during which he learnt to play rugby and played for the Wallabies and during which the 'win percentage' for the national team rose from 40 per cent prior to 1975 to 70–80 per cent over the 'decision-making era' between 1975 and 1995:

> something was happening and evolving. Australia doesn't have a great number of players so you have to say ok we don't have a great number of players how do we get around that? So what you have to do is have great coaching . . . so up until 1995 we had a system in place, that was a decision-making system, the players that came through that were la crème de la crème. If you look at the players, some of the greatest players that ever played in this country around 1995 went right through in that era.
>
> (Int. 3, 29 November 2012)

Like Mike, Robert emphasized the differences between his country of origin (South Africa) and Melbourne and how his values and beliefs about coaching were formed in South Africa:

> Commitment in SA is a lot better than it is here. We've had a couple of instances, not too dissimilar to other clubs in Melbourne, where now and again, we would have four guys not show up to training – first grade! Two of them might send you a text, two of them you would have no idea of where they are. In SA that's unheard of, if you have to move the world and the mountains to get training you'll just do it, so the level of commitment has got to do with the culture.
>
> (Int.1, 21 August 2012)

The ways in which Mike and Robert emphasized the differences between rugby culture in their home countries and in Melbourne, and the ways in which their beliefs about coaching differed, suggest the powerful influence that socio-cultural contexts exert on the formation of their beliefs and inclinations. This study also locates the construction of their coaching *habitus*, not only within three different countries, but also within contexts ranging from a tight focus on personal experience within rugby clubs to the influence of larger social fields such as that of sport and sport as business, while also suggesting their interplay. The tighter focus on CoP emphasizes agency with the larger focus on field highlighting the influence of structure. This illuminates the complex ways in which agency and structure interact in the construction of *habitus* and challenges claims that *habitus* is reductionist (King 2000). This can be understood by using the analogy of a camera lens, which can be used to provide different understandings of the object of study.

Tightening the lens provides detail on the nature of experience and its personal influence, while opening up the lens allows us to see the broader factors influencing and shaping this experience. For example, Mike's personal experiences of playing rugby in his club in Auckland promoted an attachment to, and identity with, that club. Opening up the lens allows us to see how the construction of his coaching *habitus* is shaped by the general culture of rugby in New Zealand and is influenced by Maori culture. Opening up the lens further again to allow for a global perspective enables us to see how tensions between traditional amateur ideals and professionalization can operate to influence individual coaches' development at a personal level. Drawing on Bourdieu's concept of social fields enables the identification of how this tension is a manifestation of those between the field of 'sport for sport's sake' and sport as business created by the intrusion of the field of business into the field of sport to produce the field of professional sport. In this study it seems that it is at this level of context that the three coaches' beliefs about rugby teaching life lessons and making better people were most significantly shaped. Chapter 6 illustrated how, in game coaching, decisions made are situated within and shaped by different levels of interacting context. This study on the three Melbourne coaches also emphasizes how different levels of context from the local to the global operate to shape coaching as a complex social process.

Study 2. South African and Australian coaches' encultured beliefs about coaching

This study investigates the cultural contexts within which two coaches in the Melbourne study learnt to coach and developed their beliefs about coaching and dispositions towards it. One study was conducted in Pretoria, South Africa and one in Sydney, Australia. The Pretoria study aimed to understand the impact of the socio-cultural context on Robert's development as a coach in South Africa and the extent to which his views and values reflect those of this cultural setting. The other study was undertaken in Sydney to gain insight into the nature of the cultural setting within which Paul, the Australian coach in the Melbourne study, learnt to coach. To this point, there appeared to be a strong link to their respective cultural contexts that suggested the ways in which experience shaped the coaches' views of and beliefs about coaching and suggests why it is more powerful than formal coach education (see Cushion *et al.* 2003).

Rugby and the colonized nations

The two contexts examined in this chapter are culturally different and historically constructed over time, with knowledge of how this occurred important for understanding how things are now. In South Africa, rugby is so prominent that it acts almost as a second religion (Black and Nauright 1998). In Australia it is a major sport but does not hold the same significance, with Hickie (2007) suggesting that Australian rugby structures do not promote faithful and enduring spectatorship. Both countries were colonized by the British. During the prominence of the games ethic as belief in the important moral and social lessons to be learnt through playing team sports, over the second half of the nineteenth century, British identity, imperial manliness and 'muscular Christianity' (Christian evangelism combined with vigorous masculinity) were promoted through rugby football (Dunning and Sheard 2005). In both Australia and South Africa the value attached to what sport was seen to teach was reinforced by what were perceived as threatening natural environments for the development of civilized societies (see Black and Nauright 1998; Stoddart 1986).

In both settings, rugby developed into a more localized practice, to the point of being unique to the culture in which it is steeped (Horton 2009). Through this process rugby in South Africa was dramatically shaped by politics and specifically by the reign of the racist apartheid regime under Afrikaner ideals. In Australia it was more shaped by social class with rugby union a practice of the middle classes. Indeed, the formation of rugby league in Australia in 1908 was the result of a class split between the middle classes (rugby) and the working class (rugby league). The First World War emphasized the class differences between union and league (Horton 2009), with union shut down out of respect for the soldiers in the war but with league continued.

The local context and its influence on rugby

Grundlingh (1998) suggests that sport entrenched in traditions encourages conformity and acts as a reflection of the dominant culture, but the forces shaping rugby as cultural practice are more complex than this. The practice of rugby has been shaped by the interaction of global discourse and local contexts in both Australia and South Africa that Horton (2009) describes as being 'glocalized'. However, what is not well known is the specific impact this has on current coaching trends. As research conducted by Light and Evans (2013) on rugby coaching in New Zealand and Australia suggests, rugby coaches' pedagogical views differ significantly across cultural contexts. Like teachers, coaches' philosophies arise from 'beliefs . . . [that] reflect a tacit understanding of personal, social or professional truths that have been constructed over time through enculturation, education or schooling' (Ennis, cited in Nash and Sproule 2009, p. 133). Unfortunately, there is a lack of research investigating the origins of beliefs that are reflected in such tacit understandings and that, constructed over time, influence a coach's practice. Indeed, there is evidence that they are interwoven (Nash and Sproule 2009).

South African rugby

Black and Nauright (1998) argue that the role rugby played in shaping Afrikaner identity cannot be overestimated, but it is important to understand that this does not imply that it is strictly a game played for Afrikaners in South Africa. In fact, rugby has a long history within both white-English and black (this term is used to describe non-white ethnic groups) populations. It was only during the mid-twentieth century that rugby started to align itself with Afrikanerdom as a result of the Afrikaner community seeking independence, power and identity (Grundlingh *et al.* 1995). From 1948, under the rule of the National Party, rugby developed as a privileged sport that symbolized racial superiority within the apartheid regime. While rugby was promoted as a vehicle for the promotion of sportsmanship and gentlemanly conduct by the British, the Afrikaners, in their search for identity, focused more on qualities such as 'ruggedness . . . forcefulness and determination' (Grundlingh 1998). As a result of the political situation in which rugby was immersed, it has come to be linked synonymously with Afrikanerdom. In addressing this problem the first black head coach of the Springboks (the national rugby side) was appointed to take 'into account the issue of transformation in rugby' (Gallagher 2008). This transformation is a legislative decision known as the 'quota', wherein a number of non-white players are required to be included in the national squad. There are mixed feelings concerning quotas across all the ethnic groups, often due to an ethical dilemma about the reality of the transformation of sport in post-apartheid South Africa (Höglund and Sundberg 2008) that suggests the residual effects of apartheid and the ongoing political battle in sport.

Australian rugby

The New South Wales Rugby Union (NSWRU) was at the forefront of rugby's development and shaped its wider diffusion in Australia. The entrenched amateur ethos was promoted up until the 1990s in Australia and was characterized by a game described by Fenton (as cited in Horton 2009, p. 1622) as being 'attractive to both player and spectator and an exhibition between friendly sportsmen'. This attractive style is often characterized as the Australian way of play (SANZAR News Service 2013). In contrast to South Africa, where rugby union dominates the sporting landscape, Australian rugby union has to compete against the other well-established football codes of Australian rules football, rugby league and Association football (soccer), with rugby union struggling to stamp its authority in a professional era marked by 'an expanding consumer culture. Thus . . . [it is] also a business that craves for media attention, corporate support and audience interest' (Skinner *et al.* 2003). This would suggest why the current head coach of the national team, Ewen McKenzie, is determined 'to play entertaining, attacking rugby' (Harris 2013), to keep supporters faithful and to develop rugby union as one of the main national sports.

The huge changes in Australian rugby that have been brought about by professionalism, including the increased emphasis on developing an entertaining 'product', have operated in tension with traditions of sport as a way of building character that have been so emphasized in the schools of the privileged, where rugby has formed a feature of the schooling experience (see Light 2007; Light and

Kirk 2000). During the amateur era Wallabies' teams were full of highly educated players who moved into prestigious post-rugby, professional careers, but the emergence of fully professional rugby careers has changed this dramatically. This has led to the increasing influence of the values of rugby as business and the need to entertain the public.

Methodology

Data presented in this chapter are from three completed individual cases conducted in Melbourne (Australia), Pretoria (South Africa) and Sydney (Australia) with all names used being pseudonyms. The methodology for all three studies is outlined at the beginning of this chapter.

Participants

Robert and *Paul* in the Melbourne study came from South Africa and Australia respectively, with studies in South Africa and Australia aimed at getting a better understanding of where and how their beliefs and dispositions were developed and to what extent they were a reflection of a dominant cultural practice (Light and Kirk 2000). *Isaak*, *Bob* and *Collin* made up the Pretoria case, and *Seth*, *Cameron* and *Josh* the Sydney case. Details of methodology are presented at the beginning of the chapter.

Results

Enculturation in coaching is a process of developing understandings and dispositions towards coaching over long periods of time through immersion in a particular culture (Light and Evans 2013). In the two cases reported on in this study (Study 2), and the Melbourne study reported on in Study 1, these coaching dispositions began developing from the individual coach's introduction into the sport and its culture as a young player. The majority of the coaches had an extensive playing career that begun so early that in Robert's case (Melbourne) he felt as if he had been 'born with rugby balls in [my] hands. I think I started when I was probably about six or five.' In Paul's case (Melbourne) he started late but he had started at an early age in rugby league, 'because it was basically a rugby league area and there were no other games' and he eventually switched to rugby union. It is this long engagement in particular socio-cultural contexts that led the three coaches in Melbourne to reflect on their upbringing and the differences between Melbourne rugby and what they were used to, or brought up with.

Robert is South African and had played all of his rugby in South Africa. He also coached for a couple of years in South Africa before moving to Australia ten years prior to the study. Yet, he feels that there is a marked difference between rugby in Melbourne and South Africa, terming it as a cultural difference:

> Yeah, there's a massive difference, it's a cultural difference in terms of, not motivation, what's the word I'm looking for; commitment! Commitment, yeah commitment in South Africa is a lot better than it is here.
>
> (Int. 1, 21 August 2012)

Mike had played all of his rugby and coached for a few years in New Zealand prior to coming to Australia. In interviews with him he emphasized the spiritual nature of rugby in New Zealand:

> I'm a Kiwi and in New Zealand the influence of the Maori culture on all of us and in particular on rugby. Rugby is spiritual in New Zealand, you know more than anything else it's spiritual.
>
> (Int. 1, 21 August 2012)

This view of rugby seems to be so connected with the person he is that, although he had been coaching in Australia for a longer period of time, he identifies with the club in which he played most of his rugby in New Zealand, calling Melbourne a 'surrogate home'. These views suggest a broad, strong cultural attachment, but for Paul the influence of a more localized context formed a powerful influence upon his views of coaching. He grew up in an Australian country town and because rugby league was the only sport offered he initially played league until the age of seventeen, when he switched to rugby union. He was critical of the Wallabies and their style of play (at the time of the study), which he contrasted with what he felt was the traditional style of play, characterized by flair, open, instinctive running rugby and creativity: 'We came through a decision making process, it was all about decision making, so you were la crème de la crème; the decision makers came into the full, they were the best decision makers on the field.' He termed it the 'decision-making era', and it had a very strong influence on his views of coaching. This was the era in which he learned to play and played his rugby and which he argues differs from his experiences.

It was these reflections on the part of the coaches that provided insight into the impact of the broader cultural context, such as Robert and Mike learning to play rugby in the respective countries of South Africa and New Zealand, and the more localized context of a particular era for Paul. It is at this point that theoretical sampling provided more understanding of the similarities between Robert and his counterparts in Pretoria and between Paul with his counterparts in Sydney. As Light (2007) argues, by drawing on Bourdieu, people who traverse similar sociocultural contexts express similar dispositions. This seemed to be strikingly evident with coaching rugby union. It seems that a dominant culture of Rugby, within a particular cultural context, fundamentally shapes the views these coaches have of coaching.

Pretoria and the influence of Afrikaans patriarchy

Robert's emphasis on developing respectful, disciplined players was very evident in Pretoria. He felt that a coach has to be 'permissive democratic' and be respected for his ability to make tough decisions for the team and not risk this respect to be popular with the players. Black and Nauright (1998) suggest that views like this arise from the role that rugby plays in reproducing a dominant culture in the form of Afrikaans patriarchy. Robert and Pretoria coaches Bob and Collin are all Afrikaans but Isaak is one of the few black coaches in the Pretoria league. It seems that learning to play rugby at an Afrikaans club has developed similar dispositions and views of coaching to those of Robert, Bob and Collin. This further suggests how an entrenched culture influences coaches' beliefs about coaching, beyond the scrutiny of the rational mind (Christensen 2009).

Bob was quite explicit in emphasizing a sense of order and a power hierarchy in the team, with the coach holding the power. He suggested that, not only should players respect the coach, but they should also fear him: 'you know someone once said to me your coach is like your father, you must love him but you must still be afraid of him'. This view on authority and the role it plays in the balance of coaching is well summed up by Bob:

> Respect must be earned, players must believe in you, if players don't believe in you they are quickly going to test you, you know what, you don't get a better example than like with lions. Lions will always go and test the highest authority to see if this guy really is who he says he is.
>
> (Int. 1, 11 April 2013)

Belief in the need for a patriarchal power hierarchy was evident not only in coach–player relationships but also in leadership roles within teams. Collin suggested that the same level of authority and respect is required as captain of the team because leaders set the example:

> If you've got a captain and he doesn't have the respect of other players, how can he captain a side, particularly if this bloke doesn't believe in him or that bloke doesn't believe in him or he doesn't even believe in me [the coach] or what I'm trying to achieve? So getting that respect is believing what they're saying, and following their lead.
>
> (Int. 2, 27 March 2013)

Collin felt that the emphasis on discipline in rugby had declined when compared to his experiences of growing up in rugby, possibly reflecting the 'collective discipline in the prosecution of a general cause' as a feature of Afrikaans culture (Archer and Bouillon, cited in Black and Nauright 1998, p. 10). For Collin, discipline had to be taught in the home, but its emphasis was declining:

> Discipline comes from the house and from the home that you stay in, so I mean the discipline that you create in your own home that becomes a part of your kids as well, that's a big issue for me as well . . . discipline doesn't come from school or anywhere else it comes from the home, but at times it seems to be lacking actually.
>
> (Int. 2, 27 March 2013)

South African rugby has been shaped by Afrikaner ideals in South Africa, with Grundlingh (1998) suggesting that the focus changed from British imperial ideals of Christian masculinity to one that emphasizes 'ruggedness . . . forcefulness and determination' (p. 114). Isaak picked players for their determination above any other attributes:

> I like hard workers and I like committed players, and never mind talent. I think there is where talent ends and I think there is where you have to be loyal to the people who are loyal to you. So most of the time, I prefer to use players who are very much committed understand me . . . when I pick my players I look at firstly who's committed before talent.
>
> (Int. 1, 22 February 2013)

The similarities between the attitudes of these coaches suggests that their dispositions towards coaching have become embodied as sets of deeply held beliefs, which are difficult to change (Bourdieu 1980; Light and Evans 2013). Although Robert had been in Australia for ten years at the time of the study, he retained strong views developed from his past experiences as a player and coach in a country where rugby is profoundly shaped by Afrikaans culture.

Robert's, Bob's and Collin's cultural upbringing and growing up in Afrikaans rugby were pivotal in shaping their beliefs about coaching. For example, Robert had this to say when asked about why he felt he valued discipline and commitment:

> Discipline and commitment that's the two things that we had when I was at school and that was one of the big things that I learned at a very early age, that discipline and commitment can do a lot of things for you in life; and not just sport you know, your personal life, your work life, whatever. If you have discipline and you have commitment you can achieve just about anything. And I've always lived my life according to that – business, sport and personal and I've instilled those sorts of values into my kids as well. If you're committed you can do anything.
>
> (Int. 1, 21 August 2012)

In Isaak's case it was the rugby club as a community of practice (CoP) (Lave and Wenger 1991; Wenger 1998) that most shaped his beliefs and dispositions, because his entry into the sport occurred comparatively late and the recognition required to thrive in a politically charged sporting system may have deeply influenced his views as he increased his participation in the core practices from a position of legitimate peripheral participation:

> You know I've realized one thing, even playing for Police when I was playing; if you are black most of the time you had to, you had to be extra special to be recognized. You have to be, if it's a hundred percent you have to be two hundred percent you understand. We have to work harder and that is where I think the discipline came from . . . but in terms of now, it so happens that you find yourself in the same situation when you are a coach . . . where I'm coaching now you find yourself in a situation whereby you have to be convincing so that the people can see that you are on the same par as the other coaches, it's because of the cultural difference, mostly for Afrikaners, rugby is a culture.
>
> (Int. 2, 22 March 2013)

Sydney and the influence of professionalism

The most prominent feature of the Sydney study was the impact of professionalism on coaching in a sporting environment within which there is pressure on rugby union to entertain. Rugby clubs in Sydney are now becoming a pathway to professional rugby, with players required to take more responsibility in their club rugby career as Seth suggested: 'First grade has to have fifteen guys that all want to go to super rugby because that's the pathway that is inherent in that route that they've put themselves on' (Int. 1, 27 May 2013). While the South African coaches saw the coach as a director of learning, suggesting a coach-centred approach (Light 2013b), the Australian coaches favoured empowering players and taking up a more player-centred pedagogy.

The views of Melbourne coach, Paul, were very similar to those of Josh, Seth and Cameron in the Sydney study. They all contrasted with the South African coaches' emphasis on the coach holding a position of authority and their preference for a more coach-centred, top-down, knowledge transmission approach, as is evident in Josh's views on coaching:

> I think the most successful coaches are the ones that allow the players to feel as if they've got a part of it. So you know, you get a lot of dictators who come along, scream and shout and tell everyone we have to do things my way, and it will work for a little while but sooner or later people will get the shits and bail out of it.
>
> (Int. 1, 28 May 2013)

Cameron also favoured a player-centred approach. He emphasized the need to have players understand what they are doing and why they are doing it, rather than just do what the coach asks them, and wanted them to be able to think for themselves on the field:

> I guess a good coach is someone that teaches people along the way, it's not spoon fed to people where they just do and they don't even think about it. So coaching to me, especially in rugby, is getting players to understand why they are doing things in the game rather than just doing things in the game if you know what I mean.
>
> (Int. 1, 24 May 2013)

This bears close resemblance to Paul's beliefs and the stress he places on players being able to think for themselves on the field:

> All I want [players] to do is to start thinking about what [they]'re doing, I don't want [them] to take it as gospel from me. I want [them] to think about how [they] can break down the opposition, I want [them] to think about things, I want [them] to think about how best we can beat them, start giving me ideas, I'm not the one out on the field [they] are.
>
> (Int. 2, 13 September 2012)

There is a clear pedagogical preference evident here among the Australian coaches from Sydney and Melbourne that is situated within a tradition of running rugby and the need to develop rugby as an entertaining product within the commodification of rugby on a global scale. When asked to outline the playing style of his team Seth emphasized open, running rugby:

> In terms of style you know; I coach a pretty open style of rugby which is forwards using skills, teaching the guys 1–8 you can have an effect with the ball in hand, you can run the ball and you can utilise all those attributes like breaking tackles, tackle bust, offloads and all that kind of stuff as a tight 5, you don't always need to be hitting rucks. So I try and teach my style, which is play with the ball, have a bit of fun with it, have fun with the ball in hand and play some open style rugby.
>
> (Int. 1, 27 May 2013)

When asked how he came to adopt this style he highlighted his playing experience in the Super Rugby tournament as an elite-level competition played at provincial level by teams in Australia, New Zealand and South Africa and one that relies on playing entertaining rugby due to its funding from television rights:

> There's a mixture of being taught it myself, from super rugby being coached in different elements and taking that into how I coach. I played for all super rugby teams except for the Rebels so I've had many coaches and many influences as such, a lot of what I've done in coaching has been taking the strengths of those guys and giving it my twist you know the [*Seth*] twist on how I want to play the game and then utilising that.
>
> (Int. 2, 3 June 2013)

This hints at a tradition of Australian rugby characterized by open, running and expansive play that pre-dates the professional era (from 1995) but which is strongly influenced by the commercialization of rugby and increasing competition between rugby and the other three football codes. The links between sport and business are clear here and were confirmed by Cameron, who said that sport and business are linked and that it is an essential element of the entertainment industry. He felt that because of this he had an obligation to provide an entertaining product that can compete against other football codes:

> I like to think that we're an attacking team and I think in Australian rugby we've got an obligation to be that way because otherwise our code is in danger, because of the strength of rugby league and AFL, soccer is getting stronger, rugby needs to be an entertaining product!
>
> (Int. 2, 31 May 2013)

The Sydney case provided some insight not only into the differing ideological perceptions of coaching in Afrikaans South Africa and Australia, but also into the impact of professionalization on rugby union. Of the three coaches, Cameron was the only full-time professional coach in any of the studies drawn on in this chapter. Seth and Josh had part-time positions and supplemented their roles as Director of Rugby with a day job that involved running youth coaching clinics in and around Sydney. In Melbourne, Paul, Robert and Mike were all volunteering their time.

In 2007, the Australian Rugby Championship (ARC) was introduced to provide a bridge from club rugby to the Super 15 competition, but it lasted only a year due to financial difficulties. This leaves playing premier club rugby as the only pathway for players aspiring to a professional career and particularly so in the states of Queensland and New South Wales. This is very different from the South African situation and seems to have shaped the role of the coach of today as a service provider. At the same time it has diminished volunteerism, which Taylor and Garratt (2010) argue is part of the culture of coaching on a global scale. Seth said that they had asked for volunteers to help with logistics but only one volunteer turned up, which he said was different from his playing days:

> We put out a call to our members last week for volunteers to go up to Birdswood stadium to help us with the logistics. We had 1 person come back say they would help . . . like we used to have managers coming out of everywhere just to help out the group you know; it's a bit different when you get up to a professional level . . . So yeah I think once again comparing it to at Eagles 2001 through to 2005 there were managers all over the place, there were people willing to help out, running water and making the club vibrant you know and I'm not seeing it anymore, it's difficult.
>
> (Int. 3, 12 June 2013)

This seemed to be common across the clubs of these coaches, with Josh saying that this is a reflection of modern society, the division of labour and the various tasks and roles required to field a competitive team in the professional era:

> Overall when you look at all clubs, volunteers are null and void now. I think the world has become so quick that a lot of people just don't have the time or the energy and there's a lot of things that have to be done in the club, a lot of tasks and roles that I think have increased over time because of the professional era. And it's hard to find those people to fill those roles.
>
> (Int. 3, 13 June 2013)

The Australian coaches in the two studies drawn on in Study 1 and Study 2 suggest that there was a long tradition of playing open, running rugby in Australia that has been further encouraged by the professionalization of rugby.

New Zealander, Robbie Deans, was the first foreigner to have coached the Wallabies, but in 2013 Australian Ewen McKenzie replaced him among speculation that it was his Australian coaching style that gave him the edge over South African, Rugby World Cup-winning Jake White. Bill Pulver, who is CEO of the Australian Rugby Union (ARU), was quoted as saying that, 'Arguably the most important (criterion) is that he has the ability to coach the way the Australian public wants the Wallabies to play – smart, creative running rugby' (ABC News 2013).

Discussion

This study links with Study 1 to locate the beliefs and practice of rugby coaches in experience over time, with an emphasis on the importance of the socio-cultural context. The enquiry into the two different contexts of Afrikaans rugby in Pretoria and rugby in Sydney illuminates vastly different socio-cultural environments and starkly different beliefs about coaching that provide convincing evidence of how context shapes practice. In doing so it provides valuable insights into the complex, interacting forces shaping rugby coaching at a local and global level and the interaction of individual agency and structure.

The cultural and political influence of Afrikaans culture on the coaches' approaches to coaching in Pretoria is remarkably strong and helps explain Robert's approach to coaching in Study 1. What is surprising here is the apparent lack of influence of rugby's professionalization and its commodification on a global scale in club rugby in Pretoria and particularly when compared to the Sydney study. This was not specifically explored in the study but the changes in the structure of rugby in South Africa and the way in which it seems to separate club rugby from the pathways from school into Super rugby are likely to contribute towards this.

In the Sydney study (Study 1) the global discourse of sport as a commodity and a valuable media product had a powerful influence on the need for coaches to entertain the public with open, running rugby. However, this is assisted by a tradition of playing with flair and playing running rugby in Australia as emphasized by Paul in the Melbourne study. Unlike Pretoria, club rugby in Sydney still forms part of a pathway into professional rugby and its emphasis on entertaining in the southern hemisphere. This seems to contribute towards the emphasis the Sydney coaches and Paul placed upon playing open, creative, running rugby and the need to employ player-centred coaching to achieve this.

Chapter conclusion

This chapter provides detailed understandings of how experience within particular cultural contexts shapes rugby coaches' beliefs about, sets of dispositions towards, and practice of, coaching. It makes a valuable contribution to our knowledge about what and how rugby coaches learn through experience as players and as coaches. It draws on research that takes on the challenge of providing understanding about what and how coaches learn through long-term experience without attempting to reduce the inherent complexity of this learning. It identifies the ways in which social structures and economic forces shape coaching at individual levels, but is balanced by the insights into agency it provides by examining individual experiences of playing rugby and coaching over long periods of time.

In terms of building an understanding of how coaches learn through experience it highlights the profound influence of particular social and cultural contexts upon their learning but across different levels that range from a very local level such as in a local club to the culture of Afrikaans rugby and the traditions of the Australian way of playing. It also suggests that these contexts do not operate autonomously but that they interact with other CoP and social sub-fields and intersect with the global discourses of professional, commodified rugby. While providing some answers to questions about how coaches learn through experience the chapter also asks more questions by highlighting the complexity of coach learning and the dynamic nature of the interacting contexts within which it takes place.

8

ELITE-LEVEL RUGBY COACHES' INTERPRETATION AND USE OF GAME SENSE IN AUSTRALIA AND NEW ZEALAND

This chapter draws on a study that enquired into the ways in which elite-level rugby coaches interpreted Game Sense and how this shaped the ways in which they used it (see Evans 2006b, 2011, 2012; Light and Evans 2010, 2013). The study involved eight coaches working at the highest levels of international rugby, including four head coaches of national teams. The details of the study are outlined below, after which the chapter is divided into Study 1 and Study 2, which present and discuss two different foci in the analysis of the larger project. Study 1 draws on Bourdieu's concept of *habitus* to identify the dispositions of the eight coaches towards Game Sense and how they were developed over time. Study 2 then focuses specifically on the four Australian coaches to enquire into their views on, and beliefs about, human learning and how this specifically influenced their views on Game Sense and the extent to which it influenced their coaching.

Methodology

The larger research project this chapter draws on adopts a multiple case study approach in Australia and New Zealand. Case studies provide the most appropriate strategy for examining practice within broader social contexts (Yin 2003) and are particularly useful in small-scale research where the study of practice is the goal, as is the case here (Tight 2003).

Participants

The participants were purposively selected at both sites (Wilson 2011) and include coaches working at provincial and national levels with all but one coaching a national team before, during or since the study was conducted. Pseudonyms for people and places have been used to protect anonymity with *Arnold*, *Paul*, *Walter* and *Rodney* the names used for the participants from New Zealand and *Ellery*, *Elvis*, *Joseph* and *Lincoln* used for the Australian coaches.

Data generation

Data used in this chapter were generated through three rounds of semi-structured interviews of 40 to 60 minutes each before or after training sessions at the ground used for training by each coach. The first round focused on the participant's life experiences as a player and coach, and the contexts within which these occurred, to identify how his beliefs about, and dispositions towards, coaching had been formed and what had influenced them. The second round of interviews sought to identify characteristics of their 'coaching *habitus*' (Light and Evans 2013) by enquiring into their views on aspects of coaching and learning but without directly asking such questions. It was aimed at identifying characteristics of a coaching *habitus* that structured their interpretation and use of Game Sense. The third round of interviews focused more directly on the coaches' articulated views on, and knowledge of, Game Sense and how they use it in, or adapt it to, their coaching. The structuring of the second and third rounds of interviews was also influenced by analysis of data generated by the previous interview. While reference is made to some data from the first round of interviews, the data used in this chapter were primarily generated through the second round of interviews, which were structured around Lau's (2004) three categories: (1) fundamental beliefs, un-thought premises or taken-for-granted assumptions, (2) perception and appreciation or understanding and (3) a descriptive and prescriptive practical sense of objective possibilities.

Analysis

The study used interpretive content analysis in which the data generation and analysis and the formation of theory are grounded in, and sensitive to, the context of the data and is an ongoing process (Piggott 2012; Silverman 2006). Content analysis focuses on matters in everyday social life and human communication (Krippendorff 2004; Neuendorf 2002) and can produce a 'systematic and comprehensive summary or overview of the data set' (Wilkinson 2004, p. 182). Interview data were reduced by close reading and rereading of the interview transcripts to identify and code chunks of the transcripts that could be related, or linked, to one of Lau's (2004) three themes. The data were then read through within each of Lau's themes to identify and code sub-themes. This resulted in the emergence of themes that were strong across all four participants at each site as first-order themes and second-order themes that might have been very strong with two or even three participants but not with all four (Miles and Huberman 1994).

Study 1. Dispositions of elite-level Australian and New Zealand coaches towards Game Sense

As is evident throughout this book the beliefs and sets of dispositions towards coaching that coaches develop through experience exert a powerful influence on how they interpret innovations in coaching. In school-based physical education and sport coaching this contributes to the misinterpretation of game-based approaches (GBA) that makes them difficult to implement authentically (see, for example, Jarrett and Harvey 2014; Light and Evans 2010) and the subsequent abandonment of them by coaches. The dispositions that coaches have towards coaching innovation are thus of critical importance for any attempt to implement them at individual or institutional levels because they shape interpretation of innovation.

By dispositions, we refer to the powerful influence of embodied experience, operating at a non-conscious level beyond the scrutiny of the conscious mind (Bourdieu 1990). Experience exerts a powerful effect upon coaching practice through the implicit yet powerful influence that 'tacit' and 'craft' knowledge have on practice and the ways in which the social histories of coaches shape their dispositions towards coaching (Jones *et al.* 2003; Light and Evans 2013; Nash and Collins 2006; Nash and Sproule 2011). At the same time, there is growing recognition of coach development as a learning process and the influence that social and cultural contexts have upon it (Côté 2006; Cushion 2007; Gilbert and Trudel 2000).

Study 1 in this chapter reports on research that enquired into the dispositions of elite-level Australian and New Zealand rugby coaches towards Game Sense using Bourdieu's concept of *habitus* to conceptualize how dispositions are embodied through experience over time. Like Chapter 7, it uses *habitus* to identify the coaches' dispositions and taken-for-granted sets of assumptions and beliefs by operationalizing it as a methodological tool. Although Chapter 5 was devoted to discussing the concept of *habitus*, we include a brief outline of it as used in this study.

Habitus

Bourdieu's key analytic concept of *habitus* refers to 'one's disposition, which influences the actions that one takes' (Dumais 2002, p. 46) and is structured by our past social experiences while it structures our immediate responses to emerging circumstances (Bourdieu 1977). There has been some confusion about the formation or construction of *habitus* in Bourdieu's work, but Lau (2004) suggests that it is possible to specify the mechanisms that link structural conditioning to social practices and regularities. With reference to the work of Merleau-Ponty and Husserl, he provides a framework for identifying *habitus* as it emerges from experience. Furthermore, he contends that: 'This interpretation is congruent with the argument that *habitus* is non-reductionist' (Lau 2004, p. 370). The vagueness of *habitus* is a strength, yet provides a challenge for its application with Lau's (2004) suggestions for operationalizing it offering a useful way of meeting the challenges of 'putting it to work' (Light and Evans, in press) to generate data. In the study we report on in this chapter it was used to identify the coaches' sets of beliefs and dispositions that structure their interpretation and implementation of Game Sense.

The study sought to identify the coaches' 'fundamental beliefs, un-thought premises or taken-for-granted assumptions' (Lau 2004, p. 377) by seeking their views on good coaching. To identify their perception, appreciation and understanding they were asked questions about what they thought made good rugby players and, to get a sense of their 'descriptive and prescriptive practical sense of objective possibilities', were asked questions about their attitudes towards innovation in rugby coaching (Lau 2004, p. 377).

Results

The results of the study are presented for the Australian site and then for the New Zealand site, followed by a discussion.

The Australian site

Belief-premises: views on good coaching

The participants were asked to suggest what they thought were the characteristics of a good rugby coach. In analysing data arising from their responses four consistent characteristics were suggested by the coaches as being those of a good coach, indicating their beliefs about coaching. Listed in order of importance these characteristics were that good coaches:

1 earn respect from players;
2 possess extensive knowledge;
3 display a strong work ethic, commitment and enthusiasm;
4 manage people well.

These characteristics were interrelated but are discussed under separate headings.

Earning respect from players. The most consistent mark of a good coach nominated by the four Australian coaches was that his/her players always respect him/her. For them, good coaches have a level of respect generated from being fair and honest with people in the organization, and through the display of personal traits valued by players. These were typically associated with an enthusiasm and a passion for rugby and for their work as a coach. They also valued fairness and strong leadership skills, such as being decisive about making difficult decisions and taking full responsibility for them as part of leading through example. In other words, a good coach had to display the characteristics s/he expected her/his players to show in training and in matches. The participants also felt that good coaches earn respect from players by having superior technical knowledge about the game and more specifically knowledge in the areas in which they are experts. The importance of not only having extensive knowledge, but also making it explicit, features as a means of generating player respect for coaches. In responding to a question about the traits of good coaches, Joseph said:

> I think just respect. I guess the players have to respect the coach. And as I said before, I said working with the players to get a result. The coach has to be the one leading the show and the players have to go down the path

> that he wants them to go down. But the players also have to be sitting beside him in the driving seat to get there, if that makes sense.
>
> (Int. 1, 9 February 2007)

In a later interview Ellery felt that it was important for players to respect the coach's knowledge. When describing his relationship with players he said:

> Yeah, well I think that there is mutual respect, I respect their individuality and they respect my knowledge and hopefully what I bring to the table in terms of helping to improve them as players because a coach's main job is to improve players.
>
> (Int. 1, 6 February 2007)

Possessing extensive knowledge. All four coaches felt that a good coach needs extensive, superior knowledge about both the game and training as well as in coaching approaches and techniques. For most of them this superior knowledge was what fostered the most respect for a coach among his players. Ellery said that a good coach is knowledgeable and respected and that players want to be coached by knowledgeable coaches; 'I think you have to have knowledge. I think players want to come to a coach and be sure that they know what they're talking about in most parts of the game' (Int. 1, 6 February 2007). Lincoln expressed exactly the same opinion about the need for coach knowledge and the respect for the coach that this generated, adding that they needed to be at the 'cutting edge' of developments in coaching to stay at the top. Lincoln confirms this when he makes the following statement about knowledge:

> Well I reckon you've got to be knowledgeable, you've got to know your sport, and I reckon that's a you've got to have the respect of the players, and what the players first and foremost respect is that you know your stuff. You don't have to know everything about the game, but you've got to have a handle on everything, and if you're coaching a particular area, like, that they want you to be at the cutting edge, so that's if you know your stuff, then you have the respect of the players.
>
> (Int. 1, 9 February 2007)

Elvis was less specific about knowledge but was of the opinion that his progress towards becoming a head coach had been helped over a period during which he was an assistant coach, which required a greater depth of knowledge on technical aspects of rugby. He said:

> Assistant coach is more for me is more of a technical pursuit. I've done that as well so that's far more technical the way I do it anyway. They're more technically orientated and probably have a closer relationship with the players face-to-face.
>
> (Int. 1, 28 February 2007)

He felt that becoming a good head coach required acquiring specific technical knowledge and that this knowledge came from the coach's own experiences as a player and coach and from keeping up with recent developments in coaching and the physical and psychological preparation of players.

Displaying a strong work ethic, commitment and enthusiasm. Ellery, Lincoln and Elvis consistently emphasized being enthusiastic, working hard and showing a passion for rugby as being important for getting results, earning the respect of players and being a good coach. Ellery said:

> I think you have to be extremely enthusiastic and with that comes a very high work ethic because, mate, this is one of the most wearying jobs in the world. You've got to be able to stick at it.
>
> (Int. 1, 6 February 2007)

He felt that coaching was difficult and the ability to be enthusiastic and work hard would allow you to get through the tough times associated with coaching. Lincoln had a similar view about the role of a work ethic and passion and how they were important ingredients in being successful, when reflecting on a previous coach he admired:

> You know, and it's not just that he hated losing, but he just was really, really passionate about people doing well, and performing as best they can, and I reckon you know, in anything you do in life, if you're really passionate about that, particularly about being successful, doesn't matter if it's rugby or something else, then you're half way there.
>
> (Int. 1, 9 February 2007)

The important traits of a good coach were the traits of coaches that the participants had respected as players. Elvis thought that a good coach needed to model the behaviours and that being prepared to undertake 'hard work' was high on the list of essential behaviours. Observations of training sessions conducted by the coaches suggested that Ellery, Lincoln and Elvis were indeed enthusiastic and even passionate in the ways that they approached their coaching. Ellery worked long hours and was extremely upbeat at the three sessions observed. Lincoln was also animated and excited at sessions encouraging his players to seek out excellence. Elvis described his job as having an 'extensive brief' and said that he had to constantly 'work on many fronts' (Int. 1, 28 February 2007). However, it was difficult to draw the same conclusion about Joseph due to his reserved style of interaction with the players and an approach to coaching that was more one of managing the coaching staff rather than rolling up his sleeves and becoming directly involved in coaching. Much like a very successful former national coach of the Wallabies, Rod Macqueen, Joseph saw himself more as the manager of a team of coaches rather than being a 'hands-on' coach.

Managing people well. All four coaches commented on the need for effective people management skills and the ability to lead by example, but this was least emphasized by Lincoln. Elvis felt that, 'Coaching's all people management' and that good coaches had to be able to make hard decisions such as decisions on team selection that lead to being respected by the players (Int. 1, 28 February 2007). He also suggested that it is important for good coaches to lead by example to generate respect and that this is achieved by decisive action that may not always please all players, but that should always earn respect from them for being prepared to make hard decisions and for being consistent. He said that this involved him empowering some players by delegating them some leadership responsibility, but observations indicated that the majority of training sessions were coach driven.

Joseph emphasized effective management skills more than the others did and was of the view that working with players requires understanding the type of person that you are working with to get a result. He said that a good coach needed to be aware of the different traits and personalities of his players to be able to effectively manage them and get the best out of them:

> I think working with the players to get a result. I think being very conscious that you are in the people business. Understanding the different traits of personalities of a person to get the best out of them. Understanding the strengths and the weaknesses of a player's ability, so he plays within those boundaries at times.
>
> (Int. 1, 9 February 2007)

Joseph also saw good coaching as involving the business of managing people, which included making decisions and understanding personalities. Ellery emphasized the importance of knowing players' personalities to be able to effectively manage them as a team. However, Elvis's views were very similar to Joseph's in that the latter felt, 'coaching's all people management' (Int. 1, 9 February 2007).

The New Zealand site

Belief-premises: views on good coaching

In analysing data on the participants' views on the characteristics of a good coach, two consistent themes emerged from interviews with the four New Zealand coaches. They were that a good coach:

1 fosters good relationships with players;
2 has a passion for rugby.

Fostering good relationships with players. For these four coaches there was an overarching concern with players as people and the need for coaches to build close relationships with them. This involved trying to understand players' emotions and feelings in order to foster strong bonds among players and coaching staff with the notion of care a constant theme. There was a concern with seeing the players as whole people with a life outside rugby, and the need for coaches to build strong, close relationships with them and to understand how they feel and see things. Paul said:

> I think one of the biggest things is probably even more so than it was even five years ago is and I'm not saying I've got it either is empathy, seeing the world through the young guys' eyes I think is a really powerful trait to have.
>
> (Int. 1, 5 September 2007)

Paul felt that being empathetic was an important goal for his future development as a coach and he said that it was the best way to get results because it developed better relationships between players and the coach, allowed for a more 'humanistic' environment, building team harmony and commitment: 'Because that's the best, and I've always known it's the best way to get the results out of the players and the buy-in and the commitment from your players' (Int. 1, 5 September 2007).

Paul felt that it was no longer important to be a highly technical coach because the needs for good coaching were changing: 'and a lot of it's moving away from just purely being really highly skilled technically and tactically to being a manager of people and environment' (Int. 1, 5 September 2007). Arnold said that it is important to establish a personal relationship with his players and he felt he had to understand them because the players came from a different generation from him with different needs. He said:

> The other thing about it is also the different generations of players that we've got. So I'm 54 and if I had a conservative nature and it wasn't accepting of change and able to embrace it and use it then, I think the players would probably – you wouldn't be able to relate to them. So if you like, you've got to have a young mind.
>
> (Int. 1, 4 September 2007)

Rodney has a similar view about the traits of a good coach and emphasized the importance of caring about the players beyond training sessions. He felt that caring for players was an imperative if you wanted them to learn:

> Well firstly, caring is the first prerequisite. If you don't care then you got no show 'cause people generally don't care what you know and how much you've got to offer until they know how much you care.
>
> (Int. 1, 6 September 2007)

He followed this up by saying that it is important to develop a relationship with his players and other staff so you can develop self-awareness in the coach and in the players in order to identity the individual needs of players and self. Rodney said that it was important to:

> actually connect with your people but also probably the most important skill is to be able to identify or build an awareness of what the need is. An awareness within yourself and awareness within your people. Because if they don't recognise that there is a need then you've got some challenges.
>
> (Int. 1, 6 September 2007)

In initial conversations with Paul, Walter and Rodney and outside the interviews, they regularly commented on the value of caring and regularly used this expression to describe how caring was important: 'Players don't care what you know unless they know you care about them' (Rodney, Int. 1, 6 September 2007).

Having a passion for rugby. All the coaches said that having a passion or love for rugby was important in becoming a successful coach. Walter said that passion and a love of the game were critical if you wanted to be successful at the elite level of rugby. He also felt that passion and love of the game was linked to the work ethic:

> For me anyway, I think love of the game is pretty critical. I don't think I'd do it if I didn't have that. And I think work ethic. You know, you've got to put the hours in if you want to be successful as a professional coach anyway.
>
> (Int. 1, 19 October 2007)

Paul, Rodney and Arnold were enthusiastic at training sessions, with Paul appearing excited when the players arrived and being quick to engage with them on a personal level. His passion for rugby was also reflected in how he spoke to players about the team's upcoming matches and his desire for them to be successful. Rodney was a little more reserved but was visibly interested in the players and spoke to them with passion. During observations of his training sessions, Arnold was prepared to spend additional time with players at the end of the sessions to discuss issues with them. All the coaches worked long hours and were keen to demonstrate their commitment to a range of people by always making themselves available.

Discussion

As is to be expected with a close-focus study with eight participants, there was significant variation between them with suggestions of contradiction and tensions in the beliefs and dispositions of some coaches. However, analysis of the data from the Australian site suggests sets of dispositions among the four coaches that lean more towards a coach-centred approach than towards player-centred approaches such as Game Sense. In general, they felt that coaches should be respected for their possession of knowledge and a range of personal characteristics valued by players such as strength, passion and a strong work ethic. They saw a good coach as being someone who is respected for his/her personal qualities, knowledge and experience. For them, a good coach is someone who displays character by making the tough decisions and taking full responsibility for them while displaying qualities that they expect their players to have. On the one hand, their beliefs in what makes a good coach suggests some friction with the principles of Game Sense, such as empowering the players and coaching indirectly by managing a learning environment and relying on questioning instead of telling players what to do. On the other hand, Ellery, in particular, was inclined towards the Game Sense approach but for problems with handing over power and responsibility to the players.

As with the Australian coaches there was considerable variation between the New Zealand participants, but data suggest that the four participants were favourably disposed towards Game Sense. Their views on what makes a good coach reflected a humanistic view of coaching and the value placed on developing relationships with players as is suggested in other research on New Zealand rugby (see Kidman 2005). They were moving away from an emphasis on developing superior technical knowledge towards developing the relationships they had with players and how this shaped learning (see Evans 2012). This is reflected in the importance placed on caring for players, having empathy for them and the contribution this made towards improving performance and developing self-awareness in players. This also provides a good example of how the positive coaching suggested in Chapter 2 can be successfully adopted at the most elite levels of world rugby and why it has been described as being 'humanistic' (Kidman 2005).

The Australian participants tended to display dispositions towards hierarchical power relationships between coach and players that were tied into their views on coaching as being a process of knowledge transmission. This would likely work against the uptake of Game Sense because it emphasizes monologue from the coach to players over dialogue between them that generates knowledge (Light and Fawns 2003). The *habitus* of the participants at the Australian site appears to dispose them towards what Tinning (1996) describes as a technocratic approach in which they see knowledge as an object and value both technical expertise and the ability to manage.

Predisposed towards a coach-centred approach, they see their role as one of transferring information to players and developing personal 'character' and preferred moral traits. This does not align with the principles of Game Sense as well as the *habitus* of the four New Zealand coaches seems to. The dispositions and beliefs of the participants at the New Zealand site suggest that they have, or are moving towards, a focus on establishing and maintaining relationships with players that are more humanistic. They tend to feel that caring and having empathy for a player or players is as important, if not more important, than possessing technical knowledge, which suggests a more holistic approach to coaching. The Australian participants value the ability to manage the 'work environment' and display valued personal characteristics seen as being important in generating respect from players and which they learnt to value growing up in the sub-field of Australian rugby.

The New Zealand coaches place significant value on establishing relationships with players and this resonates strongly with the humanistic intentions of Game Sense. Kidman (2005) argues that athlete-centred coaching constitutes a humanistic approach and that Game Sense has humanistic qualities. The emphasis placed on caring for players also seems to reflect what could be seen as a humanistic approach to coaching, with Jones (2009) suggesting that caring for athletes can promote empowerment and encourage them to explore situations and to find solutions to problems. The co-production of new knowledge through a partnership between the coach and players that rests upon an equitable and democratic relationship (Light and Fawns 2003) in Game Sense can be seen as another humanistic feature.

Sirna *et al.* (2010) argue that the culture of the environment contributes strongly to the pedagogical decisions made by teachers, with recent studies and writing confirming the pivotal role that context plays in shaping the implementation of game-based approaches (GBA) such as Game Sense and TGfU (see, for example, Curry and Light 2014; Quay and Stolz 2014). The positive dispositions of three of the four New Zealand coaches towards Game Sense was the result of years of change in their practice within changes in the larger environment of New Zealand rugby characterized by an organizational shift towards a Game Sense-type approach. From what we know about the influence of context, it would seem that the context of rugby in New Zealand at the time of the study would have encouraged, or at least supported, individual coaches to move towards a Game Sense or similar, player-centred, holistic approach.

While the four Australian coaches in the study had dispositions towards Game Sense that seemed less favourable than those of the New Zealand coaches, Ellery saw the possibilities offered by game-based coaching with this positive disposition towards GBA and this was strongly influenced by his experiences of sport while at school and having a teacher who used games to coach rugby. Many features of his *habitus* align with the philosophical foundations of Game Sense as suggested by his plans to introduce his 'flow' approach into his coaching, but he was less inclined to 'let go' with a preference for direct coaching and being in control. While he appreciates the benefits of a GBA, the expectations placed on rugby coaches working at his level seem to have thwarted its earlier introduction.

Conclusion

In this study there were significant differences between the Australian and New Zealand participants that have implications for the ways in which they might approach innovations in coaching. In this case it was Game Sense, but the identification of sets of dispositions among them has relevance and significance for rugby coaching more generally. It is also important for us to recognize the limitations of being able to generalize from such a small number of participants at either site but, of the eight participants, five have experience of coaching the Wallabies or All Blacks. There was also some variation between participants *within* either site, with one Australian coach more disposed towards the principles of Game Sense than the other three and one New Zealand coach less well disposed towards them than the other three. A closer focus also suggests that there is some tension and contradiction at work for each coach, but this is to be expected.

Rather than reduce the social complexity of coaching and coaches' dispositions, this chapter tries to make sense of it to provide insight into the powerful influence of a lifetime of experience in the sub-field of rugby on coaches' embodied knowledge, beliefs and dispositions towards an innovation in coaching. It draws attention to the powerful ways in which unarticulated and embodied experience structures coaches' practice and their interpretation of innovation. The use of *habitus*, and using it to generate data in particular, also offers an example of one way in which researchers might begin to investigate *how* and *what* learning occurs in coach development through experience and the important influence of context as is demonstrated in Chapter 7.

Study 2. Elite-level coaches' views on learning and the implications for coaching pedagogy

One of the main features of holistic approaches to coaching is the shift from a focus on what the coach does (coach behaviour) to a focus on what the players are learning and how. This is a very major change in thinking about coaching and player learning that has very clear implications for the coaching pedagogy adopted. Pedagogy is concerned with shaping and influencing learning that occurs at both explicit and implicit levels and is based upon particular perspectives on learning. Game-based coaching approaches sit upon assumptions about learning and notions of what knowledge is and how it is acquired (epistemology) that are very different from those that underpin more traditional, directive and skill-focused coaching.

Research on GBA in physical education teaching and sport coaching consistently identifies the ways in which the epistemology and assumptions about learning that underpin them can present problems for coaches (and teachers) interested in adopting them (see Butler 1996; Jarrett and Harvey 2014; Light 2004) and impede their wider uptake (see Curry and Light 2014; Light 2004; Roberts 2011). There has, however, been little *specific* attention paid to coaches' beliefs about learning, how they are developed and how they shape their interpretation of GBA. This chapter redresses this oversight by investigating the four Australian coaches' views on learning.

Game Sense pedagogy

The features of Game Sense pedagogy described and discussed in Chapters 1 and 2 sit upon constructivist perspectives on learning. These see it as something constructed by the individual through interpretation of learning experiences that is shaped by past experience, knowledge and dispositions and which contrasts with objectivist views of knowledge as an object that is transmitted from coach to players.

This typically challenges more traditional beliefs that coaches tend to hold about learning as being the transmission of knowledge that this chapter investigates. Given the earlier attention paid to Game Sense we restrict our discussion of it here to its particular pedagogical features that are relevant to the coaches' views on human learning.

The use of the term 'pedagogy' in this chapter refers to a broad and inclusive notion of it as being 'any conscious activity by one person designed to enhance learning in another' (Watkins and Mortimore 1999, p. 3). While many rugby coaches use games in practice sessions they typically do not use Game Sense pedagogy and this seems to be largely due to the ways in which it challenges their beliefs about how players learn and what good coaching involves (see Light and Evans 2010). The core idea of Games Sense is the use of a game as a context for learning along the lines of the pedagogy suggested by Dewey (1916/97), in which learning occurs through interaction with the environment rather than through direct instruction from the coach.

This pedagogy shifts the focus from the coach to the players by taking a problem-solving, player-centred approach. Encouraging players to think about what they are or should be doing places them at the centre of the learning process as active learners. The distinctive features of Game Sense (see Light 2013b and Chapters 1 and 2 in this volume) reflect a very different notion of learning to that which underpins more directive and coach-centred approaches to coaching that are based upon an objectivist and behaviourist view of learning as a process of knowledge transmission. From a constructivist perspective, Game Sense sees knowledge, the learner and the learning as being inseparable (Light and Fawns 2003). Owing to the fact that the coach is learning while guiding player learning, he/she can be seen as a partner in learning with learning conceived as an ecological process inseparable from the environment (Davis *et al.* 2000; Dewey 1916/97; Lave and Wenger 1991; Light and Fawns 2003). From this perspective learning does not involve adding on new knowledge, but, instead, transformation and adaptation (Davis *et al.* 2000; Prawat 1999).

Results

The pedagogy physical education teachers and coaches adopt is strongly influenced by their sets of unarticulated and unquestioned assumptions about learning (Light 2008a). If it is accepted that learning is an interpretive process shaped by the learner's past experience and sets of embodied dispositions, then coaches' responses to innovation or change in coaching are also shaped by their often unquestioned and unarticulated assumptions about learning.

Four interrelated themes emerged from the analysis and are listed below in order of importance, with coaches believing that:

1 learning is a process of internalizing knowledge as an object;
2 players have a preferred learning style;

3 players learn best when motivated through hard work;
4 players learn from their peers.

Learning is a process of internalizing knowledge as an object. The interviews with all coaches suggested an objectivist view of learning, but with Ellery there was some suggestion that he partially accepted the idea that players could construct their own knowledge by drawing on experience and prior knowledge. Overall, there was a strong view of learning as being a process of internalizing knowledge, with Elvis suggesting that learning was a process of 'absorbing' information:

> But I think yeah they're going to hear it, see it or do it, pretty much. So it's going to be one of those three or a combination of those three. So it's absorbing information that way.
>
> (Int. 2, 18 July 2007)

The dominant view among the coaches was that knowledge is an object that is transmitted or 'injected' by the coach and digested or absorbed by the players. Three of the coaches mentioned that, as the game of rugby union was a professional sport, coaches were required to transmit a larger volume of 'information' than previously, which players were required to absorb and process, but Elvis also felt that this is in some part learning through experience:

> So you know I think as the professional game's allowed us to inject a large quantity of information in terms of analysis and some people are better at digesting it than others so I think initially it's by doing it.
>
> (Int. 2, 18 July 2007)

Players have a preferred learning style. The notion of distinct learning styles is now over sixty years old in education. Yet to be supported by research, it has been criticized by many academics (see Reynolds 1997), but informed the views of the four coaches on learning. Ellery, Lincoln and Elvis felt that players have a particular learning style and this should form the basis for determining how to organize information and training for players. Ellery felt that the learning style can be tested and used as the basis for developing training programmes and that players had a dominant learning preference, which was mainly kinaesthetic or visual. In a response to a question on how players learn Ellery said:

> Well I think with players, you have to firstly find out their sensory preference of how they best learn and particularly in professional rugby now, we're getting guys coming through, the greater percentage of players are kinaesthetic and visual. And that increasingly a lower percentage of players who read and write, learn. We've just done some testing on them. So for each of those players, then you have to find out what their main medium is.
>
> (Int. 2, 19 April 2007)

Lincoln said it was important to find out how players learned. He felt that players had a learning style and that there were a number of styles players could access or to which they could be exposed. He said that coaches had to:

> Try and find out, get a feel for how the guys like to learn, and some guys get very little out of what's on a bit of paper or what's on video, but they need to get out there and do it, but if there's five or six different learning styles, like you're exposed to all of them.
>
> (Int. 2, 20 April 2007)

Lincoln also felt that it was important for players to understand their own learning style in order to learn: 'what the player's got to do is understand his own learning style' (Int. 2, 20 April 2007). Elvis thought that players needed to learn by watching and listening because of rugby union's reliance on the use of video recordings in coaching. He talked about how he used learning styles or preferences in his approach to coaching. He said that players learn:

> By knowing what their best [learning preference is], knowing how they absorb information for a start and then obviously trying to give them the information or tutoring in that context.
>
> (Int. 2, 18 July 2007)

Ellery, Lincoln and Elvis felt that their approaches to training reflected their understanding of learning styles and that the coaching they implemented took into account the learning styles of players. Lincoln pointed out that he and his coaching staff, 'try and use as many stimuli as we can' to ensure players get the information. He also mentioned that it was important not to rely on just one particular learning style for training:

> I'm not about the people who just say oh, no, f**k it, I'll learn just by doing, you know? And we'll have a crack at learn by watching, learn by listening as well, and we'll add to that.
>
> (Int. 2, 20 April 2007)

Observations indicated that these coaches primarily use verbal descriptions (as monologue) and demonstrations of skills in their coaching. This suggests that while the coaches said that they saw the need to use a range of stimuli in their sessions it was not reflected in the practices that were observed.

Players learn best when motivated through hard work. Each coach felt that hard work and motivation were necessary for players to improve at the elite level of rugby union. By this they meant that players needed to be intrinsically motivated to improve, and learnt best when involved in training that was physically and emotionally demanding. They expressed a belief in the need for players to sacrifice and suffer a little at training to prepare them for the rigours of matches and believed they needed the self-motivation to do so. They felt that players had to be motivated enough to succeed at, and profit from, this 'hard work'. When asked what was required for players to learn Ellery said: 'it's just hard work in simulated games situations' (Int. 2, 19 April 2007), suggesting a belief not only in hard work but also in the need to contextualize this within physical environments that replicate match conditions. Of the four coaches Ellery was most convinced of the value of games as an important part of training for elite-level players, as is reflected in the above quotation, but he also stressed the importance of hard work for players learning: 'If you don't have work ethic, you don't get improvement, so you've got to make sure that's non-negotiable, and you've got to create it' (Int. 2, 19 April 2007).

Lincoln stressed the role of motivation in players' learning but saw a commitment to hard work as an important means of stimulating this motivation. More broadly, he emphasized the need for many hours of hard work through hours of practice for players to improve:

> The quality of your learning requires motivation, so if you're not really motivated, you aren't learning. It's about doing. It's about making mistakes, well that's just you know, the hours of practice that are required.
>
> (Int. 2, 20 April 2007)

Lincoln also made reference to the need to make mistakes to learn but not to the reflection that Light (2013b) suggests is part of the Game Sense approach. Joseph was perhaps the strongest advocate of the need for hard work to help players improve and learn. He also stressed the need for hard work to involve 'repetition' for effective learning to take place. When asked about how players learn best he said that they learn: 'By mainly repetition on the [training] field' (Int. 2, 18 December 2007).

Players learn from their peers. The fourth theme in the coaches' views on how players learnt best was a belief that learning to play elite-level rugby union involved players learning from each other, which was strong among Ellery, Lincoln and Elvis. Ellery went as far as to suggest that players were the 'best teachers' and the coach's role was to facilitate this interaction when creating the training environment. Reflecting upon his own experience as a player Ellery gave the following response to a question about the role that he felt players should take to help each other learn:

> Generally the best teachers are the best players, and I think players learn best from other players, and we again, our coaching role is to create an environment so that can happen, and at the same time, ensure the standards doesn't drop.
>
> (Int. 2, 19 April 2007)

Ellery suggested that more informal interaction was also an important way in which players learned from each other. He lamented the reduction in opportunities to do so in contemporary rugby union:

> When we played, we used to go down the pub after a game and talk about it. That was a great learning experience. They don't do that anymore, because that's not society anymore, so they don't do it. So they get changed, they go to a nightclub and they don't talk.
>
> (Int. 2, 19 April 2007)

Lincoln felt that his organization had been successful in creating an environment where players learn from each other, with him emphasizing the need for junior players to learn from senior players and not only about how to play the game. He also said that they needed to learn the cultural elements of rugby and how to do a range of things associated with the practice of being a professional rugby union player. These included their approach to training and the quality of their training. Lincoln valued the individual specific knowledge about their position and the importance of having a 'feel for the game' among senior players but also thought that they should be passing on some of the culture of the team and organization in terms of values and attitudes towards training, playing and being in the team or organization. In response to a question about the capacity of players to learn from each other Lincoln said:

> I reckon players learn not so much about the intricacies of the game, but they learn a lot about how to train from their peers, and that's one of the major focuses with our younger players, particularly your academists [academy players] with it's not so much what you do, it's how you do it, learning to train, learning to be professional . . . I think they learn about being professional players, about being one and what it takes off their peers.
>
> (Int. 2, 20 April 2007)

Elvis felt that players learned more from each other than they did from coaches about certain aspects of technique and how to play and acknowledged how certain players in his team knew more about their position than he did. When asked about the capacity of players to teach each other Elvis cited the example of one of his players who is a teacher:

> Des Taylor for me is one of our best coaches because he's one of the world-class players and I say to my second rowers all the time, the best way for you to improve is to play with Des Taylor. I can tell you all I know about lineouts but playing with Des Taylor you'll learn more than I'll ever be able to tell you or show you or whatever because he'll be in your ear the whole time. He's holding on to you and you're scrummaging and he'll be able to

> do it better and you'll be able to watch him too, you can do all those things, you can hear it, see it and do it.
>
> (Int. 2, 18 July 2007)

Views on the use of games for learning

Asking the coaches about the place of game-based training in their coaching approaches provided some useful insight into their views on learning with three strong themes emerging. They were that (1) training games create similar pressure to the actual game and test players equally, (2) games are important for the development of spatial awareness and decision-making and (3) there was a need for skills to be developed *before* games are used. The following section will address each theme.

Applying pressure and testing players' skills

Ellery, Lincoln and Elvis felt that games were an opportunity for players to be tested under similar pressure to that experienced in a game. Ellery said that games were an important part of his approach to training and that they created similar conditions to those in a match, which meant that players' skills were tested in match-like conditions. Ellery made the following comment in response to a question about the role of games in the learning process for players:

> They're the test, they're the most important thing for them, because that's where they've got to execute everything under the conditions, and they're undoubtedly the best learning format.
>
> (Int. 2, 19 April 2007)

Lincoln felt that games provided an opportunity to create pressure that was similar to that in the actual game, although it was not possible to replicate a game exactly. He felt that practice games helped players learn to execute moves under pressure because there was an opposition, which was part of the contest: 'It is the pressure of a result, and the pressure of opposition' (Int. 2, 20 April 2007). Elvis felt that the contextual nature of training games was similar to that of the competition match and that, if the design of the game met certain spatial criteria, then players would feel match pressure. In a response to a question about the contribution of games to learning, Elvis said:

> I think if it's spatially right and it's a microcosm of the game you can see if they're getting the message, be it a skill message or a tactical one, yeah you can see it. Seeing it gives it relevance. This is how it fits in. They're not going to say it to you but you can see it in their eyes, I understand. So when they play the game they'll feel that environment.
>
> (Int. 2, 18 July 2007)

Ellery placed more emphasis on using games to develop decision-making and tactical knowledge than the others, but games were seen by the other three coaches primarily as a means of testing skills, game plays and tactics under match-like conditions rather than as media for learning skills, tactics and decision-making.

Developing spatial awareness and decision-making

Ellery, Lincoln and Elvis felt that training games provided an opportunity for players to understand the spatial requirements of rugby union and to improve their decision-making ability. In response to a question about what type of learning takes place during practice games, Lincoln said:

> It's about vision, spatial awareness, decision-making, all those things you do with ball in hand, as the game is played, so they're what we're trying to get out of our games.
>
> (Int. 2, 20 April 2007)

However, Lincoln felt that the benefits of using games for improving spatial awareness and decision-making were contingent upon the development of skills prior to the use of a game rather than learning skills in and through games:

> What you might be able to get out of the game in terms of spatial awareness and decision-making is sorely limited by their [the players'] lack of capacity to execute the skill. So I say got to get them to a certain skill level, and then you can grow the player, and if you can't get them to that skill level, see you later mate.
>
> (Int. 2, 20 April 2007)

Ellery was the strongest proponent of using games in training and felt that playing games improved the game sense of players. Indeed, he firmly believed that exposure to unstructured games during childhood was where game sense was developed, lamenting the decreased exposure of young players to such informal games:

> I think we train too much to play, you know, kids have got to play, and that's why I suppose we've had such good game sense, because our players used to play so much. Now we don't have good game sense.
>
> (Int. 2, 19 April 2007)

Elvis felt that training games provided an opportunity for improving decision-making and problem solving. Scrummaging is an area that is typically seen as being very technical, but Elvis was aware of the learning that emerges from actual match play and from simulated match conditions in training. While convinced of the central importance of technical work in scrummaging, he also outlined the need for problem-solving ability and experience in matches or match-like environments for improvement in scrummaging:

> What I learn in the game is about, I learn about my opponent and about how I can generate pressure and relieve pressure and that. In training if I'm doing a technical session it mightn't actually have anything to do with that opponent, it might be a general thing about maybe how we're going to engage our hips and things like that. So it's different and you've got time to talk about that . . . Whereas on the field I'm just actually dealing with that problem, I'm dealing with that situation. Might be familiar with my opponent I might never have played against him. So I've actually got to come up with solutions, so you know that's probably quite a specific example but that's how I look at it you know.
>
> (Int. 2, 18 July 2007)

Joseph used games for warm-ups and saw a role for them in training but was not convinced of their importance. However, he did recognize the important implicit learning that arises from playing games, suggesting that Australian players were more skilful than their counterparts due to playing touch football:

> Australians have always seemed to have great skills and I'm sure that's not because [of] the skill work they do. It's because since they've grown up, they've always played touch [touch football]. Before training, after training, they've played touch.
>
> (Int. 2, 18 December 2007)

Developing skills before games

All four coaches felt that skills had to be learnt before playing any training games. Ellery and Lincoln both indicated that there were advantages in using practice games, but were of the opinion that skills had to be developed to a certain level before a game can be used in training. Ellery valued the use of games as part of a training regime for developing skills, but was equally clear in his conviction that skills had to be adequate before playing the game and there had to be a progression from a focus on technique through to their application in match-like conditions with a gradual increase in pressure:

> When you want to improve your skills, got to lead to using it in the game, so I think the continuous skill practices you do, technique, skill, no pressure, skill under pressure, and then skill in the game, and you rotate through that continuum, and you jump. Sometimes you start with a skill in the game, go back to technique, go to skill with no pressure, and you keep moving through that, and that's the way to make the learning permanent. 'Cause what we're

> after is not performance at training, we're after learning at training, you know, it's a . . . it's a big thing. Like our training today, the last part was more about performance to get a bit of confidence.
>
> (Int. 2, 19 April 2007)

Ellery used a progression to develop skills in which skill execution in games was the last step and gradually developed it in increasingly complex environments accompanied by increasing pressure. Lincoln held similar views about the development of skills and their use in games. Lincoln held strong views about the role of games in training and was concerned that skills be developed in a sequential manner before the introduction of games. When asked how to improve his players' skills Lincoln said: 'Well my general theory is you need a baseline of core skill, so that I'm a strong believer in doing closed skill primers, and then moving into a more open environment' (Int. 2, 20 April 2007). Lincoln felt that when players do not have the required skill levels this can interfere with the training and learning of more experienced and skilful players:

> I believe if you don't have the skill in the open environment, then all you're doing is getting in f**king other people's way, and f**king up the learning experience for other people.
>
> (Int. 2, 20 April 2007)

Discussion

Despite significant variation between the coaches' views on how players learn they all seem to be influenced by common-sense assumptions about learning as a process of transmitting knowledge (Davis and Sumara 1997; Light 2008a). They tended to see knowledge as being an object that can be transferred from the coach to the players and believed in the notion of people having a particular learning style. That is to say, they do not see learning as a complex, whole-person process but, instead, as a linear and relatively unproblematic process. Davis and Sumara (2003) argue that the notion of learning styles proposes an artificial separation of modes of learning into specific designated 'styles' that overlooks how learning is a complex process that always involves a range of interacting senses. Slotting players into different categories of learning styles is reductionist and oversimplifies learning. Socio-cultural constructivist perspectives see learning as a process of interpretation through which the learner constructs new knowledge specific to his/her existing knowledge and inclinations (see Davis and Sumara 2003; Gréhaigne *et al.* 2005; Kirk and Macdonald 1998; Light and Kentel 2013).

The participants' stress on the need for hard work to learn is not necessarily at odds with the philosophy underpinning GBA, with Ellery, in particular, feeling that hard work is best done in the sort of practice games used in Game Sense coaching but with appropriate intensity. It would certainly be incorrect to suggest that, when using a Game Sense approach at elite levels, it should not be demanding or physically testing. Indeed, the continuity provided through practice games pitched at the appropriate level of challenge can replicate or exceed the intensity of competition matches as we have suggested for sevens rugby in Chapter 3. It can also provide the positive learning experiences promoted by positive coaching/ pedagogy when players are empowered to meet these challenges through interaction and collaboration with their peers. The importance placed upon players learning from each other through social interaction in and out of training sessions by three of the four coaches suggests they would be reasonably well disposed towards this approach.

Views on learning through games

The four coaches had generally positive views about the role of games in their coaching sessions. They all valued games, with Ellery in particular seeing them as being a very important medium for learning but not in the same way suggested in GBA. The prime difference here between their beliefs and the common features of GBA was the coaches' belief in the need to develop skills *before* playing practice games instead of learning them *through* games (see Light 2013b). Typically they employed the language of motor learning and followed a pattern of working on 'closed' skills out of context, then developing them by using practice games that progressively increase in complexity and the pressure on players until approximate levels experienced in a competitive match are reached. This suggests a belief in many of the ideas of Game Sense and other GBA around learning in contexts that resemble or replicate real game conditions, but also reflects a view of skills as being separate from tactical knowledge, decision-making and other aspects of game play. This is reflected in their views on the role of games as providing a means of testing skills and tactics (to a lesser extent) under pressure. They also valued games as a way of developing spatial awareness and decision-making in players but still with the proviso that skills were developed *before* the game and not *during* the game.

Game Sense approaches tend to be player-centred and focused on learning through engagement with the learning environment (see Light 2013b; Slade 2010). In these approaches players reflect upon and discuss their experiences within the context of the training environment and with dialogue between players and coaches central to the development of new knowledge (Evans 2012). Lincoln valued using games to develop skills and tactics but did not see value in discussion by, or with, his players. In fact, he viewed this as being detrimental to the coaching process. While it appears that the deep beliefs about learning of the coaches in this study do not align with the epistemology and assumptions about learning that underpin Game Sense, it is more complex than that. There was variation between the coaches and some contradictions and tensions for each coach. For example, Joseph seemed the least inclined towards Game Sense pedagogy, but Ellery held firm beliefs that align well with player-centred approaches to coaching yet seemed reluctant to empower players.

Chapter conclusion

This enquiry into New Zealand and Australian rugby coaches' dispositions towards Game Sense suggests a significant difference between the New Zealand and Australian coaches that is shaped by the contexts within which they learnt to play and coach. At the same time, it identifies variation between the coaches at either site, with the tighter focus on the four Australian coaches' beliefs about learning in Study 2 providing more detailed insight into contradictions between different beliefs at an individual level. It identifies aspects of coaches' beliefs that create tension with the pedagogical features of Game Sense and the ideas underpinning it. This suggests that we need more detailed understandings of what coaches' beliefs about learning and coaching actually are, and to avoid categorizing them as traditional or progressive coaches whose beliefs align with, or oppose, player-centred coaching approaches.

We suggested in Chapter 1 that it would be naive and unproductive to see coaches as being either traditionalists using direct instruction and focusing exclusively on technique or progressive coaches wholly adopting Game Sense and other GBA and this is supported by the results of the study reported on here. Case studies such as those drawn on in this chapter are difficult to generalize from but help in developing understanding of how experience influences coaching practice. The influence that unarticulated beliefs about coaching have on coaches' responses to innovation in coaching, and the complexity of this, also has implications for any programme of coach education that attempts to encourage significant changes in practice. From a social contructivist perspective, pre-existing knowledge and dispositions shape the ways in which the learner interprets the learning experience to construct his/her individual knowledge. For large organizations such as the RFU, this suggests that in attempting to make significant changes in how rugby is coached across England (examined in the following chapter) this awareness and understanding could be invaluable for achieving successful outcomes but would require a significant programme of research on coaches.

9

THE INTERPRETATION AND MISINTERPRETATION OF GAME SENSE IN ITS IMPLEMENTATION BY THE RFU

(with Paul Reid)

Some of the basic ideas of Game Sense have influenced the English Rugby Football Union (RFU) approach to coach education over the past decade (Light 2013b), with the term 'Game Sense' first appearing in its coaching resource materials and on its award courses in its Level 2 *Handbook* in 2001. This was well before the RFU had formally decided to align its coach education courses with the expectations of the United Kingdom Coaching Certificate (UKCC) and its emphasis on pedagogy, and on learner-centred pedagogies such as Game Sense in particular. At its most basic level Game Sense:

> involves designing a sequence of games to achieve particular outcomes, asking questions to stimulate thinking and reflection, and ensuring there are opportunities for group discussion, collaboration and the formulation of ideas/solutions that are tested and evaluated.
>
> (Light 2013b, p. 48)

Despite a significant body of research suggesting the challenges involved in switching from a directive and skill-focused coaching approach to game-based, player-centred approaches such as Game Sense (see, for example, Light and Evans 2010; Roberts 2011), the transition to a Game Sense coaching approach seems to have been perceived to be a straightforward process by the RFU, with inadequate consideration of the significant challenges involved in successfully implementing such a radical change in coaching. Although the use of games in practice is not uncommon in rugby coaching and other team sports, the player-centred Games Sense pedagogy presents a major problem for coaches (see Light and Evans 2010; Roberts 2011). These include, but are not limited to, a shift from coach-centred to player-centred coaching, the different role and positioning of the coach, the challenges involved in using questioning and the different relationships between players and between the coach and his/her players (see Evans 2014; Light 2004; Light and Evans 2010; Roberts 2011). This then presents a considerable challenge for any National Governing Body (NGB) that sets out to implement coach education programmes that actually lead to lasting and significant changes in practice (see Jarrett and Harvey 2014) because it confronts, not only coaches', but also coach educators' unarticulated beliefs and assumptions about learning and what good coaching is.

This chapter draws on a recent study on the implementation of a Game Sense-influenced coach education programme by the RFU to identify and discuss some of the challenges involved in overseeing such a significant change in the way rugby coaches coach. It examines the experiences of coaches and coach educators as learners of a new approach to coaching. It also examines coach educators' interpretation of the approach and their efforts to teach coaches so they could begin to implement it.

How coaches learn

Experience exerts a powerful influence on coaches' beliefs about coaching but research on their embodied assumptions about learning and how they shape interpretation of any coaching innovation is still limited. The research that has been completed in this area has mostly been conducted in rugby (see Evans 2012, 2014; Light and Evans 2013), with Chapter 7 reporting on an ongoing study on Australian, South African and New Zealand rugby coaches. Research conducted thus far suggests that coaches interpret Game Sense in different ways that are reflective of their coaching 'philosophies' and current practice (Harvey *et al.* 2010a; Kidman 2001; Light 2004; Roberts 2011), which, in turn, presents a huge challenge for coach educators and coach education more broadly. Moreover, there is a dearth of studies that have examined the perspectives of coach educators in empowering coaches to adopt constructivist approaches to learning such as Game Sense.

Formal coach education courses continue to be taught along traditional, didactic lines (similar to what we have suggested in Chapter 1 are traditional coaching sessions), where coach educators are perceived as knowledgeable experts who transfer knowledge to coach candidates as willing learners. Criticism of formal coach education provision sometimes describes it as 'coach training' and 'indoctrination', due to the lack of consideration given to the process of learning, and the greater focus placed upon the educational endeavours of the governing body than on the learners (coaches) (Nelson *et al.* 2006). As Light (2014) suggests, one of the more significant features of constructivist-informed coaching approaches such as Game Sense is their focus on what the players learn instead of on the coach's behaviour. The inability of formal coach education courses to successfully capture the situational variability within which coaches operate is seen as another reason why such courses are ineffective in shaping coaches' future practice and/or philosophies

(Chesterfield *et al.* 2010) and why these courses have little or no long-term, significant effect on actual coaching practice (Trudel *et al.* 2010).

This traditional approach to coach education is at odds with the underpinning epistemology of Game Sense and its learner-centred pedagogy, which sees learning as a social and complex process involving the whole person across a wide range of contexts (Light and Evans 2010; Light *et al.* 2014a; Trudel *et al.* 2010). As Dewey (1916/97, p. 19) suggests, we do not 'educate directly, but indirectly by means of the environment'. This holistic view of learning rejects objectivist views of learning to see knowledge as being inseparable from the learner (Light 2013b). In this way, Game Sense pedagogy sits on the assumption that learners learn by constructing meaning from their experiences rather than a predetermined, objectivist viewpoint.

Increasing attention is being paid to practical epistemologies (Quennerstedt 2013) within the physical education and sport field as a way of understanding the nature of knowledge and knowing in the world. Practical epistemologies promote ideas of learning as being shaped over time through participation in practice, with, and alongside, others, and through reflection in and on action. Learning is seen as being socially constructed and deeply embedded within social and cultural contexts, including the relationships between the coach, the player and the environment (Cushion 2011). Practical epistemologies allow researchers to consider a critical analysis of how knowledge, power and politics influence athlete/player learning and his/her constructions of knowledge. This view is well suited to the study of coach candidates learning about Game Sense pedagogy, as formal coach education courses are situated within particular social and cultural contexts where knowledge is developed through participation in practice within these contexts (Light 2008a).

Light and colleagues (see Light 2008a, 2013b; Light and Kentel 2013) draw on complex learning theory (CLT) to explain and understand learning in and through Game Sense and other learner-centred, enquiry-based coaching. Davis and Sumara (2003) first proposed CLT as an attempt to circumnavigate contradictions between social and psychological constructivism by drawing on complexity theory and identifying three common features. They suggest that: (1) learning is active, (2) learning is social and (3) learning is a process of interpretation (see also Light *et al.* 2014a). Unlike TGfU (Teaching Games for Understanding) there is no model for Game Sense but, drawing on CLT, Light (2013b) suggests a loose framework for Game Sense pedagogy by suggesting that Game Sense coaching (and teaching) should display four pedagogical features that are explained in the following section. One of the problems in initiating a large-scale change to a Game Sense-informed approach to coaching seems to be identifying what Game Sense actually is.

Game Sense

The loose framework suggested by Light (2013b) for Game Sense pedagogy (see Chapter 2) comprises four features that should be present in Game Sense coaching. These are that it involves:

1 the design and manipulation of practice games and activities;
2 the use of questioning;
3 the provision of opportunities for dialogue, collective development and testing of solutions for tactical problems;
4 building a supportive socio-moral environment.

The first feature involves coaches and coach educators designing the learning environment so that learners can engage with the environment and not through direct instruction (see Turner 2014). For coach candidates, this means educating players through modified and/or conditioned games where there is an interaction between techniques and tactics within the context of this game. There is, therefore, no requirement to have a prerequisite list of techniques/skills to play the game. From a coach educator perspective, this would mean supporting coach candidates in designing modified and/or conditioned games, affording coach candidates with the opportunities to 'plan, do and review' their coaching sessions, and offering advice and support along the way. The second feature is that coaches (and coach educators) should use questioning to stimulate dialogue and reflection. Within their coaching sessions coach candidates would therefore utilize open or divergent questions to stimulate players' thinking and dialogue (see Forrest 2014; Wright and Forrest 2007). Similarly, coach educators could also use a questioning approach to stimulate dialogue between themselves and the coach candidates and between the coach candidates themselves to generate deeper thinking and reflection. This does not come without its challenges as many players and/or coach candidates may become resistant to this approach as they, like the students in Roberts' (2011) study, 'just want the answer'.

The third feature of Game Sense coaching suggested by Light (2013b) is the provision of opportunities for arriving at collaborative ideas and solutions to game problems that are tested and evaluated. In terms of the coaching sessions, coach educators could let coach candidates deliver a short coaching session, stop it, provide opportunities for debate and discussion between the coach candidates about what went well, what needed improving and so on, and then make the necessary amendments and allow the coach to go back and continue to deliver the session. It might be that one coach candidate suggests a rule modification to the game, the coach and his/her coaching group would test this, and then there would be some time to reflect on its impact, before coming up with a new action project (Gréhaigne *et al.* 2005). The fourth feature of Game Sense pedagogy requires coaches and coach educators to provide a supportive learning environment in which making mistakes is seen as an essential part of learning and players are encouraged to take risks, be creative and engage in active learning.

Methodology

Participants and setting

A non-probability, convenience sampling strategy was employed (Singleton and Straits 1999) to identify coach candidates on UKCC RFU Level 2 courses in the northwest of England over a period of two years between 2010 and 2012. The Level 2 coach candidates who consented to participate in the study had all undergone the RFU Level 1 course within the five years prior to them undertaking their Level 2 course. Some had additional continuing professional development (CPD) units offered by the RFU to bridge the gap between the Level 1 and Level 2 courses.

Typically, the RFU Level 2 course is a four-day course offered over two weekends and in this case there was a month between each weekend. The course is a mixture of indoor, theoretical, module delivery and outdoor, practical modules. Candidates are asked to prepare and deliver sessions throughout the course, either individually, in pairs or in small groups, with all sessions formatively assessed by their course tutor who provides feedback. Coach educators generally work on a 1:8 ratio with candidates throughout the duration of the course and often join another group to deliver sessions when numbers are needed to make sessions realistic and relevant, such as unit or team plays and simulated game play. On day three there is a one-hour theory session on Game Sense that is delivered by the course leader, but the learner-centred pedagogical principles are introduced and reinforced throughout the entire course with coaches encouraged to deliver using this approach and adopt Game Sense, as and when appropriate. Summative assessment is awarded against a set of competencies that include subject knowledge and practical, coaching ability.

Data generation

Data were generated through (1) paper and electronic versions of an open-ended, self-administered questionnaire, (2) non-participant observations and informal conversations with coaches and coach educators, which were transposed into field notes, and (3) semi-structured interviews conducted on a one-to-one basis.

Questionnaires. Questionnaires were guided by a framework of focused questions borne out of observations and themes identified by the guest author and respondents from observations of previous courses. They were distributed at the end of the Level 2 courses and follow-up copies were sent out via e-mail to all candidates following the completion of the course. Sixty questionnaires were distributed with twenty-two returned. Four main questions were asked of the coaches:

1 What is your understanding of the term 'Game Sense'?
2 Have you used Game Sense with your players and if so how and when have you used it?

3 Outline the level and type of support that has been provided to you as a coach in your understanding and development of Game Sense.
4 What are the challenges of adopting Game Sense in your coaching?

Further prompts were also given to the coaches to which open-ended responses were provided. For example, for question 2, coaches were asked to respond to the prompt: How do you promote and develop game understanding and/or game awareness in your players?

Field notes. Field notes focused upon coach and coach educator interactions during sessions where Game Sense was highlighted and were gathered over the duration of each course and recorded in a field journal. The field notes were then used to promote questions to coaches and coach educators during observations of sessions.

Interviews. Observations formed the basis of questions to coaches in the semi-structured, one-to-one interviews that were conducted in a conversational tone and aimed at exploring and testing the emergent theories developed from analysis of the questionnaire data. Interviews with coaches and coach educators tended to be conducted after the delivery of a session by the coach or coach educator to gauge their views and triangulate these with observations of the researcher.

Data analysis

The questionnaire responses, field notes and semi-structured interview data were analysed using a constant-comparative approach (Bryman 2004). To achieve familiarization with the data questionnaire responses, field notes and the interview transcripts were read and reread. In line with the grounded theory approach taken (Glaser and Strauss 1975), data were analysed using the following two-step process: (1) reducing it down into meaningful units and (2) collating units that had similar properties to form broader categories. The purpose of this process was to organize the unstructured, qualitative data, which in turn helped with interpretation. From this process emerging themes and ideas were identified and tested in subsequent rounds of data generation, using the different methods outlined to arrive at a number of substantive theories that are presented in the results section of this chapter.

Results

The results of the study are collated under four main themes that are presented in order of importance. They provide insight into the experiences of the coach candidates and coach educators in their utilization of Game Sense pedagogy as it was interpreted by the RFU and in the delivery of RFU Level 2 courses. While these four themes are presented separately, they are in some sense interdependent, connecting readily to the holistic focus of Game Sense pedagogy presented in this book. The four themes are (1) the overlooking of pedagogy, (2) inconsistency of messages from coach educators, (3) limited opportunities to develop a practical 'sense' of Game Sense and (4) the quality and effectiveness of resources.

The overlooking of pedagogy

Game Sense was initially adopted as a new way of thinking by members of the RFU Coaching Department in a 'top-down' approach and was soon integrated into coach education resources and delivery to trainee coaches. In this study there appeared to be some confusion and differences in interpretations of Game Sense between the RFU coach education literature and the on-course delivery. There was, however, a common view of Game Sense as being primarily concerned with the use of modified games for practice as is evident in the following quotations from two coach candidates:

> The term game sense means that training sessions are tailored around games rather than drills. For example, the training session should involve activities which involve the participants playing games and actually learning the 'in and outs' of rugby through playing game specific games rather than drills. For example, when learning how to carry out back play, it may be more beneficial to just play a game and let the backs play what is in front of them rather than just run through moves without opposition.
>
> (Coach 5, interview)

> Game sense is teaching through modified games and game related/game realistic drills. It can be about setting a challenge for learners to solve through experimentation and guidance from a coach. The drills being realistic to game situations allow the players to have the correct tools to react to these situations in games. If they are set up correctly they can be very simulating environments for learners to be stimulated and learn.
>
> (Coach 10, interview)

As these quotations suggest, there is awareness of what Game Sense means for the coach candidates but this is focused predominantly on content to the neglect of its pedagogy. Light and Evans (2010) found the same problems with Australian rugby coaches' interpretation of Game Sense, reporting that they viewed it as being limited to the use of practice games while ignoring its player-centred pedagogy. This shallow interpretation contrasts with the view that pedagogy is central to effective Game Sense coaching in the sport coaching and physical education literature (see Evans 2012; Light 2013b; Roberts 2011). It also contrasts with the view that it should be approached from a situated, humanistic perspective that considers the pivotal importance of learning through the physical and socio-cultural context and the relationships between players, coaches and their environment (see Evans 2014; Kidman 2005; Quay and Stolz 2014).

Nelson and Cushion (2006) argue that a certain amount of 'filtering' of information occurs if the main points for consideration are not clearly identified or articulated in coach education and this seems to have been the case in this study. This can lead to the simplification of the key messages and a misunderstanding or misinterpretation of their true meaning (Roberts 2011). Rossi *et al.* (2007) also reported problems with understanding of key concepts of the Games Concept Approach (GCA), partly blamed on the 'top-down' nature of its implementation in Singapore. In the RFU study reported on here the use of largely direct instruction, and out of context, seems to have contributed strongly to the overlooking of Game Sense pedagogy and the lack of consideration of it by the coach candidates. Coaches like to learn through experience and it is the most influential way in which they learn, but despite how the articulation of Game Sense coaching should be they did not experience it.

Inconsistency of messages from coach educators

Interviews with coaches and coach educators suggest variation in the understandings that the coach educators had about what Game Sense was. The different approaches adopted by the coach educators and a lack of consistency in their message added to the challenges involved in moving coaches towards Game Sense pedagogy. Many seemed to misinterpret Game Sense, overlook its distinctive pedagogy, and see it as being merely the use of games: 'Game Sense is a style of coaching through the use of games. The games can be normal rugby style games or they can be modified to suit the needs of the situation or context' (Coach Educator 2, interview).

When asked what the main aim of Game Sense is the responses of coach educators suggested that, although they had some understanding of Game Sense, a clear message was lacking. For coaches struggling to understand a new approach that challenges their past practices and beliefs, this lack of a consistent message about the nature of Game Sense and this lack of clarity and consistency on the part of the coach educators, as is evident in the following two quotations, made learning a new way of coaching more challenging than it need have been:

> The idea of Game Sense is that players develop better when they are in a realistic learning environment, for example, if a coach wanted to develop the long/miss pass they might put this into a drill which isn't using maximum participation and although may be working on the technique is not developing the player's ability to use that pass when in a game situation.
>
> (Coach Educator 1, interview)

> As long as they (the coaches) start off at a particular point, ask questions and develop to a full game scenario then they are using Game Sense. They just need to make sure that the game is conditioned so that they can get their outcome.
>
> (Coach Educator 4, interview)

While there is some similarity in these responses from coach educators there was enough confusion about what Game Sense is and what its purpose is to affect the coach candidates' understanding of it. The coaches in the study were quick to articulate their concerns with this problem:

> I'm finding it very hard to keep track of what they are saying because they keep changing their minds and using different words. Just when I think that I have got it they keep throwing something else into the mix. I'm not even convinced that they know what they are on about themselves.
>
> (Coach 4, interview)

This perceived lack of a clear and consistent 'message' in the course combined with the use of a direct instruction approach to coach education combined to reduce the coaches' confidence in the coach educators' knowledge of Game Sense and their ability to help the coaches learn. Adopting the 'transmission model' of teaching requires having enough knowledge of what is being taught to foster confidence in the learners and belief that the teacher knows what s/he is talking about, but this did not seem to be the case:

> They keep banging on about Games Sense but then when another tutor takes over he changes his message! If they are going to teach us what to do then they need to have a common message. I think Game Sense, as I understand it, is just good coaching . . . making them (the players) think and taking responsibility for their own actions. I don't know if that's Game Sense but I always coach that way.
>
> (Coach 3, interview)

The data did not suggest that the coach educators were 'wrong' about Game Sense but that the programme needed more consistency and a more clear and consistent message. When asked about his thoughts on what these might be for Game Sense, one of the Level 2 Course Leaders said that 'it's asking questions, getting players involved, challenging players to think, making it relevant to the game, problem solving' (Coach Education Course Leader, August 2012). While this might not exactly match up to the features of Game Sense suggested by Light (2013b) and outlined in the introduction to this chapter, there is some close alignment with what Evans (2006b) calls its essence, but this did not seem to help the coach candidates in understanding 'the message'.

Limited opportunities to develop a practical 'sense' of Game Sense

Most coaches felt that they needed more time to work through the ideas in Game Sense in a practical setting and were frustrated by not having time available to do so. At least nine coaches outlined how they struggled to see a 'model' of Game Sense 'in practice' with comments from Coach 8 indicative of those coaches, specifically noting the limited support offered during some practical elements of the Level 2 course:

> Some support [was given] through the practical sessions when a comment was made as to how the particular skill practised was related to a decision making situation, but I wasn't given any time to develop this further.
>
> (Coach 8, interview)

Coaches learn and understand in practical ways and it is not surprising that the coaches in this study wanted more 'hands-on' time to learn how to coach using Game Sense. The message that in Game Sense players learn through experience in modified games and reflecting upon it seems to have come through, but the coaches wanted more time and opportunity to practise this. Coach 3 understood the importance of learning through the experience of playing practice games designed to facilitate certain learning but bemoaned not having sufficient time on the courses to develop his Game Sense practice:

> There has been an emphasis of using player[s'] experiences to communicate ideas, especially mid practical, which does allow an element of what I believe is 'Game Sense'. I don't think there was enough opportunity to explore the idea fully, but it was, on reflection, utilized in parts.
>
> (Coach 3, questionnaire)

All coaches received a review from their coach educators and were partnered with another coach to encourage dialogue between them, but most felt that they did not have enough time to reflect upon their pedagogical practices and to engage in the dialogue that the Game Sense approach promotes. The idea of having a partner coach was a step in the right direction but the coaches felt it was not enough because reflection in pairs was seldom encouraged or facilitated by the coach educators. Consequently, these reflections often became superficial and limited to discussion of session content rather than session delivery or pedagogy (field journal). This lack of dialogue, debate and reflection is paradoxical given that this process is a cornerstone of Game Sense pedagogy (Light 2013b).

Having most of the on-course learning conducted in classroom environments and other out-of-context practical settings was also seen as a weakness in the course by most coaches because it was too far removed from the real context of coaching, with Coach 12 saying that 'The course isn't realistic enough. I don't coach like this back in my club.' Coach 9 (interview) was more pointed in his criticism of the lack of learning experiences that were close to the real practice of coaching when he asked the following rhetorical question: 'How can they really tell anything about my coaching from an unrealistic scenario with nine players all of different ability and experience?'

Not providing practising and developing coaches with sufficient support and opportunities 'to coach' and reflect on this 'realistic' experience has been a common criticism of coach education courses in the past (Cassidy *et al.* 2004). Cushion (2006, cited in Jones 2006, p. 144) calls for greater support for developing coaches, and highlights the role of coach education in facilitating the 'construction of knowledge through experiential, contextual and socio-cultural methods in real world communities'.

As chapters 7, 9 and 10 demonstrate, coaches tend to develop their knowledge from sources such as coaching and playing experience and informal networks rather than from formal coach education courses and this was apparent among the coaches in this study:

> On the rugby Level 2, I had very little support apart from being told what it was on my PGCE and given some ideas for modified games. My main experience of the subject has come from personal experimentation when teaching and coaching and from working alongside other coaches who have been using this approach.
>
> (Coach 10, interview)

Analysis of the data collected on the coaches in this study indicates that they gained a significant amount of their professional development from sources other than those provided by the RFU as a form of social capital (Putnam 2000) rather than through formal coach education such as the RFU courses in this study (see also Williams and Kendall 2007). A problem with this is that innovation such as Games Sense coaching loses its authenticity or 'fidelity' (Jarrett and Harvey 2014) because the coaches taking it up have not gained a full understanding of it. Thus, the gaps in their knowledge are easily permeated and what ends up being offered is not Game Sense, but a 'version' of it that was not intended to be delivered.

The quality and effectiveness of resources

The final theme developed from the analysis of data is criticism by coaches of the resources provided by the RFU and the ways in which they were used. This was not as strong as the other three themes but was closely tied into them. For example, Coach 1, who is a physical education teacher, explained how he felt that 'From the RFU courses [the materials] are a fairly poor standard, and my main influence and knowledge about Game Sense is from industry and my professional career.' The importance of developing a 'coach-friendly' literature (coach manuals) is highlighted in a study by Irwin *et al.* (2004, p. 433) in which they note that, 'information [given to coaches] was in some cases too specialized and not practical enough'. While elite coaches might well have the knowledge to make sense of the material published in sport science journals they are not always capable of dealing with the complex, academic jargon that accompanied the material and that can alienate coaches of all levels (Williams and Kendall 2007).

As we have outlined above, there was inconsistency in the messages passed on to coaches by coach educators, which created confusion among the coaches who were frustrated by a lack of practical, 'hands-on' engagement in learning the Game Sense approach to coaching and being taught using pedagogy that was at odds with

Game Sense pedagogy. Having resources delivered at an inappropriate level for the coaches in this study seems to have further alienated them. This then links back to the points made earlier about coaches who are interested in the Game Sense approach being forced to develop their knowledge independently through their informal networks, which has the potential to widen the gap between knowledge and delivery of Game Sense pedagogy and the learning theories and epistemology that underpins it.

Discussion

This chapter identifies four aspects of the RFU coaching programme that appear to detract from its successful implementation of an authentic Game Sense approach to rugby coaching and that derive from conceptual, pedagogical and socio-cultural challenges. Of the four themes presented in this chapter the first three were stronger and more significant and of more relevance to improving knowledge that can help in the implementation of Game Sense coaching, with the last theme seeming to arise from existing frustration.

What seems to be incomplete conceptual and pedagogical understanding of Game Sense by coach educators was translated to coaches in the course to create confusion among them about what it is and how to do it. One of the major misinterpretations by coach educators and coaches is seeing Game Sense as just being the use of practice games and led to neglect of the distinctive Game Sense pedagogy, which is an issue raised elsewhere in rugby (see Light and Evans 2010). Despite the emphasis of the UKCC on athlete-centred pedagogy, both coach educators and coaches focused on *what* to coach rather than *how* to coach it. As Roberts (2011) cautions, when trying to oversimplify typically complex processes, greater clarity and support from the NGB, both on and post courses, are required for successful implementation of GBA such as TGfU and Game Sense. As we have suggested throughout this volume, deep understanding is essential for successful change to occur in coaching practice from the level of the practising coach to coach educators and those making important decisions about the nature of coach education. This is, in itself, a very challenging task for any NGB that requires considerable investment, commitment and monitoring.

While the first problem identified relates to coaches' practice and to coach education, the second problem identified is specifically related to coach education. Despite the emphasis of Game Sense on dialogue, reflection, collaboration, enquiry and equal relationships (see, for example, Evans 2014), the coach educators adopted a directive, transmission model approach to teaching that was not related to the 'knotty' and complex realities of coaches' practice (Jones *et al.* 2011). This is a case of asking coaches to 'do as I say and not what I do' for learners who typically value the practical aspects of learning. These require coaches to 'plan, do and review', with the review critical in aiding coaches to reflect on their own practice, possibly with support from a critical friend (Light and Evans 2013). Although coaches were put into pairs and encouraged to engage in reflection during the course, this was often rushed, undirected, uncritical and largely without support from a coach educator knowledgeable about Game Sense and the learning theory and epistemologies that underpin it. Few, if any, of the reflections were linked to how the coaches could adapt Game Sense to the demands of their own contexts or, indeed, explore how they would overcome challenges when trying to do so. In summary we suggest that, ironically, coach educators were trying to teach coaches a new method using the precise method they were seeking to challenge.

Game Sense pedagogy entails providing opportunities for collaborative formulation, testing and evaluation of solutions, all of which seem to be lacking in its delivery by the RFU (Light 2013b). This suggests that perhaps the RFU needs to consider ensuring clarity on what Game Sense pedagogy involves. Attention to providing coaches with a continued support network post the Level 2 course could also help by ensuring that they are involved in an ongoing process of learning as reflective practitioners (Schön 1983; see also Chapter 4 in this volume) and less likely to revert to the comfort and safety of their own personal or professional environment/networks to learn about Game Sense and/or simply reject it. Coach candidates should be made aware of the challenges of employing Game Sense pedagogy, such as changes to the aesthetics of training (Light 2004), and 'space' should be provided for coach candidates to engage in dialogue about, and reflection on, their implementation of Game Sense. This would at least be one way of supporting coach candidates on the Level 2 course, as they embark on the challenge of integrating Game Sense Pedagogy into their practice.

Conclusion

As Evans (2012) suggests, the use of Game Sense involves not only an awareness of the pedagogical principles specific to it but also an appreciation of what this looks like and feels like in practice when relating to the learners' own context of delivery. He also raises the issue of how uncertainty about, and variation in, the terminology used and muddy ideas about what Game Sense is can lead to misinterpretation and misunderstanding that interferes with the 'fidelity' of the approach (Jarrett and Harvey 2014). This seems to have been a problem in this study.

In addition to these misinterpretations and misunderstandings by coaches, adequate support was not provided to them post course to encourage learning as an ongoing process. This becomes even more important for the practising coach when the on-course messages and examples provided by the coach educators are divorced from their own contexts of delivery. In this instance, critical support and guidance from experienced coach educators is fundamental to learning and currently not accessible to learner coaches post course, something that is in urgent need of addressing.

The coach education research identifies the non-linear and complex process that learning new ways of coaching entails (see Davids 2010; Harvey *et al.* 2010a). Further research on NGB-level implementation might explore how this could be offset with the provision of context-specific learning situations where messages and practical examples are realistic and relevant, language is consistent and comprehensible and where opportunities to practise, make mistakes, and reflect on and learn how to remedy these, are both provided and valued. As Armour and Yelling (2004) suggest, professional bodies such as NGBs should focus more on professional 'learning' rather than professional 'development' and we need to recognise and value a variety of learning activities that exist along a spectrum from formal to informal settings.

The RFU clearly recognizes the considerable benefits that implementing a Game Sense-influenced approach to coaching nationally can produce. We applaud this foresight and commitment to improving coaching across all levels of rugby in England. Shifting coaching on such a large scale from what we have described earlier in this volume as 'traditional' directive and skill-focused coaching to player-centred, enquiry-based coaching represents a massive challenge for the RFU that this study suggests it may well have underestimated. It might well be time for the RFU to engage in some assessment of how the task is progressing and critical reflection on where it needs to 'lift its game'. We wholly support the idea of implementing a Game Sense-influenced approach to coaching on a national scale but would be deeply disappointed to see it flounder due to poor implementation strategies.

10

BRIDGING THE GAP BETWEEN THEORY AND PRACTICE THROUGH COLLABORATIVE ACTION RESEARCH

As suggested in Chapters 4 and 9 coach accreditation courses and other professional development, training or education typically take the form of short interventions that the sport coaching literature suggests are limited in their capacity to meet the development needs of coaches and enhance the development of expertise (Cassidy *et al.* 2004; Cushion 2007; Dickson 2001; Jones 2006). Busy coaches are also hard pressed to find the time to read or even locate relevant research findings that can also be difficult to access due to the use of academic jargon, with theory often too removed from practice to engage them. These challenges have encouraged researchers in sport coaching to look at alternative approaches to developing coach expertise and have stimulated interest in education theory and practice (see, for example, Jones 2006, 2007). Within this development some have suggested looking at how action research (AR), as used for teacher development, could promote coach development in a way that can focus on the specific interests of the coach (Ahlberg *et al.* 2008; Butler 2005; Cassidy *et al.* 2006).

Undertaking AR is one way in which coaches can focus on their particular needs and interests, but for coaches unused to research and unfamiliar with the research literature this may not be an attractive option. This chapter presents an approach developed for coaching that redresses this problem. Collaborative action research (CAR) is an innovative approach that makes a link between practising coaches and developments in research and theory in sport coaching through collaboration between a coach and an academic working in the field (Evans and Light 2008). The academic collaborates by sharing professional knowledge, providing suggestions for relevant reading and leading in designing and conducting the research as areas where s/he could be expected to have more expertise. This chapter outlines CAR and provides an example of its application through collaboration between one of the authors and a rugby coach in Australia, which is preceded by a brief discussion of how coaches learn.

The development of coaches' beliefs and practice

Coaches develop their beliefs about coaching through ongoing participation in the practice of coaching (Lyle 2002) and over lives of involvement in their sport from their first experiences of it (see, for example, Evans 2011). They recognize the central role that experience plays in their development with recent research suggesting the ways in which it is embodied over extended periods of time through participation in their sport and how it shapes their practice and beliefs (Abraham *et al.* 2006; Culver and Trudel 2006; Gilbert and Trudel 2000; Light and Evans 2013).

Learning through experience is the major avenue through which coaches develop expertise and, as such, certainly deserves more research attention. However, as important and influential as it is, learning through experience alone cannot adequately prepare coaches to deal with the demands of modern professional coaching, community coaching or youth coaching:

> It would be a relief to believe that one need only spend a certain amount of time teaching or coaching, and the lessons learned in the experience would elevate one to the next level of expertise. Unfortunately, that is not the case. To become better skilled at one's professional practice, a novice teacher or coach needs to do more than simply spend time on the job.
>
> (Bell 1997, p. 25)

Experience needs to be complemented by some form of structured learning for coaches to develop expertise and this is the aim of accreditation programmes and professional development. Attempts to structure coach education and disseminate developments in coaching have thus seen the widespread growth of formal coach education programmes but these are rarely integrated with experience. Typically, these involve short intensive courses of study leading to formal qualifications in the form of coach accreditation qualifications from introductory to state or national coaching accreditation. It is through these intensive courses that recent developments and ideas in coaching are disseminated in the hope that they will improve coaches' practice but this has been questioned in the literature (Cassidy *et al.* 2004; Gilbert and Trudel 2000; Jones 2006). For example, in his examination of the Australian coach accreditation scheme, Dickson (2001) suggests that it is actually unclear whether or not formalized accreditation leads to the development of confidence, competence or improvements in coaching.

Action research

Suggestions for coach development through AR (see, for example, Ahlberg *et al.* 2008; Cassidy *et al.* 2006) draw on a long tradition in the education field. AR was first proposed by social psychologist Kurt Lewin in 1948 as research with an emphasis on its capacity to address practical problems in specific situations (Dick 1999; Street 2004). This certainly makes it attractive for rugby coaches looking for an edge or to just keep improving. AR conducted in schools usually involves the teacher actively involved in his/her own development of practice by systematically and critically reflecting upon it and initiating pedagogical changes as a result of this reflection. It is claimed that AR promotes critical and reflective teaching in physical education (Noffke and Brennan 1991), with it also having been used to reveal inequalities and injustices in physical education (see, for example, Law 1994; Stanley 1995).

AR typically involves an intervention or change in practice that is centred on the teacher's or coach's practice and managed by him/her. It involves a learning process in which there is change in what people do, how they interact with others in their work situation, and the meanings and interpretation they draw from the experience (Carr and Kemmis 1983). It thus links research, theory and practice at a personal level and is research that can be very meaningful for coaches (Evans and Light 2008). AR generates knowledge about teaching and learning, increased understanding of practice, and improvements in teaching and learning (Kemmis and McTaggart 1988) that is specific to the particular contexts and situations within which it is undertaken. While this might be seen as a problem because of the difficulty in making broad generalizations about teaching and learning, from a practitioner's perspective it is one of its strengths. This is because AR is so specific to the teacher's or coach's situation and needs, giving it clear relevance, meaning and usefulness. As is the case with teaching more broadly, published AR in physical education tends to focus on the improvement of individual teachers' practice or understanding the impact of interventions in teaching school students or pre-service (PETE – physical education teacher education) teachers. It has been suggested that it offers a very effective means of improving practice in physical education (see, for example, Gore 1991; Kirk 1995) and specifically of developing a game-based approach to teaching games as demonstrated by Gubacs-Collins' (2007) research on the effectiveness of a Tactical Games approach for teaching tennis (see also Kirk 1995).

Kirk (1995) suggests that for AR to be successfully undertaken it should: (1) involve collaboration, (2) be self-managed, (3) have action that is based on data, (4) involve practitioner reflection, (5) be situated in practice and (6) focus on reforming practice. The use of reflection in the process of AR produces new knowledge about teaching (or coaching), increased understanding of practice and improvements in teaching and learning. This emphasis on reflection is a prominent theme in the work of Dewey in the philosophy of education and in the recent development of constructivist-informed approaches to teaching such as Teaching Games for Understanding (TGfU) and the Tactical Decision Learning Model (see, for example, Butler 2005; Gréhaigne *et al.* 2005; Light and Fawns 2003; Quay and Stolz 2014).

The role of experience in action research

While experience is central to learning, Dewey (1963) argues that immediate reflection upon experience (as a second experience) is required to enhance and shape that learning. This is because learning occurs through the original experience *and* through the experience of reflecting upon that experience (Dewey 1916/97, 1963). Reflection through the use of language provides a means of linking concrete experience and abstract learning (Light and Fawns 2003; Light and Wallian 2008). Learning through experience must also form part of learning as an ongoing and continuous process linked to other experience and learning, as Dewey explains:

> Scientific study leads to and enlarges experience, but this experience is educative only to the degree that it rests upon a continuity of significant knowledge and to the degree that this knowledge modifies or 'modulates' the learner's outlook, attitude and skill.
>
> (1963, p. 10)

The reflection involved in action research in the education field produces new knowledge about teaching, increases understanding of practice and enhances improvements in teaching and learning (Kemmis and McTaggart 1988). Reflective practice forms a central concern of AR as a process that enables professionals to plan and implement activities that are well thought out and based upon previous experience. Enhancing learning through experience thus sits upon the principles of continuity and interaction, leading to ongoing growth and development, and this forms part of the AR process.

AR has been used extensively in education and in physical education (see, for example, Dick 1999; Gubacs-Collins 2007). In sport coaching it may provide a valuable, structured way of using coaches' experience to contribute to their professional development but, although it has been used in sport coaching (Ahlberg *et al.* 2008; Barker-Ruchti 2002; Kidman and Carlson 1998), its use is limited.

Reflection on experience is a key idea of AR and enables professionals to plan and implement activities that are well thought out and based on previous experience. Kruse (1997, p. 47) suggests that, 'Meaningful strategies are not isolated random actions, but carefully coordinated and independent tactics designed to achieve important and valued goals by the participants in the action.'

Collaborative action research

Action research can be conducted individually, in pairs or in small groups of teachers or coaches who share the workload between them. It typically involves reading and being up to date with relevant literature on the intervention or change in practice that is planned. Teachers have typically been through three- to four-year teacher education programmes in which they have been exposed to research relevant to their profession and have had some experience in research methods. Despite growth in the availability of degree programmes in universities, many coaches have not had the same exposure to research or to the relevant literature and this can make it difficult for them to undertake AR.

Collaborative action research (CAR) introduces a 'sport pedagogue' who collaborates with the practitioner in an equal partnership and through which they both learn something about coaching practice. In CAR the coach is the expert in coaching practice, with the research focused on improving his/her practice and the sport pedagogue bringing expertise in pedagogy and in the theories informing it. This does not, however, preclude him/her from also being an experienced practitioner, as was the case in this study. Either the coach or the sport pedagogue can initiate the research but they work in an equal partnership through which they develop knowledge about coaching and player/athlete development. In CAR there is a strong emphasis on the relationship between practice and theory as mutually informing entities that are essential both for the development of knowledge and for the improvement of the coach's practice and confidence in his/her coaching.

In the study reported on in this chapter the coach knew the sport pedagogue as a former rugby player and coach who was working in sport pedagogy with a focus on rugby. The coach wanted to change his practice and had a little knowledge about what might be possible but felt he needed some assistance so approached the sport pedagogue. He expressed an interest in using some of the Game Sense ideas as a means of making his coaching more 'dynamic' and of introducing some innovation. He wanted to improve communication between himself and his players to get better feedback from them on his coaching, make practice sessions more dynamic, encourage his players to be more independent and to make his coaching more player-centred. Through discussion between the coach and the sport pedagogue they agreed to change the coach's approach by drawing on ideas from the Game Sense approach.

Methodology

Aims

The study aimed at investigating the influence of implementing a change in coaching pedagogy over an eight-week period as perceived by the players and by the coach and gaining an understanding of the coach's experience of the change. The intervention involved (1) introducing coaching that was more relevant to match conditions, (2) engaging the players more in dialogue with the coach and, (3) involving the players more in decision-making about practice. The coach utilized the sport pedagogue to collaboratively develop his practice and as a critical friend who assisted in his reflection upon practice.

The site and participants

Pseudonyms have been used to protect the identities of the coach, the players and their club. The coach (*Max*) was Director of Rugby for a Premier club in Sydney. He had been a professional rugby coach for over twenty years and coached successfully in Australia, the United Kingdom and Europe. He entered coaching after a long period as a player and then as a part-time coach before taking up a professional appointment when rugby became a professional sport. He has a Level 3 coaching accreditation with the Australian Rugby Union and coaches a first division team in the NSW Shute Shield competition, referred to in this chapter under the pseudonym 'the Eagles Rugby Club'.

Five rugby players aged between 20 and 29 years (M = 25.4 yrs) participated in the study and were selected by the coach. The five players included both professional and semi-professionals who train up to five times per week. Three were age-group national representatives when younger. *Oscar* is an outside back who has represented Australia in under-age teams; *Colin* is an inside back and has been a fringe player in a Super 14 training squad; *Roger* is a prop forward who had been a long-term first-grade player and junior representative player; *Sam* is a lock forward who had been a long-term first-grade player; and *Roy* is a loose forward who represented Australia in the national seven-a-side team.

The sport pedagogue has an extensive background in rugby as a player and coach, having coached a national youth team at the world championships for that age level. He generated data through observation, conducting interviews with the coach and players and videoing practice for the coach to review. He also drew on his knowledge of Game Sense pedagogy and the constructivist theories of learning that have been used to understand how learning occurs, to inform discussions (see Gréhaigne *et al.* 2005) with Max. The term 'sport pedagogue' was adapted from Culver's experience as a pedagogy consultant and sport psychologist and as a facilitator in teams or sport clubs (Culver and Trudel 2006, p. 105). The sport pedagogue facilitated the coach's pedagogical development by providing relevant journal articles and books on player-centred coaching to help in developing a Game Sense pedagogical approach. He also engaged with Max in discussions on the meaning and application of theory to practice, on constructivist ideas of how people learn and on his experiences of changing his practice.

Procedure

The research involved collaboration between the rugby coach, Max, and the sport pedagogue as an informed 'critical friend'. The coach's interest in being involved in the research was driven by his desire to improve his coaching. He had a particular interest in getting authentic feedback from his players through improving communication with them and empowering them to be more active in learning within a broader desire to develop a more player-centred approach to coaching that was more relevant to game conditions. The process began with discussions between the coach, referred to using the pseudonym Max, and the sport pedagogue. After this the sport pedagogue provided Max with readings on player-centred pedagogy that could inform his practice and was available for discussions about any issues that arose from the readings. He then worked in collaboration with

Max to set out how he would implement a new approach to coaching and to plan the research. Before Max began to change his coaching approach the sport pedagogue interviewed each of the five players whom the coach had selected to participate in the study.

Max kept a reflective journal over the duration of the study and was interviewed by the sport pedagogue before, and at the end of, the study. The data generation utilized the coach's reflection across the planning, action, assessment and evaluation/review stages. After Max had completed his readings, discussions between him and the sport pedagogue, collaborative analysis of the CBS-C (Coach Behaviour Scale for Coaches) surveys and videos of practice and the pre-intervention interviews, an action plan was formulated for implementation by the sport pedagogue and Max. This focused on achieving two key objectives.

The first objective was to alter training to make practice sessions more relevant to match conditions and to increase player motivation at training that included the use of modified games. These modified games involved the creation of game scenarios that focused on particular tactical aspects, decision-making and contested drills conducted in contexts that required some decision-making. The second objective was to involve players more in decision-making about training and to empower them by (1) providing individualized feedback through viewing video footage of matches, using open-ended questioning to stimulate their input into the analysis, and (2) organizing player meetings for competition match reviews based upon reduced video footage. These were aimed at providing more interaction and giving the players more input into strategic and tactical decisions made for the next game.

Max and the sport pedagogue agreed that achieving both objectives required the development of Max's questioning technique. Midway through the eight-week intervention they met to discuss his experiences of the intervention and the CAR process to date. This discussion centred upon how successful Max thought the changes in pedagogy had been and what he saw as the benefits of the CAR process. At the completion of the eight-week intervention Max and the sport pedagogue analysed and discussed the video footage and field notes taken from the last training session. The sport pedagogue then interviewed Max to determine whether or not he could identify any changes as a result of the process. The sport pedagogue also interviewed the five players to enquire into whether or not there were any perceived changes in practice and, if so, what benefits, if any, they thought had resulted from the intervention.

Data generation

Data were generated through the use of five methods: (1) noted observations made by the sport pedagogue; (2) the coach's written reflections, stimulated by coach–sport pedagogue dialogue and viewing of video recordings of practice; (3) semi-structured interviews conducted with players and the coach by the sport pedagogue; (4) the completion of a Coaching Effectiveness Self Analysis sheet; and

(5) players' completion of the CBS-C. The sport pedagogue conducted the interviews before and after the intervention programme. In these interviews the players were asked for their views on the relevance of training to matches, the adequacy of feedback from the coach, the specificity of training and their relationships with the coach.

The choice of research methods reflects the research requirements (Branigan 2003, p. 1) with the CAR method being a rich and full approach that takes into account the coach's normal professional situation. The AR method (and by implication the CAR method) is participative, qualitative and oriented towards action (Dick 1999).

Analysis

Content analysis was used to identify major themes emerging from the comparison of pre-intervention data and post-intervention data within the three areas focused on. Content analysis focuses on matters in everyday social life and human communication (Krippendorff 2004) to produce a 'systematic and comprehensive summary or overview of the data set' (Wilkinson 2004, p. 182). Interview data were reduced by close reading and rereading of the interview transcripts to identify and code chunks of the transcripts leading to the identification of developing sub-themes. This process resulted in the emergence of the themes presented in the results within each area of enquiry.

Results

The analysis of data was conducted within three areas: (1) the players' perceptions of the intervention; (2) the coach's experience of the intervention and its efficacy; and (3) the coach's views on the CAR process to identify major themes within each of these areas.

Player perceptions of changes in practice

Player perceptions of the effects of the change in coaching practice by Max suggested three major themes: (1) increased player motivation; (2) an increased sense of player autonomy; and (3) improvements in the relationship between the players and the coach.

Increased motivation

Noted observations, video footage of training before and during the changes in coach practice and player interviews suggested increased player enjoyment and motivation resulting from changes in training. The changes introduced were aimed at making training more relevant to match conditions and comprised the introduction of practice games, game scenarios and contested drills all aimed at introducing levels of competition, decision-making and the need to read conditions. Data strongly suggest that these changes lifted the intensity of training sessions and increased their connectedness with match conditions. This increased relevance to competitive match conditions raised motivation during training and enjoyment of it by the players, as Colin suggests: 'training is more free flowing, we're enjoying training'. The players saw the new approach to coaching as being more active and less static than it had been, recognizing how the use of games had contributed to this. As Roy said in an interview: 'training is more active and dynamic with an emphasis on games'. The changes to training also created what some players saw as a level of training specificity. For example, in response to being asked what he saw as the positive aspects of the changes Oscar said, 'the structure of training is geared towards the following game, more specific'.

Increased player autonomy

Max's aim of involving players more in training and empowering them involved the use of three strategies: (1) providing individual feedback to players on a one-to-one basis with the coach; (2) having regular meetings between the coach and the players to assess performance in matches and to discuss how training might address any problems identified; and (3) the coach using questioning in training instead of direct instruction to stimulate thinking and intellectual engagement.

All the players interviewed reported a strong sense of increased player autonomy and felt they had moved into a position of having more power in decision-making about training and match strategy and tactics. When asked about what, if any, the benefits of the change in coaching were, Roger said that it was the increased involvement in decision-making by the players: 'reviews are run by the players . . . a lot more of the problem solving done by the players'. This was a common response among the five players interviewed that was captured by Colin, who said that it, ' feels like we have more input now'. They also felt more autonomy because Max had worked at having them understand the aims of different activities and drills and why he was taking a particular approach. The players felt that individual feedback on performance and group discussion sessions helped them develop a deeper understanding and awareness of training, with Roy feeling that this helped the team understand the *why* of training: 'now we get feedback on performance and for me the why has been addressed'.

Coach–player relationships

Coach–player relationships play an important part in establishing an environment that is conducive to player satisfaction, positive experiences and learning (Ahlberg *et al.* 2008) and are of particular importance for coaches taking up a Game Sense and similar approaches (Evans 2012). The players saw the change in relationships between them and the coach as a positive outcome of the intervention. Communication had moved from a monologue of information passed from the coach down to the players towards a meaningful dialogue between them that the players felt involved them more in practice and gave them more input into match strategy and tactics and responsibility for their performance on the field. Max scored a high 5.8 for positive rapport with players in the CBS-C survey, but the responses from players in interviews suggest a more significant improvement in this area from their perspectives. The intervention fostered a new coach–player relationship with more interaction between the coach and the players and a more equal distribution of power in the relationship. This was not restricted to the three strategies Max implemented but extended to relationships in, around and outside training, suggesting that the changes led to somewhat of a cultural change in the squad.

The players suggested that Max was more approachable and personable in his dealings with them. When asked to comment on the impact the changes implemented by Max had, Sam said, 'Max's been listening to players and physios (physiotherapists) about our training especially after a couple of tough games.' The feedback provided by Max to players on a one-to-one basis and the opportunities for them to provide feedback on his coaching as part of the CAR process were also well received, as Colin's response to the same question suggests: 'I think it is really good how he takes players aside and works with them.' This change in relationships extended to interaction beyond training, as Oscar explained: 'he spends personal time with players . . . social nights, not just rugby stuff'.

Coach perceptions of changes in practice

During the evaluation phase Max pointed out how he felt he had been able to change his coaching practices by (1) working with the sport pedagogue to develop training activities that better replicated match conditions; (2) taking time to explain the aims and rationale of his coaching to players and introducing individual and group feedback sessions; and (3) using player questioning instead of direct instruction. To make training more relevant to match conditions Max used game-based training, specific match scenarios and contextualized skill development activities to develop perception and decision-making, as suggested by Light (2013b), in a competitive environment. This involved his drawing on the knowledge of the sport pedagogue of Game Sense pedagogy and working collaboratively to design appropriate practice games and activities.

Over the eight-week period of the intervention Max said that he was pleased with the raised levels of intensity exhibited by the players in practice. He was also pleased with the ways in which practice had become more dynamic and in which he had been able to establish a 'flow' in each session. During the pre-intervention stage of the research collaborative analysis of video footage of practice allowed Max to identify a problem with the flow of his training sessions. He was concerned with the progression from the warm-up using a modified game, to skills work that resulted in a loss of flow. He suggested that this was due to poor progression from the dynamic nature of the warm-up game to a static, uncontested skill exercise. He decided to use game-based training and specific match scenarios to maintain the flow that his warm-up games established, while still being able to focus on particular tactical and skill aspects of play.

While many coaches use game-based training they typically do not adopt Game Sense pedagogy within which questioning is a key feature (Light 2006a; Light and Evans 2010). The player-centred nature of Game Sense and its emphasis on questioning makes it an innovation and this was an aspect of the intervention that Max felt he struggled with. He said that he had been working on improving his questioning but was not sure of the extent to which he had improved it over the eight-week period. Developing effective questioning forms a common challenge for coaches (Roberts 2011) and physical education teachers (McNeill *et al.* 2008) adopting player/student-centred approaches such as Game Sense. This is partly due to the change in the positioning of the coach that takes him/her off centre stage because Game Sense coaching involves a change from the coach directing learning to facilitating and enhancing it (Light 2004, 2013b). The significant changes Max introduced during a competitive season presented a few problems for him in regard to the use of questioning and his repositioning as the coach and this is to be expected. He said that he had not felt completely comfortable with the changes but felt that they had been successful and was interested in building on what he had learned for next season.

The coach's views on the CAR process

In analysing Max's experience of the intervention it is difficult to separate it from his experience of being involved in the CAR process. In fact, interviews and casual conversation over the period of the research suggested that he had difficulty separating the intervention from the research process. Central to this was the key role that the sport pedagogue played in the research through collaboration, his theoretically informed input and the ways in which he facilitated Max's critical reflection upon his practice. Max was not only pleased with the experimentation that he and the sport pedagogue conducted in order to improve his coaching, but also with his involvement in the research process and the information it provided on his own coaching. This is seen in his response to being asked what the benefits of the CAR process were, to which he replied that it, 'provides a process to get feedback on my coaching' through which 'You get honest answers, instead of players telling you what you want to hear.'

For Max, the process of having a sport pedagogue as the critical friend provided an important link with developments in, and research on, coaching pedagogy and provided the opportunity for reflection upon his practice and professional interaction. When responding to a question about the benefits of the process and the role of the researcher/pedagogue, Max said, 'by having a third person (sport pedagogue) it provides a forum for players'. He was also pleased with how the CAR experience allowed him to achieve his aims of building better relationships with his players and engaging them more in decision-making about practice, saying that, 'it's also about meeting some of the needs of players'.

Discussion

There are two aspects to this study that have implications for rugby coaching: (1) the results of the Game Sense intervention and (2) the coach learning through the CAR process. The success of an intervention based on the Game Sense approach suggests the ways in which it can contribute to improvements in coaching rugby. Max's experience of being involved in the CAR process suggests that it may offer a useful means of facilitating self-directed coach development in which academics in coach education can make a valuable contribution towards both coach development and the grounding of research in the day-to-day practices of coaches. This alone is a significant finding because it offers a way of redressing the huge gap between research and practice in coaching.

The opportunities offered by Game Sense

This case study suggests that the intervention in the coach's practice was successful in achieving his aims. Despite some difficulty in adapting to a more player-centred approach as a facilitator rather than an instructor, Max was satisfied with his experiment and was looking to employ some of it in his future coaching. He was pleased with the ability of the changes to maintain the flow of intensity, dynamism and player motivation established with his warm-up games through the use of game-based learning and with the ability of his changes to involve players more in decision-making about practice. Max was particularly pleased with the feedback he was able to get from his players on his change in coaching. Light's (2004) study on coaches' experiences of working with a Game Sense approach across a range of sports in Australia highlights the challenges involved in moving from a technical, direct instruction approach to a player-centred, enquiry-based coaching approach. In light of this and other similar studies it is not surprising that Max felt he needed more time to develop this approach. The player responses suggest that they also saw the changes in a positive light and were particularly happy with the more dynamic nature of game-based training that they saw as being more like match conditions and with the improved communication between them and the coach. Guided by the Game Sense approach to coaching the success of these changes suggests that elements of Game Sense can be used effectively in elite-level rugby coaching.

Contribution of CAR to coach development

This study suggests that CAR might have the potential to meet a number of challenges in coach development identified in the introduction. Certainly it seems to have met the needs of the coach in this study. In combining research with coach development it supports open learning and allows for coaches to take up professional development activities in their day-to-day work environment. Although there is justifiable criticism of coaches relying entirely on experience for their development (Abraham *et al.* 2006), they valued it highly with it exerting a profound influence on their beliefs about coaching and their practice. However, it does not figure prominently in formal coach education programmes, which tend to be shorter and invariably ineffective interventions (see, for example, Cushion 2007; Jones 2006).

Dewey's (see 1916/97) work in the philosophy of education recognizes the centrality of experience in learning but emphasizes the central role that reflection must play in this learning. This suggests that for coach education and coach experience professional development programmes might profit from making a link between the content of courses and experience by emphasizing reflection. In some ways this is what CAR seems to achieve. In this study CAR offered a means of providing coach development in which experience is a central concern yet which is informed by developments in coaching research through the role of the sport pedagogue. In CAR the sport pedagogue provides the opportunity for collaboration and interaction through which the coach learns and a supportive learning environment.

Conclusion

The sort of collaboration reported on here could be instrumental in exposing coaches to theory that can inform their practice and give them the opportunity to test it within their work environment. CAR may also offer an effective way through which researchers can be involved in coach development activities that are authentic and participative and that offer them a chance to test their ideas and theories in real practice. Of course it has its limitations due to the time and effort needed from the sport pedagogue to commit to one coach. This could be partially redressed through having the sport pedagogue work with a number of coaches in a club. It could also possibly be used in coaching degree programmes by having students in their senior years work with coaches of an appropriate level in a collaborative arrangement from which both learn something about coaching. Certainly, this approach offers researchers in coaching an opportunity to conduct research that is highly relevant to coaches and which provides valuable insight into the profession and the efficacy of theories and ideas developed for coaching.

REFLECTIONS AND CONCLUDING THOUGHTS

Learning

The holistic approach that we adopt in this book highlights the need to account for, consider and make sense of coaching as a complex and deeply situated practice in preference to reductionist conceptualizations of it as a non-problematic and linear process. One of the features of this book is the overarching emphasis on learning. This includes a focus on (1) what the players learn through practice and playing in competitive matches instead of what the coach does and (2) how coaches learn to coach as they do.

Focusing on player learning instead of coach behaviour represents a profound change in thinking about coaching and the role of the coach. While it is likely that this could be hindered by the association of 'learning' with schools and teaching by many coaches, we want to confirm our broad use of the term learning that attempts to transcend schools and classrooms to include not only player improvement in sport and coach development over time, but also the concept of lifelong learning, which all humans experience whether they realize it or not. Seeing player development and improvement as a process of learning (see Kirk 2010) opens coaching up to a range of theories of learning that provide valuable ways of understanding how and what players learn with concomitant attention drawn to how the coach shapes, influences, fosters or enhances this learning. Again, this is a significant departure from views of seeing the coach's role being the transmission of knowledge and direct instruction, informed by the separation of technique and skill from the game, and the quest for the ideal execution of skills for skills' sake.

Seeing coach development as a process of learning encourages a sophisticated conception of how it takes place over time through both conscious and non-conscious learning and can take into account their interaction. Developments in player-centred coaching approaches such as Game Sense strongly emphasize the role of the physical environment (modified practice games or contextualized skill work) in learning. Looking at coach development facilitates identifying and exploring the role that context plays in coach development. This can be institutional context such as schools or an NGB (see Chapter 9), or socio-cultural contexts that, over longer periods of time, can profoundly shape ideas and beliefs about coaching and that can operate at a non-conscious level and beyond conscious consideration (see, for example, Chapter 7). Chapter 7 illustrates the powerful influence of socio-cultural context on coaches' development of beliefs about coaching that shape their approaches to practice, with a marked contrast between the beliefs of the three coaches from Pretoria and the three coaches from Sydney.

The holistic approach adopted for research presented in this book attempts to make sense of the complexity of learning to coach and this involves recognition that learning is not an isolated process but, instead, part of a lifelong learning process that constructivism sees as a process of constant change and adaptation that is social and interpretive (see Bruner 1987; Davis and Sumara 2003; Fosnot 1996). This then suggests that, as suggested in Chapter 4, short-term coach education programmes should link to coaches' life experiences and involve some reflection upon their beliefs about coaching to have any hope of initiating change in practice. In Chapter 8, Study 2, there is clearly tension between the beliefs of three of the four Australian coaches about human learning and the epistemology that Game Sense sits upon. This prior learning would likely need to be addressed to move them towards a Game Sense approach.

There has been a number of suggestions for theorizing learning in and through sport, but the writing and research presented in this book is underpinned by constructivism as a branch of epistemology with its particular perspective on what knowledge is and how we acquire it. We use this theory to help us understand, or 'see', what is happening but are careful to not just champion one theoretical framework over others for the sake of theory alone. Instead, we have worked at making practice and theory mutually informing with this relationship evident throughout the book. A constructivist learning theory perspective suggests how learning is interpretive and how this interpretation is shaped by prior knowledge and experiences, for both players and for coaches. Our focus on how coaches shape and influence player learning and how coaches learn to coach as they do also highlights the profound significance of context on player and coach learning. This context includes physical contexts such as competition matches and practice games designed to prioritize certain aspects of play, the context of the match within which the coach must make decisions and communicate with players, and how this is influenced by macro, meso and macro levels of context (Bouthier and Durey 1995; and Chapter 6 in this volume). To understand how larger social and cultural contexts play a part in shaping learning we turn to the social theory of Bourdieu with a focus on *habitus* (Chapter 5) that is, in turn, put to work in research on coaching reported on in Chapters 7 to 10 in particular.

A heuristic for considering coach learning and growth

Although coaching is significantly different from teaching a focus on learning underlines some of the overlap between them. The constructivism that underpins this book has a long history in education with the challenges of teachers implementing constructivist-informed teaching approaches resonating with some of the same problems identified in the studies on coaching in this book (see Davis and Sumara 2003). Here we draw on the work of Windschitl (2002) on the problems teachers experience when attempting to implement constructivist approaches to teaching, in order to frame our thinking about holistic coaching.

Windschitl (2002) argues for a 'constructivism in practice', which 'involves phenomena distributed across multiple contexts of teaching' (p. 132), with an interest in the 'intellectual and lived experiences that prevent the theoretical ideals of constructivism being realized in practice' (p. 132). He suggested that there are four 'dilemmas' facing teachers who seek to integrate constructivist practices into their teaching: conceptual, pedagogical, cultural and political. In offering this 'heuristic' Windschitl (2002) acknowledges that separating these dilemmas offers a somewhat 'tidy compartmentalization' of the issues facing teachers, but suggests that each one is 'intimately connected to the other in the context of the teachers' own lives' (p. 157) and that 'The overlaps between the four categories are loci for identifying how understanding and experience in one area can be combined with understanding and experience in another area to foster conditions for the vitality of constructivist learning environments' (p. 157). When perceived as a 'dilemma' each of the four constructs is necessarily problematic and negative, but Windschitl provides for a positive approach by 're-casting' them as 'conceptual understanding, pedagogical expertise, cultural consciousness, and political acumen' (p. 160). By doing this he suggests that they provide insights into the intersections of 'conditions that must be realized for constructivist teaching to flourish in a classroom – conditions that are best realized when teachers draw on multiple dimensions of experience' (p. 160). This resonates with Antonovsky's (see 1979) work on the social conditions that foster positive well-being. It also aligns with Positive Psychology (Seligman and Csikszentmihalyi 2000) and the concept of Positive Pedagogy outlined in Chapter 2. Given the prominence of Game Sense and the related concept of Positive Pedagogy in this book, we feel that this heuristic offers a fitting way of making sense of the messages arising from this book. In this reflection we use these four constructs to think about how we might move towards developing and implementing more holistic approaches to coaching rugby and other sports.

Conceptual understanding

Conceptual understanding relates to beliefs and epistemologies that shape and influence the formation of concepts in coaching. In this book we have explored how embodied personal experience in particular contexts over time embed unquestioned beliefs and dispositions towards ways of coaching that can make it difficult for coaches to understand and adopt innovative practice such as Game Sense. Many in the physical education field argue for a models-based approach to overcome the limitations of 'traditional' practice in physical education (see Kirk 2013). Instead, we favour providing a stronger foundational comprehension of how learning occurs and how it can be shaped by pedagogy that coaches (and teachers) can draw on to meet the range of challenges that confront them when trying to implement innovation. This aligns well with the emphasis of player-centred coaching approaches such as Game Sense on the fundamental concepts of play, which are the manipulation of space and time. That is to say that we would argue for a conceptual approach to educating coaches in preference to a more detailed set of steps and procedures for adopting a particular model of coaching.

The Singaporean Game Concept Approach is another GBA that emphasizes the central role that developing a conceptual understanding of team games plays, with research also emphasizing the challenges involved in its authentic implementation (see Fry and McNeill 2014). Study 2 in Chapter 8 provides a good example of the importance of a conceptual understanding to see change through in coaching. Its enquiry into four Australian rugby coaches' beliefs about learning and the impact this seems to have on how they interpret Game Sense identifies some conceptual understandings of learning and suggests how these shape the ways in which they coach and interpret the Game Sense approach. The comparison of Australian and New Zealand coaches in the previous study (Study 1) also describes conceptual differences between the two groups of coaches and within each group that influence their interest in Game Sense and the ways in which they use practice games.

Davis and Sumara (2003) suggest that to encourage teachers to take up constructivist approaches to teaching their professional education courses should encourage them to reflect upon their beliefs about teaching and learning in order to bring it to consciousness. Once this has been done Davis and Sumara suggest they can consider the concepts they base their thinking on and critically evaluate them in regard to the core concepts of constructivism. The approach proposed by Davis and Sumara for teacher education is similar to the approach they want to encourage them to adopt in the classroom and this would seem to make sense in coach education as well. However, Chapter 9, on the RFU's implementation of Game Sense pedagogy in its coach education courses, revealed limited opportunities for the coach candidates to reflect and challenge their deep beliefs about coaching through interaction with coach educators and to develop conceptual understandings of new pedagogy. The lack of deep knowledge about, and conceptual clarity of, what Game Sense *pedagogy* is by the coach educators made the task of developing coach candidates with a conceptual understanding far too difficult.

Pedagogical expertise

At the heart of a GBA is not simply the notion of modified games but, instead, the teachers' use of 'skilful and progressive instruction' (Hopper 2002, p. x). Indeed, the notion of the ability to progress learning tasks and/or practice games is possibly the most challenging task facing the Game Sense coach – despite the common identification of the challenges involved in developing effective questioning technique (see Roberts 2011). Certainly, it is critical for optimizing learning in and through practice games by maintaining both an appropriate level of challenge and intensity and the prioritization of the practice game as suggested in Chapter 2 on positive coaching (see Light 2014; Turner 2014).

The ability of a coach or teacher to step back, observe and analyse performance, know when to ask and when to tell (Chen and Rovegno 1998) and know when and how to listen (Suzuki 2013) is important for quality coaching. GBA encourage participants to develop a deep understanding of the game through engagement in situated practice, supported by teacher questioning and their facilitation of discussion, dialogue and debate (Light 2014; Wallian and Chang 2007).

Chapters 2 and 3 offer concrete examples of the application of this approach in rugby where quality coaching is seen to provide players with the opportunity to engage in the ongoing conversation of games. Stepping back off centre stage encourages the coach to think more about setting and managing an optimum environment for learning so that players can make decisions 'in the moment' about the appropriate action, but have opportunities to reflect on, and engage in, dialogue with others about the efficacy of their decisions. This is because coaches must recognize that 'in the moment' decisions are predicated on the decisional background (agreed team strategies) as well as the local context (the score). This is why 'designer games' (Charlesworth 2002) offer a way for coaches and players to work together to solve the game's problems and collectively arrive at strategies formulated to overcome them.

Cultural consciousness

The approaches to coaching and conducting research on coaches that we have presented in this book not only sit upon particular philosophical foundations but also sit within a particular culture of coaching that is different from that which shapes approaches at the traditional end of the coaching spectrum. There is a very resilient culture that pervades coaching, characterized by direct instruction and the transmission of knowledge as an object from the coach to the players (Kirk 2010). The player-centred, 'learning approach underpinned by social constructionist theory' (Cushion 2013, p. 68) challenges the pervasive 'traditional' beliefs of coaches and their players about a 'type' or 'form' of coaching and coach education dominated by coach-led instruction and learners/players as empty vessels waiting to be filled with knowledge (Harvey *et al.* 2010a).

By covering this ground again here in 'Reflections and concluding thoughts' we want to emphasize how cultural consciousness can intersect with conceptual understandings and pedagogical expertise to provide the positive conditions for holistic coaching to flourish. A resistant and reproductive culture dominated by coach-led instruction and belief in coach-centred coaching will be more challenging to change or modify than a culture, which is 'open' to change such as that which supports a Game Sense, Play Practice or TGfU approach. This is strongly influenced by the dominant pedagogical approach and its epistemological assumptions. Having knowledge of the culture within which particular coaching pedagogies operate and develop is thus very helpful for assisting in moving towards the type of holistic coaching we have promoted in this book.

Coaches who possess cultural consciousness can have some agency over what they are doing and act as 'change agents' by providing positive examples about how one can change one's practice and provide glimpses of an alternate culture. This also relates to our earlier point about providing coaches with deep, conceptual knowledge of coaching approaches, the learning theory it sits upon and the culture that shapes them. Resisting or rejecting the pervasive culture expressed in behaviouristic coaching practices opens up possibilities for coaches to be seen as positive role models that others may be encouraged to follow. An excellent example in this volume is the coaches from New Zealand who were enacting a seemingly constructivist (or empowerment/athlete-centred) approach to their rugby coaching. While this approach may have been challenged initially by traditional beliefs about coaching in New Zealand, victory by the All Blacks in the 2011 Rugby World Cup and being ranked by the IRB as the premier team in world rugby for four consecutive years offers highly valued and much warranted 'validation' of the game-based approach to coaching rugby.

Further validation of this approach is suggested by the offer made to All Blacks assistant coach Wayne Smith to join the coaching staff for England for their 2015 RWC campaign. Smith could be considered to be the pre-eminent Game Sense rugby coach in the world (see Kidman 2001, 2005) and, in addition to being 'one of the masterminds behind the All Blacks World Cup triumph' (Mairs 2012), has had a very positive impact upon the New Zealand Super Rugby team, The Chiefs, with them winning back-to-back titles, which contrasts to an underachieving past. What seems to have assisted in the adoption and development of Game Sense-type approaches was the fact that the New Zealand culture more broadly was built around this more 'open' approach. Nonetheless, these changes are a result of individual coaches changing their practice and acting as 'change agents' within a culture that supports it and is evident with the New Zealand coaches in Study 1, Chapter 8.

A change in culture also seems to provide an explanation for the differences between the attitudes of Australian coaches towards player-centred coaching in Study 2, Chapter 7, and in Chapter 8. We would suggest that significant development in the commercialization of rugby at a global level over the five to six years between these two studies has influenced this. Perhaps more specifically, a particular culture of playing entertaining rugby that seems to have been emphasized so strongly since professionalization in 1995 in Sydney is at work here as well. The influence that culture has on coaching and beliefs about coaching is particularly evident in the stark contrasts between the beliefs and practice of coaches in Pretoria and coaches in Sydney. These appear to be shaped not only by the coaching culture, but also by the larger culture within which they have developed and global discourses of rugby that are tied into its history and that of sport more generally. Chapter 7 in particular highlights the situated nature of coach development, the importance of the socio-cultural contexts within which coaches learn to coach and the complex interaction of socio-cultural, political and economic forces operating at local, national and global levels.

Political acumen

Progressive and culturally responsive coaches and coach education programmes can work to develop curricula that reflect the creative, innovative and holistic practice that we promote in this book. However, as Cushion (2013) argues, political systems can run counter to these practices, in that they seek to limit and remove freedom and autonomy for practitioners as coaches seek to meet a range of benchmarks, standards and levels in order to demonstrate the fidelity and efficacy of their, in this case, coach education programmes.

A very good example of this is provided in Chapter 9 (with Paul Reid) where the top-down approach to the implementation of Game Sense contradicted the ontology and epistemology upon which Game Sense pedagogy rests. Any governing body of sport considering integrating Game Sense pedagogy into its coach education would be well advised to critically examine the problems faced by the RFU in Chapter 9. Learning from this chapter should lead to thinking about offering a more progressive coach education programme that is underpinned by the tenets of Game Sense pedagogy. Inviting one of the most prominent proponents of Game Sense coaching, Wayne Smith, to join the England coaching staff (Mairs 2012) and deciding to move coach education towards a Game Sense approach suggests recognition in the RFU of what Game Sense has to offer, but the contradictions evident in Chapter 9 could arise from political problems. Here, curriculum requirements might be negotiated rather than regulated and those offering support to coach candidates would be those well versed in Game Sense pedagogy with the deep conceptual knowledge we have argued for and changes in institutional culture to support such a significant change.

Where to now?

Windschitl's (2002) four constructs provide a framework for thinking about developing more holistic approaches to coaching in ways that are very positive and encourage coaches to be positive and proactive instead of negative and reactive. This framework also connects with a positive strand weaving its way through the book, particularly in Chapter 2 with its proposal for positive coaching by drawing on the concept of Positive Pedagogy (see Light 2014). We would thus like to take the opportunity of finishing on a positive note – despite this being unusual in academic writing.

In an article on keeping children in swimming clubs in Australia, France and Germany, Light *et al.* (2013) chose to investigate the positive aspects of being in swimming clubs that contributed to keeping children aged 9–12 years engaged instead of focusing on 'barriers' and dropping out. With two of these authors on the writing team for this book it is probably not surprising that we want to finish on a positive note.

Windschitl's (2002) 'recasting' of four 'dilemmas' to 'conceptual understanding, pedagogical expertise, cultural consciousness, and political acumen' involves a significant shift from a negative to a positive approach. It moves from identifying problems and what is wrong to a positive approach that identifies 'conditions that must be realized for constructivist teaching to flourish in a classroom' (p. 160). As we noted earlier in this chapter, this is very similar to Antonovsky's (1979) approach to promoting good health and well-being, in which he identifies the affective and social conditions from which positive well-being emerges. He challenges the dichotomy of health and disease to propose that for people to enjoy good health and positive well-being their lives must be *comprehensible*, *manageable* and *meaningful*. Instead of looking for what makes people unhealthy and unhappy he focused on what conditions led to them being healthy and enjoying positive well-being.

Positive Psychology is probably a far better known concept than Antonovsky's (1979) Sense of Coherence (SoC), which has had a significant influence upon psychology and upon making schooling a more positive experience through which students learn positive personal traits such as resilience, tolerance, empathy, courage and creativity. It aims to build 'thriving individuals, families and institutions' and make 'normal life more fulfilling' (Seligman and Csikszentmihalyi 2000, p. 5). It strives to redress a preoccupation of psychology with the worst aspects of life by promoting what is good about life. Chapter 2 invites coaches to consider taking up positive coaching by adopting Positive Pedagogy as a concept that draws on Positive Psychology and Antonovsky's (1979) SoC to suggest how to further enhance the positive aspects of Game Sense pedagogy and apply them beyond team games. All these positive concepts involve far more than just using positive language and have great potential for continuing and enhancing the two prominent features of research in sport coaching over the past few decades that we identified in the introduction. These are the growth in (1) interest among both researchers and coaches in GBA such as Game Sense and (2) recognition of the complexity and situated nature of coaching and coach development.

We close by encouraging coaches, coach educators, academics and researchers to consider what holistic approaches to coaching have to offer at all levels of coaching, in rugby and other sports, and in research on coaching and coaches. We also ask them to consider moving towards a more positive approach to coaching (at all levels from children's first experiences of sport to sport at the most elite levels), research, lecturing and development of coaching in rugby and any other sport – an approach that is proactive and can make a positive difference.

REFERENCES

ABC News (2013) 'Ewen McKenzie replaces Robbie Deans as Wallabies coach', *ABC News*, 9 July. Online at www.abc.net.au/news/2013-07-09/ewen-mckenzie-unveiled-as-wallabies-coach/4808328 (accessed 9 February 2014).

Abraham, A. and Collins, D. (1998) 'Examining and extending research in coach development', *Quest*, 50(1): 59–79; doi: 10.1080/00336297.1998.10484264.

Abraham, A., Collins, D. and Martindale, R. (2006) 'The coaching schematic: validation through expert coach consensus', *Journal of Sports Sciences*, 24(6): 549–64.

Ahlberg, M., Mallett, C.J. and Tinning, R. (2008) 'Developing autonomy supportive coaching behaviors: an action research approach to coach development', *International Journal of Coaching Science*, 2(2): 3–22.

Alexander, K. and Penney, D. (2005) 'Teaching under the influence: feeding games for understanding into the sport education development-refinement cycle', *Physical Education and Sport Pedagogy*, 10(3): 287–301; doi: 10.1080/17408980500340901.

Allison, S. and Thorpe, R. (1997) 'A comparison of the effectiveness of two approaches to teaching games within physical education: a skills approach versus a games for understanding approach', *British Journal of Physical Education*, 28(3): 9–13.

Almond, L. and Launder, A. (2010) 'A critical dialogue between TGfU and play practice: implications for practice and the research agenda', paper presented at the TGfU Seminar, 26 October, AIESEP World Congress, La Coruña, Spain.

Antonovsky, A. (1979) *Health, Stress, and Coping*, San Francisco, CA: Jossey-Bass.

Araújo, D., Davids, K. and Hristovski, R. (2006) 'The ecological dynamics of decision making in sport', *Psychology of Sport and Exercise*, 7(6): 653–76; doi: 10.1016/j.psychsport.2006.07.002.

Araújo, D., Davids, K., Chow, J.Y., Passos, P. and Raab, M. (2009) 'The development of decision making skill in sport: an ecological dynamics perspective', in D. Araujo, H. Rippoll and M. Raab (eds), *Perspectives on Cognition and Action in Sport*, New York: Novo Science Publishers, pp. 157–69.

Armour, K.M. and Yelling, M. (2004) 'Professional "development" and professional "learning": bridging the gap for experienced physical education teachers', *European Physical Education Review*, 10(1): 71–93; doi: 10.1177/1356336X04040622.

Atkin, C. (2000) 'Lifelong learning-attitudes to practice in the rural context: a study using Bourdieu's perspective of habitus', *International Journal of Lifelong Education*, 19(3): 253–65.

Auerbach, C.F. and Silverstein, L.B. (2003) *Qualitative Data: An Introduction to Coding and Analysis*, New York and London: New York University Press.

Bakhtine, M. (1984) *Esthétique de la création verbale*, Paris: Gallimard.

Barbier, J.M. (2000) *L'Analyse de la singularité de l'action*, Paris: PUF.

Bardin, L. (1993) *L'Analyse de contenu*, Paris: PUF.

Barker, D., Quennerstedt, M. and Annerstedt, C. (2013) 'Facilitating group work in physical education: working with post-Vygotskian ideas', *Physical Education and Sport Pedagogy* (ahead of print); doi: 10.1080/17408989.2013.868875.

Barker-Ruchti, N. (2002) 'A study journey: a useful example of action research', *Journal of Physical Education New Zealand*, 35(1): 12–24.

Becker, A.J. (2009) 'It's not what they do, it's how they do it: athlete experiences of great coaching', *International Journal of Sports Science & Coaching*, 4(1): 93–119.

Bell, M. (1997) 'The developmental of expertise', *Journal of Physical Education, Recreation and Dance*, 68(2): 34–8.

Berg, B.L. (2007) *Qualitative Research Methods for the Social Sciences* (6th edn), Boston, MA: Pearson & Allyn Bacon.

Bernstein, N.A. (1967) *The Co-ordination and Regulation of Movements*, Oxford: Pergamon Press.

Birks, M. and Mills, J. (2011) *Grounded Theory: A Practical Guide*, Los Angeles, CA: Sage.

Black, D. and Nauright, J. (1998) *Rugby and the South African Nation*, Manchester: Manchester University Press.

Bloom, G.A., Crumpton, R. and Anderson, J.E. (1999) 'A systematic observation study of the teaching behaviors of an expert basketball coach', *The Sport Psychologist*, 13: 157–70.

Bloomer, M. (2001) 'Young lives, learning and transformation: some theoretical considerations', *Oxford Review of Education*, 27(3): 429–49.

Bourdieu, P. (1977) *Outline of a Theory of Practice* [Esquisse d'une théorie de la pratique, précédé de trois études d'ethnologie Kabyle] (R. Nice trans.), Cambridge: Cambridge University Press.

Bourdieu, P. (1980) *Le Sens pratique* [The Logic of Practice] (R. Nice trans.), Paris: Minuit.

Bourdieu, P. (1983) 'Forms of capital', in J.C. Richards (ed.), *Handbook of Theory and Research for the Sociology of Education*, New York: Greenwood Press.

Bourdieu, P. (1984) *Distinction: A Social Critique of the Judgement of Taste* [La Distinction] (R. Nice trans.), Cambridge, MA: Harvard University Press.

Bourdieu, P. (1990) *The Logic of Practice* [Le Sens pratique] (R. Nice trans.), Cambridge: Polity Press.

Bourdieu, P. and Passeron, J.C. (1990) *Reproduction in Education, Society and Culture* [La Reproduction: eléments pour une théorie du système d'enseignement] (R. Nice trans.), London: Sage.

Bourdieu, P. and Wacquant, L.J.D. (1992) *An Invitation to Reflexive Sociology*, Chicago, IL: University of Chicago Press.

Bouthier, D. and Durey, A. (1995) 'La compétence d'un entraîneur de rugby', *Education Permanente*, 2(123): 65–78.

Branigan, E. (2003) '"But how can you prove it?" Issues of rigour in action research', *Journal of the Home Economics Institute of Australia*, 10(3): 37–8.

Breed, R. and Spittle, M. (2011) *Developing Game Sense Through Tactical Learning: A Resource Book for Teachers and Coaches*, Melbourne, Vic.: Cambridge University Press.

Brewer, C.J. and Jones, R.L. (2002) 'A five-stage process for establishing contextually valid systematic observation instruments: the case of rugby union', *Sport Psychologist*, 16(2): 138–59.

Bringer, J.D., Brackenridge, C.H. and Johnston, L.H. (2006) 'Swimming coaches' perceptions of sexual exploitation in sport: a preliminary model of role conflict and role ambiguity', *Sport Psychologist*, 20(4): 465–79.

Brooker, R. and Abbott, R. (2001) 'Developing intelligent performers in sport: should coaches be making more sense of Game Sense?', *Journal of Sport Pedagogy*, 7(2): 67–83.

Brubaker, R. (1993) 'Social theory as habitus', in C. Calhoun, E. LiPuma and M. Postone (eds), *Bourdieu: Critical Perspectives*, Cambridge: Polity Press, pp. 212–34.

Bruner, J. (1987) 'Prologue to the English edition', in L.S. Vygotsky (ed.), *The Collected Works of L.S. Vygotsky: Problems of General Psychology, Including the Volume Thinking and Speech*, New York: Springer, pp. 1–16.

Bryant, A. and Charmaz, K. (2010) 'Grounded theory research: methods and practices', in A. Bryant and K. Charmaz (eds), *The SAGE Handbook of Grounded Theory* (paperback edn), Los Angeles, CA: Sage, pp. 1–28.

Bryman, A. (2004) *Social Research Methods* (2nd edn), Oxford: Oxford University Press.

Bunker, D. and Thorpe, R. (1982) 'A model for the teaching of games in secondary schools', *Bulletin of Physical Education*, 18(1): 5–8.

Butler, J.I. (1996) 'Teacher responses to Teaching Games for Understanding', *Journal of Physical Education, Recreation and Dance*, 67(9): 17–20.

Butler, J.I. (2005) 'TGfU pet-agogy: old dogs, new tricks and puppy school', *Physical Education and Sport Pedagogy*, 10(3): 225–40.

Carr, W. and Kemmis, S. (1983) *Becoming Critical: Knowing through Action Research* (rev. edn), Waurn Ponds, Vic.: Deakin University Press.

Carson, F. (2008) 'Utilizing video to facilitate reflective practice: developing sports coaches', *International Journal of Sports Science and Coaching*, 3(3): 381–90; doi: 10.1260/17479540 8786238515.

Cassidy, T. and Kidman, L. (2010) 'Initiating a national coaching curriculum: a paradigmatic shift?', *Physical Education and Sport Pedagogy*, 15(3): 307–22; doi: 10.1080/174089 80903409907.

Cassidy, T. and Rossi, T. (2006) 'Situating learning: (re)examining the notion of apprenticeship in coach education', *International Journal of Sports Science and Coaching*, 1(3): 235–46.

Cassidy, T., Jones, R. and Potrac, P. (2004) *Understanding Sports Coaching: The Social, Cultural and Pedagogical Foundations of Coaching Practice*, London: Routledge.

Cassidy, T., Potrac, P. and McKenzie, A. (2006) 'Evaluating and reflecting upon a coach education initiative: the CoDe of rugby', *Sport Psychologist*, 20(2): 145–61.

Cassidy, T., Jones, R. and Potrac, P. (2009) *Understanding Sports Coaching: The Social, Cultural and Pedagogical Foundations of Coaching Practice* (2nd edn), London: Routledge.

Chandler, T. and Nauright, J. (1999) *Making the Rugby World: Race, Gender, Commerce*, London and Portland, OR: Frank Cass.

Charlesworth, R. (2002) *Staying at the Top*, Sydney, NSW: Pan Macmillan.

Charmaz, K. (2006) *Constructing Grounded Theory: A Practical Guide through Qualitative Analysis*, London: Sage.

Chen, W. and Rovegno, I. (2000) 'Examination of expert and novice teachers' constructivist-oriented teaching practices using a movement approach to elementary physical education', *Research Quarterly for Exercise and Sport*, 71: 357–72.

Chesterfield, G., Potrac, P. and Jones, R. (2010) '"Studentship" and "impression management" in an advanced soccer coach education award', *Sport, Education and Society*, 15(3): 299–314.

Christensen, M.K. (2009) 'An eye for talent: talent identification and practical sense of top-level soccer coaches', *Sociology of Sport Journal*, 26(3): 365–82.

Christensen, M.K. (2011) 'Exploring biographical learning in elite soccer coaching', *Sport, Education and Society*, 9(2): 204–22.

Clot, Y. (2008) *Travail et pouvoir d'agir*, Paris: PUF.

Clot, Y. and Faïta, D. (2000) 'Genres et styles en analyse du travail: concepts et méthodes', *Travailler*, 4: 7–42.

Coakley, J. (2001) 'Sports and children: are organized programs worth the effort?', in J. Coakley (ed.), *Sport in Society: Issues and Controversies* (7th edn), Toronto: McGraw-Hill, pp. 113–46.

Cohen, E. (2010) 'From the Bodhi tree to the analyst's couch then into the MRI scanner: the psychologisation of Buddhism', *Annual Review of Critical Psychology*, 8: 97–119.

Coles, T. (2009) 'Negotiating the field of masculinity: the production and reproduction of multiple dominant masculinities', *Men and Masculinities*, 12(1): 30–44.

Collins, T. (2008) '"The first principle of our game": the rise and fall of amateurism: 1886–1995', in G. Ryan (ed.), *The Changing Face of Rugby: The Union Game and Professionalism since 1995*, Newcastle: Cambridge Scholars Publishing, pp. 1–19.

Cook, D.T. and Cole, C.L. (2001) 'Kids and sport', *Journal of Sport & Social Issues*, 25(3): 227–28; doi: 10.1177/0193723501253001.

Coombs, P.H. and Ahmed, M. (1974) *Attacking Rural Poverty: How Nonformal Education Can Help*, Baltimore, MD, and London: Johns Hopkins University Press.

Côté, J. (2006) 'The development of coaching knowledge', *International Journal of Sports Science and Coaching*, 1(3): 217–22.

Côté, J. and Fraser-Thomas, J. (2008) 'Play, practice, and athlete development', in D. Farrow, J. Baker and C. MacMahon (eds), *Developing Sport Expertise: Researchers and Coaches Put Theory into Practice*, London: Routledge, pp. 17–28.

Côté, J. and Sedgwick, W. (2003) 'Effective behaviors of expert rowing coaches: a qualitative investigation of Canadian athletes and coaches', *International Sports Journal*, 7(1): 62–77.

Côté, J., Salmela, J.H., Trudel, P., Baria, A. and Russell, S. (1995) 'The coaching model: a grounded assessment of expert gymnastic coaches' knowledge', *Journal of Sport & Exercise Psychology*, 17(1): 1–17.

Crawford, S. (1999) 'Rugby and the forging of a national identity', in J. Nauright (ed.), *Sport, Power and Society in New Zealand: Historical and Contemporary Perspectives*, Canberra, ACT: ASSH Studies in Sports History, pp. 5–20.

Crotty, M. (1998) *The Foundations of Social Research: Meaning and Perspective in the Research Process*, St Leonards: Allen & Unwin.

Culver, D.M. and Trudel, P. (2006) 'Cultivating coaches' communities of practice: developing the potential for learning through interactions', in R.L. Jones (ed.), *The Sports Coach as Educator: Re-conceptualising Sports Coaching*, London: Routledge, pp. 97–112.

Culver, D.M., Gilbert, W.D. and Trudel, P. (2003) 'A decade of qualitative research in sport psychology journals: 1990–1999', *Sport Psychologist*, 17(1): 1–15.

Curry, C. and Light, R.L. (2014) 'The influence of school context on the implementation of TGfU across a secondary school physical education department', in R. Light, J. Quay, S. Harvey and A. Mooney (eds), *Contemporary Developments in Games Teaching*, London: Routledge, pp. 118–32.

Cushion, C.J. (2001a) *The Coaching Process in Professional Youth Football: An Ethnography of Practice*, unpublished PhD dissertation, School of Sport and Education, Brunel University.

Cushion, C.J. (2001b) 'Coaching research and coach education: do the sum of the parts equal the whole?', *The New PE & Sports Dimension*, 3 September.

Cushion, C.J. (2006) 'Mentoring: harnessing the power of experience', in R.L. Jones (ed.), *The Sports Coach as Educator: Re-conceptualising Sports Coaching*, London: Routledge, pp. 128–44.

Cushion, C.J. (2007) 'Modelling the complexity of the coaching process', *International Journal of Sports Science and Coaching*, 2(4): 395–401; doi: 10.1260/174795407783359650.

Cushion, C.J. (2011) 'Coach and athlete learning: a social approach', in R.L. Jones, P. Potrac, C. Cushion and L.T. Ronglan (eds), *The Sociology of Sports Coaching*, London: Routledge, pp. 166–78.

Cushion, C.J. (2013) 'Applying game centered approaches in coaching: a critical analysis of the "dilemmas of practice" impacting change', *Sports Coaching Review*, 2(1): 61–76.

Cushion, C.J. and Jones, R.L. (2001) 'A systematic observation of professional top-level youth soccer coaches', *Journal of Sport Behavior*, 24(4): 354–77.

Cushion, C.J. and Jones, R.L. (2006) 'Power, discourse, and symbolic violence in professional youth soccer: the case of Albion football club', *Sociology of Sport Journal*, 23(2): 142–61.

Cushion, C.J. and Lyle, J. (2010) 'Conceptual development in sports coaching', in J. Lyle and C. Cushion (eds), *Sports Coaching: Professionalisation and Practice*, Edinburgh: Elsevier, pp. 1–14.

Cushion, C.J., Armour, K. and Jones, R. (2003) 'Coach education and continuing professional development: experience and learning to coach', *Quest*, 55(3): 215–30.

Cushion, C.J., Armour, K.M. and Jones, R.L. (2006) 'Locating the coaching process in practice: models "for" and "of" coaching', *Physical Education & Sport Pedagogy*, 11(1): 83–99.

Cushion, C.J., Nelson, L., Armour, K., Lyle, J., Jones, R., Sandford, R. and O'Callaghan, C. (2010) *Coach Learning and Development: A Review of the Literature*, Leeds: Sports Coach UK.

Davids, K. (2010) 'The constraints-based approach to motor learning: implications for a non-linear pedagogy in sport and physical education', in I. Renshaw, K. Davids and G.J.P. Savelsbergh (eds), *Motor Learning in Practice: A Constraints-led Approach*, London: Routledge, pp. 3–6.

Davis, B. and Sumara, D. (1997) 'Cognition, complexity and teacher education', *Harvard Educational Review*, 67(1): 105–25.

Davis, B. and Sumara, D. (2003) 'Why aren't they getting this? Working through the regressive myths of constructivist pedagogy', *Teaching Education*, 14(2): 123–40.

Davis, B. and Sumara, D. (2006) *Complexity and Education: Inquiries into Learning, Teaching and Research*, London: Lawrence Erlbaum Associates.

Davis, B. and Sumara, D. (2008) 'Complexity as a theory of education', *TCI (Transnational Curriculum Inquiry)*, 5(2): 33–44.

Davis, B., Sumara, D. and Luce-Kapler, R. (2000) *Engaging Minds: Learning and Teaching in a Complex World*, Mahwah, NJ: Lawrence Erlbaum Associates.

Day, D. (2011) 'Craft coaching and the "discerning eye" of the coach', *International Journal of Sports Science and Coaching*, 6(1): 179–96.

De Marco, G., Maricini, V., Wuest, D. and Schempp, P. (1996) 'Becoming reacquainted with a once familiar and still valuable tool: systematic observation methodology revisited', *International Journal of Physical Education*, 33: 17–26.

De Martelaer, K., De Bouw, J. and Struyven, K. (2013) 'Youth sport ethics: teaching pro-social behaviour', in S. Harvey and R. Light (eds), *Ethics in Youth Sport: Policy and Pedagogical Applications*, London: Routledge, pp. 55–73.

Demers, G., Woodburn, A.J. and Savard, C. (2006) 'The development of an undergraduate competency-based coach education program', *Sport Psychologist*, 20(2): 162–73.

den Duyn, N. (1997) *Game Sense: Developing Thinking Players*, Belconnen, ACT: Australian Sports Commission.

DeVries, R. and Zan, B. (1996) 'A constructivist perspective on the role of the sociomoral atmosphere in promoting children's development', in C.T. Fosnot (ed.), *Constructivism: Theory, Perspectives and Practice*, New York and London: Teachers College, Columbia University, pp. 103–19.

Dewey, J. (1916/97) *Democracy and Education: An Introduction to the Philosophy of Education*, New York: Macmillan.

Dewey, J. (1933) *How We Think: A Restatement of the Relation of Reflective Thinking to the Educative Process*, Boston, MA: D.C. Heath.

Dewey, J. (1938) *Logic: The Theory of Inquiry*, New York: Holt, Rinehart and Winston.

Dewey, J. (1963) *Experience and Education*, New York: Collier.

Dick, B. (1999) 'Sources of rigour in action research: addressing the issues of trustworthiness and credibility', paper presented at the Association for Qualitative Research Conference: Issues of Rigour in Qualitative Research, Melbourne, Vic., 6–10 July.

Dickson, S. (2001) *A Preliminary Investigation into the Effectiveness of the National Coaching Accreditation Scheme*, Bruce, ACT: Australian Sports Commission; doi: 10.1080/13573322.2012.665803.

Dumais, S.A. (2002) 'Cultural capital, gender, and school success: the role of habitus', *Sociology of Education*, 75(1): 44–68.

Dunning, E. and Sheard, K. (2005) *Barbarians, Gentlemen and Players: A Sociological Study of the Development of Rugby Football* (2nd edn), London: Routledge.

Dyson, B. (2005) 'Integrating cooperative learning and tactical games models: focusing on social interactions and decision-making', in L.L. Griffin and J.I. Butler (eds), *Teaching Games for Understanding: Theory, Research, and Practice*, Champaign, IL: Human Kinetics, pp. 149–68.

Ella, M. (2008) 'Coaching spotlight turns away from Tahs', *The Weekend Australian*, 24 May, p. 53.

Erickson, K., Côté, J. and Fraser-Thomas, J. (2007) 'Sport experiences, milestones, and educational activities associated with high-performance coaches' development', *The Sport Psychologist*, 21(3): 302–16.

Evans, J.R. (2006a) 'Capturing the essence of rugby through Game Sense', in R. Lieu, C. Li and A. Cruz (eds), *Teaching Games for Understanding in the Asia-Pacific Region*, Hong Kong: Hong Kong Institute of Education, pp. 71–9.

Evans, J.R. (2006b) 'Elite level rugby coaches' interpretation and use of Game Sense', *Asian Journal of Exercise and Sport Science*, 3(1): 17–24.

Evans, J.R. (2011) *Elite Rugby Coaches' Interpretation and use of Game Sense in Australia and New Zealand: An Examination of Coaches' Habitus, Learning and Development*, unpublished PhD, University of Sydney.

Evans, J.R. (2012) 'Elite level rugby coaches' interpretation and use of games sense', *Asian Journal of Exercise and Sports Science*, 3(1): 17–24.

Evans, J.R. (2014) 'The nature and importance of coach–player relationships in the uptake of Game Sense by elite rugby coaches in Australia and New Zealand', in R. Light, J. Quay, S. Harvey and A. Mooney (eds), *Contemporary Developments in Games Teaching*, London: Routledge, pp. 133–45.

Evans, J.R. and Light, R. (2008) 'Coach development through Collaborative Action Research: A rugby coach's implementation of Game Sense pedagogy', *Asian Journal of Exercise and Sport Science*, 5(1): 31–7.

Ezzy, D. (2002) *Qualitative Analysis: Practice and Innovation*, Crows Nest, NSW: Allen & Unwin.

FitzSimons, P. (2003) *The Rugby War* (2nd edn), Sydney, NSW: HarperCollins.

Ford, P.R., Yates, I. and Williams, A.M. (2010) 'An analysis of practice activities and instructional behaviours used by youth soccer coaches during practice: exploring the link between science and application', *Journal of Sports Sciences*, 28(5): 483–95.

Forrest, G. (2014) 'Questions and answers: understanding the connection between questioning and knowledge in game-centred approaches', in R. Light, J. Quay, S. Harvey and A. Mooney (eds), *Contemporary Developments in Games Teaching*, London: Routledge, pp. 167–77.

Fosnot, C. (ed.) (1996) *Constructivism: Theory, Perspectives, and Practice*, New York: Teachers College Press.

Fredricks, J.A. and Eccles, J.S. (2006) 'Is extracurricular participation associated with beneficial outcomes? Concurrent and longitudinal relations', *Developmental Psychology*, 42(4): 698–713; doi: 10.1037/0012–1649.42.4.698.

Fry, J.M. and McNeill, M.C. (2014) 'Teaching how to play and teach games in Singapore: a decade in the field', in R. Light, J. Quay, S. Harvey and A. Mooney (eds), *Contemporary Developments in Games Teaching*, London: Routledge, pp. 43–56.

Fuller, A., Hodkinson, H., Hodkinson, P. and Unwin, L. (2005) 'Learning as peripheral participation in communities of practice: a reassessment of key concepts in workplace learning', *British Educational Research Journal*, 31(1): 49–68; doi: 10.1080/014119 2052000310029.

Galipeau, J. and Trudel, P. (2006) 'Athlete learning in a community of practice: is there a role for the coach', in R.L. Jones (edn), *The Sports Coach as Educator: Re-conceptualising Sports Coaching*, London: Routledge, pp. 77–94.

Gallagher, B. (2008) 'Peter de Villiers named Boks' first black coach', *The Telegraph*, 10 January. Online at www.telegraph.co.uk/sport/rugbyunion/international/southafrica/ 2288509/Peter-de-Villiers-names-Boks-first-black-coach.html (accessed 19 February 2014).

Gard, M. and Wright, J. (2005) *The Obesity Epidemic: Science, Morality and Ideology*, London: Routledge.

George, M.G. (2006) 'The power of Positive Pedagogy', Music Learning Community. com *Newsletter*, October–November. Online at www.musiclearningcommunity.com/ NewsletterArchive/2006October.The%20Power%20of%20Positive%20Pedagogy.htm (accessed 14 July 2008).

Gibson, J. (2002) 'A theory of direct visual perception', in A. Noë and E. Thompson (eds), *Vision and Mind: Selected Readings in the Philosophy of Perception*, Cambridge, MA: MIT Press, pp. 77–90.

Gilbert, W.D. and Trudel, P. (2000) 'Validation of the coaching model (CM) in a team sport context', *International Sports Journal*, 4(2): 120–8.

Gilbert, W.D. and Trudel, P. (2001) 'Learning to coach through experience: reflection in model youth sport coaches', *Journal of Teaching in Physical Education*, 21(1): 16–34.

Gilbert, W.D. and Trudel, P. (2004) 'Role of the coach: how model youth team sport coaches frame their roles', *The Sport Psychologist*, 18(1): 21–43.

Gilbert, W.D. and Trudel, P. (2005) 'Learning to coach through experience: conditions that influence reflection', *The Physical Educator*, 62(1): 32–43.

Gilbert, W.D., Côté, J. and Mallett, C. (2006) 'Developmental paths and activities of successful sport coaches', *International Journal of Sports Science and Coaching*, 1(1): 69–76.

Glaser, B. (1978) *Theoretical Sensitivity: Advances in the Methodology of Grounded Theory*, San Francisco, CA: The Sociology Press.

Glaser, B. and Strauss, A. (1975) *The Discovery of Grounded Theory: Strategies for Qualitative Research*, Chicago, IL: Aldine.

Gore, J. (1991) 'Practicing what we preach: action research and the supervision of student teachers', in B.R. Tabachnick and K.M. Zeichner (eds) *Issues and Practices in Inquiry-oriented Teacher Education*, London: The Falmer Press, pp. 253–72.

Gould, R. (2013) 'State of Zen', *Herald Sun*, June 3, p. 58.

Gray, S. and Sproule, J. (2011) 'Developing pupils' performance in team invasion games', *Physical Education and Sport Pedagogy*, 16(1): 15–32; doi: 10.1080/17408980903535792.

Gréhaigne, J.F., Godbout, P. and Bouthier, D. (1999) 'The foundations of tactics and strategy in team sports', *Journal of Teaching in Physical Education*, 18(2): 159–74.

Gréhaigne, J.F., Richard, J.F. and Griffin, L.L. (2005) *Teaching and Learning Team Sports and Games*, New York: RoutledgeFalmer.

Griffin, L.L., Mitchell, S.A. and Oslin, J.L. (1997) *Teaching Sport Concepts and Skills: A Tactical Games Approach*, Champaign, IL: Human Kinetics.

Grundlingh, A. (1998) 'From redemption to recidivism? Rugby and change in South Africa during the 1995 Rugby World Cup and its aftermath', *Sporting Traditions*, 14(2): 67–86.

Grundlingh, A., Odendaal, A. and Spies, B. (1995) *Beyond the Tryline: Rugby and South African Society*, Johannesburg: Ravan Press.

Gubacs-Collins, K. (2007) 'Implementing a tactical approach through action research', *Physical Education and Sport Pedagogy*, 12(2): 105–26.

Hadfield, D. (2005) 'The change challenge: facilitating self-awareness and improvement in your athletes', in L. Kidman (ed.), *Athlete-centred Coaching: Developing Inspired and Inspiring People*, Christchurch, NZ: Innovative Print Communications, pp. 31–44.

Harris, B. (2013) 'Ewen McKenzie has had experience of Sydney's obsession with running rugby', *The Australian*, August. Online at www.theaustralian.com.au/sport/opinion/ewen-mckenzie-has-had-experience-of-sydneys-obsession-with-running-rugby/story-e6frg7vo-1226695171674# (accessed 25 August 2013).

Harvey, S., Cushion, C.J. and Massa-Gonzalez, A. (2010a) 'Learning a new method: Teaching Games for Understanding in the coaches' eyes', *Physical Education and Sport Pedagogy*, 15(4): 361–82.

Harvey, S., Cushion, C.J., Wegis, H.M. and Massa-Gonzalez, A. (2010b) 'Teaching Games for Understanding in American high-school soccer: a quantitative data analysis using the game performance assessment instrument', *Physical Education and Sport Pedagogy*, 15(1): 29–54; doi: 10.1080/17408980902729354.

Harvey, S., Kirk, D. and O'Donovan, T.M. (2014) 'Sport education as a pedagogical application for ethical development in physical education and youth sport', *Sport, Education and Society*, 19(1): 41–62; doi: 10.1080/13573322.2011.624594.

Hattie, J. (2008) *Visible Learning: A Synthesis of Over 800 Meta-analyses Relating to Achievement*, London: Routledge.

Henricks, T.S. (2006) *Play Reconsidered: Sociological Perspectives on Human Expression*, Urbana, IL: University of Illinois Press.

Hickie, T. (2007) 'The amateur ideal in the era of professional rugby', in M. Bushby and T. Hickie (eds), *Rugby History: The Remaking of the Class Game*, Melbourne, Vic.: Australian Society for Sports History, pp. 17–50.

Höglund, K. and Sundberg, R. (2008) 'Reconciliation through sports? The case of South Africa', *Third World Quarterly*, 29(4): 805–18.

Holt, N. (2008) *Positive Youth Development Through Sport*, London: Routledge.

Hopper, T. (2002) 'Teaching Games for Understanding: the importance of student emphasis over content emphasis', *Journal of Physical Education, Recreation, and Dance*, 73(7): 44–8.

Horton, P. (2009) 'Rugby union football in Australian society: an unintended consequence of intended actions', *Sport in Society: Cultures, Commerce, Media, Politics*, 12(7): 967–85; doi: 10.1080/17430430903053216.

Horton, S., Baker, J. and Deakin, J. (2005) 'Expert in action: a systematic observation of 5 national team coaches', *International Journal of Sport Psychology*, 36(4): 299–319.

Husserl, E. (1962) *Ideas: General Introduction to Pure Phenomenology* [Ideen zu einer reinen Phänomenologie und phänomenologischen Philosophie] (W.R.B. Gibson trans.), London: Collier & Macmillan.

Hutchinson, J. (2008) 'A saint-sational career', *Sunday Telegraph Magazine*, pp. 25–8.

Irwin, G., Hanton, S. and Kerwin, D. (2004) 'Reflective practice and the origins of elite coaching knowledge', *Reflective Practice*, 5(3): 425–42; doi: 10.1080/146239404 2000270718.

Irwin, G., Hanton, S. and Kerwin, D. (2005) 'The conceptual process of skill progression development in artistic gymnastics', *Journal of Sports Sciences*, 23(10): 1089–99; doi: 10.1080/ 02640410500130763.

Jackson, S.A. and Csikszentmihalyi, M. (1999) *Flow in Sports: The Keys to Optimal Experiences and Performances*, Champaign, IL: Human Kinetics.

Jackson, S.J. (2004) 'Reading New Zealand within the new global order: sport and the visualisation of national identity', *International Sport Studies*, 26(1): 13–27.

Jarrett, K. and Harvey, S. (2014) 'Recent trends in research literature on game-based approaches to teaching and coaching games', in R. Light, J. Quay, S. Harvey and A. Mooney (eds), *Contemporary Developments in Games Teaching*, London: Routledge, pp. 87–102.

Jenkins, R. (2002) *Pierre Bourdieu* (2nd edn), London: Routledge.

Jess, M., Atencio, M. and Thorburn, M. (2011) 'Complexity theory: supporting curriculum and pedagogy developments in Scottish physical education', *Sport, Education and Society*, 16(2): 179–99; doi: 10.1080/13573322.2011.540424.

Johnson, J.G. (2006) 'Cognitive modeling of decision making in sports', *Psychology of Sport and Exercise*, 7(6): 631–52.

Jones, R.L. (ed.) (2006) *The Sports Coach as Educator: Re-conceptualising Sports Coaching*, London: Routledge.

Jones, R.L. (2007) 'Coaching redefined: an everyday pedagogical endeavour', *Sport, Education and Society*, 12(2): 159–73.

Jones, R.L. (2009) 'Coaching as caring (the smiling gallery): accessing hidden knowledge', *Physical Education and Sport Pedagogy*, 14(4): 377–90; doi: 10.1080/17408980801976551.

Jones, R.L. and Turner, A.P. (2006) 'Teaching coaches to coach holistically: can problem-based learning (PBL) help?', *Physical Education and Sport Pedagogy*, 11(2): 181–202; doi: 10.1080/17408980600708429.

Jones, R.L. and Wallace, M. (2005) 'Another bad day at the training ground: coping with ambiguity in the coaching context', *Sport, Education and Society*, 10(1): 119–34.

Jones, R.L., Armour, K.M. and Potrac, P. (2003) 'Constructing expert knowledge: a case study of a top-level professional soccer coach', *Sport, Education and Society*, 8(2): 213–29; doi: 10.1080/13573320309254.

Jones, R.L., Armour, K.M. and Potrac, P. (2004) *Sports Coaching Cultures: From Practice to Theory*, London: Routledge.

Jones, R.L., Potrac, P., Cushion, C. and Ronglan, L.T. (eds) (2011) *The Sociology of Sports Coaching*, London: Routledge.

Jones, R.L., Morgan, K. and Harris, K. (2012) 'Developing coaching pedagogy: seeking a better integration of theory and practice', *Sport, Education and Society*, 17(3): 313–29; doi: 10.1080/13573322.2011.608936.

Kay, J. and Laberge, S. (2002) 'The "new" corporate habitus in adventure racing', *International Review for the Sociology of Sport*, 37(1): 17–36.

Kemmis, S. and McTaggart, R. (1988) *The Action Research Reader* (3rd edn), Waurn Ponds, Vic.: Deakin University Press.

Kerr, G. and Stirling, A. (2013) 'Putting the child back into children's sport: nurturing young talent in a developmentally appropriate manner', in S. Harvey and R.L. Light (eds), *Ethics in Youth Sport: Policy and Pedagogical Applications*, London and New York: Routledge, pp. 25–39.

Kidd, B. and Donnelly, P. (2000) 'Human rights in sports', *International Review for the Sociology of Sport*, 35(2): 131–48.

Kidman, L. (2001) *Developing Decision Makers: An Empowerment Approach to Coaching*, Christchurch, NZ: Innovative Print Communications.

Kidman, L. (2005) *Athlete-centred Coaching: Developing Inspired and Inspiring People*, Christchurch, NZ: Innovative Print Communications.

Kidman, L. and Carlson, T.B. (1998) 'An action research process to change coach behavior', *Avante*, 4(3): 100–17.

King, A. (2000) 'Thinking with Bourdieu against Bourdieu: a "practical" critique of the habitus', *Sociological Theory*, 18(3): 417–33.

Kirk, D. (1995) 'Action research and educational reform in physical education', *Pedagogy in Practice*, 1: 4–21.

Kirk, D. (2010) 'Towards a socio-pedagogy of sports coaching', in J. Lyle and C. Cushion (eds), *Sport Coaching: Professionalisation and Practice*, Edinburgh: Elsevier, pp. 165–76.

Kirk, D. (2013) 'Educational value and models-based practice in physical education', *Educational Philosophy and Theory*, 45(9): 973–86.

Kirk, D. and Macdonald, D. (1998) 'Situated learning in physical education', *Journal of Teaching in Physical Education*, 17(3): 376–87.

Kirk, D. and MacPhail, A. (2000) *The Game Sense Approach: Rationale, Description and a Brief Overview of Research*, Loughborough: Institute of Youth Sport, Loughborough University.

Kirk, D. and MacPhail, A. (2002) 'Teaching Games for Understanding and situated learning: rethinking the Bunker-Thorpe model', *Journal of Teaching in Physical Education*, 21(2): 177–92.

Kirk, D. and MacPhail, A. (2003) 'Social positioning and the construction of a youth sports club', *International Review for the Sociology of Sport*, 38(1): 23–44; doi: 10.1177/101269 0203031726.

Kirk, D., Nauright, J., Hanrahan, S., Macdonald, D. and Jobling, I. (1996) *The Sociocultural Foundations of Human Movement*, Melbourne, Vic.: Macmillan Education.

Kitson, R. (2005) 'How All Blacks went back to their roots', *The Guardian*, 2 July.

Knowles, Z., Tyler, G., Gilbourne, D. and Eubank, M. (2006) 'Reflecting on reflection: exploring the practice of sports coaching graduates', *Reflective Practice*, 7(2): 163–79; doi: 10.1080/14623940600688423.

Kretchmar, S. (2005) 'Teaching Games for Understanding and the delights of human activity', in L. Griffin and J. Butler (eds), *Teaching Games for Understanding: Theory Research and Practice*, Champaign, IL: Human Kinetics, pp. 199–212.

Krippendorff, K. (2004) *Content Analysis: An Introduction to its Methodology* (2nd edn), Thousand Oaks, CA: Sage.

Kruse, S.D. (1997) 'Reflective activity in practice: vignettes of teachers' deliberative work', *Journal of Research and Development in Education*, 31(1): 46–60.

Langer, B. (1992) 'Emile Durkheim', in P. Beilharz (ed.), *Social Theory: A Guide to Central Thinkers*, Crows Nest, NSW: Allen & Unwin, pp. 70–5.

Larson, R.W. (2000) 'Toward a psychology of positive youth development', *American Psychologist*, 55(1): 170–83; doi: 10.1037//0003–066X.55.170.

Lau, R.W.K. (2004) 'Habitus and the practical logic of practice: an interpretation', *Sociology*, 38(2): 369–87.

Launder, A.G. (2001) *Play Practice: The Games Approach to Teaching and Coaching Sports*, Champaign, IL: Human Kinetics.

Launder, A.G. and Piltz, W. (2013) *Play Practice: Engaging and Developing Skilled Players from Beginner to Elite* (2nd edn), Champaign, IL: Human Kinetics.

Lave, J. and Wenger, E. (1991) *Situated Learning: Legitimate Peripheral Participation*, Cambridge: Cambridge University Press.

Law, R. (1994) *After Method: Mess in Social Science Research*, London and New York: Routledge.

Le Moigne, J.L. (1990) *La Modélisation des systèmes complexes*, Paris: Dunod.

Lemyre, F. and Trudel, P. (2004) 'The learning path of volunteer coaches', *Avante*, 10(3): 40–55.

Lemyre, F., Trudel, P. and Durand-Bush, N. (2007) 'How youth-sport coaches learn to coach', *The Sport Psychologist*, 21(2): 191–209.

Lenzen, B., Theunissen, C. and Cloes, M. (2009) 'Situated analysis of team handball players' decisions: an exploratory study', *Journal of Teaching in Physical Education*, 28(1): 54–74.

Leplat, J. (2000) *La Psychologie du travail*, Paris: PUF.

Light, R.L. (2002) 'The social nature of games: Australian pre-service primary teachers' first experiences of Teaching Games for Understanding', *European Physical Education Review*, 8(3): 286–304.

Light, R.L. (2004) 'Coaches' experiences of Game Sense: opportunities and challenges', *Physical Education and Sport Pedagogy*, 9(2): 115–31; doi: 10.1080/1740898042000294949.

Light, R.L. (2005) 'Making sense of the chaos: Australian coaches talk about Game Sense', in L. Griffin and J. Butler (eds), *Teaching Games for Understanding: Theory, Research, and Practice*, Champaign, IL: Human Kinetics, pp. 169–82.

Light, R.L. (2006a) 'Game Sense: innovation or just good coaching?', *Journal of Physical Education New Zealand*, 39(1): 8–19.

Light, R.L. (2006b) 'Situated learning in an Australian surf club', *Sport, Education and Society*, 11(2): 155–72; doi: 10.1080/13573320600640686.

Light, R.L. (2007) 'Re-examining hegemonic masculinity: the body, compliance and resistance', *Quest*, 59: 323–39.

Light, R.L. (2008a) 'Complex learning theory – its epistemology and its assumptions about learning: implications for physical education', *Journal of Teaching in Physical Education*, 27(1): 21–37.

Light, R.L. (2008b) *Sport in the Lives of Young Australians*, Sydney, NSW: University of Sydney Press.

Light, R.L. (2009) 'Understanding and enhancing learning in TGfU through complex learning theory', in T. Hopper, J. Butler and B. Storey (eds), *TGfU – Simply Good Pedagogy: Understanding a Complex Challenge*, Toronto: PHE Canada, pp. 23–34.

Light, R.L. (2011) 'Opening up learning theory to social theory in research on sport and physical education through a focus on practice', *Physical Education and Sport Pedagogy*, 16(4): 369–82; doi: 10.1080/17408989.2010.535197.

Light, R.L. (2013a) 'Game Sense pedagogy in youth sport: an applied ethics perspective', in S. Harvey and R.L. Light (eds), *Ethics in Youth Sport: Policy and Pedagogical Applications*, London: Routledge, pp. 92–106.

Light, R.L. (2013b) *Game Sense: Pedagogy for Performance, Participation and Enjoyment*, London: Routledge.

Light, R.L. (2013c) 'O Game Sense como pedagogia positiva para treinar o desporto juvenil [Game Sense as Positive Pedagogy for coaching youth sport]', in C. Congalves (ed.),

Educação pelo desporto e associativismo desportiva [Youth Sport: Between Education and Performance], Lisbon: Instituto do Desporto de Portugal, pp. 111–31.

Light, R.L. (2014) 'Positive Pedagogy for physical education and sport: Game Sense as an example', in R.L. Light, J. Quay, S. Harvey and A. Mooney (eds), *Contemporary Developments in Games Teaching*, London and New York: Routledge, pp. 29–42.

Light, R.L. and Evans, J.R. (2010) 'The impact of Game Sense pedagogy on Australian rugby coaches' practice: a question of pedagogy', *Physical Education and Sport Pedagogy*, 15(2): 103–15.

Light, R.L. and Evans, J.R. (2013) 'Dispositions of elite-level Australian rugby coaches towards Game Sense: characteristics of their coaching habitus', *Sport, Education and Society*, 18(3): 407–23; doi: 10.1080/13573322.2011.593506.

Light, R.L. and Evans, J.R. (in press) 'Putting habitus to work in research on how coaches learn through experience: identifying a coaching habitus', in L. Hunter, W. Smith and E. Emerald (eds), *Fields of Physical Culture: Encounters With and Beyond Pierre Bourdieu*, London and New York: Routledge.

Light, R.L. and Fawns, R. (2003) 'Knowing the game: integrating speech and action in games teaching through TGfU', *Quest*, 55(2): 161–76.

Light, R.L. and Georgakis, S. (2005) 'Integrating theory and practice in teacher education: the impact of a game sense unit on female pre-service primary teachers' attitudes towards teaching physical education', *Journal of Physical Education New Zealand*, 38: 67–80.

Light, R.L. and Harvey, S. (2013) 'Introduction', in S. Harvey and R.L. Light (eds), *Ethics in Youth Sport: Policy and Pedagogical Applications*, London: Routledge, pp. 1–8.

Light, R.L. and Kentel, J.A. (2013) '*Mushin*: learning in technique-intensive sports as a process of uniting mind and body through complex learning theory', *Physical Education and Sport Pedagogy* (ahead of print): 1–16; doi: 10.1080/17408989.2013.868873.

Light, R.L. and Kirk D. (2000) 'High school rugby, the body and the reproduction of hegemonic masculinity', *Sport, Education and Society*, 5(2): 163–76.

Light, R.L. and Nash, M. (2006) 'Learning and identity in overlapping communities of practice: surf club, school and sports clubs', *Australian Educational Researcher*, 33(1): 145–62.

Light, R.L. and Tan, S. (2004) 'Early career teachers' experiences of implementing TGfU/GA in Australia and Singapore', in M.-K. Chin (ed.), *Global Perspectives in the Integration of Physical Activity, Sports, Dance, and Exercise Science in Physical Education: From Theory to Practice*, Hong Kong: Department of Physical Education and Sports Science, Hong Kong Institute of Education, pp. 321–30.

Light, R.L. and Wallian, N. (2008) 'A constructivist-informed approach to teaching swimming', *Quest*, 60(3): 387–404.

Light, R.L., Harvey, S. and Memmert, D. (2013) 'Why children join and stay in sports clubs: case studies in Australian, French and German swimming clubs', *Sport, Education and Society*, 18(4): 550–66.

Light, R.L., Harvey, S. and Mouchet, A. (2014a) 'Improving "at-action" decision-making in team sports through a holistic coaching approach', *Sport, Education and Society*, 19(3): 258–75; doi: 10.1080/13573322.2012.665803.

Light, R.L., Quay, J., Harvey, S. and Mooney, A. (eds) (2014b) *Contemporary Developments in Games Teaching*, London and New York: Routledge.

Light, R.L., Curry, C. and Mooney, A. (2014c) 'Game Sense as a model for delivering quality teaching in physical education', *Asia-Pacific Journal of Health, Sport and Physical Education*, 5(1): 67–81.

Lizardo, O. (2004) 'The cognitive origins of Bourdieu's habitus', *Journal for the Theory of Social Behaviour*, 34(4): 375–401.

Long, J. and Sanderson, I. (2001) 'The social benefits of sport: where's the proof?', in C. Gratton and I.P. Henry (eds), *Sport in the City: The Role of Sport in Economic and Social Regeneration*, London: Routledge, pp. 187–203.

Lyle, J. (1999) 'The coaching process: an overview', in N. Cross and J. Lyle (eds), *The Coaching Process: Principles and Practice for Sport*, Oxford: Butterworth-Heinemann, pp. 3–24.

Lyle, J. (2002) *Sports Coaching Concepts: A Framework for Coaches' Behaviour*, London: Routledge.

Lyle, J. (2007) 'A review of the research evidence for the impact of coach education', *International Journal of Coaching Science*, 1(1): 19–36.

Lyle, J. and Cushion, C. (eds) (2010) *Sports Coaching: Professionalisation and Practice*, Edinburgh: Elsevier.

McCullick, B.A., Belcher, D. and Schempp, P.G. (2005) 'What works in coaching and sport instructor certification programs? The participants' view', *Physical Education and Sport Pedagogy*, 10(2): 121–37.

McFarlane, S. (1990) '*Mushin*, morals, and martial arts: a discussion of Keenan's YogZicara critique', *Japanese Journal of Religious Studies*, 17(4): 397–420.

McNeill, M.C., Fry, J.M., Wright, S.C., Tan, W.K.C., Tan, K.S.S. and Schempp, P.G. (2004) '"In the local context": Singaporean challenges to teaching games on practicum', *Sport, Education and Society*, 9(1): 3–32; doi: 10.1080/1357332042000175791.

McNeill, M.C., Fry, J.M., Wright, S.C., Tan, C. and Rossi, T. (2008) 'Structuring time and questioning to achieve tactical awareness in Games', *Physical Education & Sport Pedagogy*, 13(3): 231–49.

MacPhail, A., Kirk, D. and Griffin, L. (2008) 'Throwing and catching as relational skills in game play: situated learning in a modified game unit', *Journal of Teaching in Physical Education*, 27(1): 100–15.

McPherson, S.L. and Kernodle, M.W. (2003) 'Tactics, the neglected attribute of expertise: problem representations and performance skills in tennis', in J.L. Starkes and K.A. Ericsson (eds), *Expert Performance in Sports: Advances in Research on Sport Expertise*, Champaign, IL: Human Kinetics, pp. 137–68.

Magill, R.A. (1998) 'Knowledge is more than we can talk about: implicit learning in motor skill acquisition', *Research Quarterly for Exercise and Sport*, 69(2): 104–10; doi: 10.1080/02701367.1998.10607676.

Magill, R.A. (2004) *Motor Learning and Control: Concepts and Applications* (7th edn), Boston, MA: McGraw-Hill.

Mahoney, J.L. (2000) 'School extracurricular activity participation as a moderator in the development of antisocial patterns', *Child Development*, 71(2): 502–16.

Mairs, G. (2012) 'Wayne Smith turns down offer of coaching role with Stuart Lancaster and England', *The Telegraph*, 1 May. Online at www.telegraph.co.uk/rugbyunion/international/england/9238518/Wayne-Smith-turns-down-offer-of-coaching-role-with-Stuart-Lancaster-and-England.html (accessed 7 June 2013).

Mallett, C.J. and Dickens, S. (2009) 'Authenticity in formal coach education: online postgraduate studies in sports coaching at the University of Queensland', *International Journal of Coaching Science*, 3(2): 79–90.

Mangan, J.A. (1981) *Athleticism in the Victorian and Edwardian Public School: The Emergence and Consolidation of an Educational Ideal*, Cambridge: Cambridge University Press.

Marsh, H.W. and Kleitman, S. (2002) 'Extracurricular school activities: the good, the bad, and the nonlinear', *Harvard Educational Review*, 72(4): 464–515.

Marshall, G. (1994) *The Concise Oxford Dictionary of Sociology*, Oxford: Oxford University Press.

Martens, R. (1982) *Joy and Sadness in Children's Sport*, Champaign, IL: Human Kinetics.

Martens, R. (1996) *Successful Coaching*, Champaign, IL: Human Kinetics.

Marx, K. (1999) 'Economic and philosophic manuscripts' (T. Bottomore trans.), in E. Fromm, *Marx's Concept of Man*, New York: Continuum, pp. 87–196.

Memmert, D. and Furley, P. (2007) '"I spy with my little eye!": Breadth of attention, inattentional blindness, and tactical decision making in team sports', *Journal of Sport and Exercise Psychology*, 29(3): 365–81.

Merleau-Ponty, M. (1962) *Phenomenology of Perception*, London: Routledge and Kegan Paul.

Miles, M.B. and Huberman, A.M. (1994) *Qualitative Data Analysis: An Expanded Sourcebook* (2nd edn), Thousand Oaks, CA: Sage.

Mitchell, S. and Oslin, J. (1999) 'An investigation of tactical transfer in net games', *European Journal of Physical Education*, 4(2): 162–72; doi: 10.1080/1740898990040205.

Mitchell, S., Griffin, L. and Oslin, J. (1995) 'The effects of two instructional approaches on game performance', *Pedagogy in Practice: Teaching and Coaching in Physical Education and Sports*, 1(1): 36–48.

Mosston, M. and Ashworth, S. (1990) *The Spectrum of Teaching Styles: From Command to Discovery*, New York: Longman.

Mouchet, A. (2005) 'Subjectivity in the articulation between strategy and tactics in team sports: an example in rugby', *Italian Journal of Sport Sciences*, 12(1): 24–33.

Mouchet, A. (2008) 'La subjectivité dans les décisions tactiques des joueurs experts en rugby', *eJRIEPS*, 14: 96–116.

Mouchet, A. (2014) 'Subjectivity as a resource for improving players' decision-making in team sport', in R. Light, J. Quay, S. Harvey and A. Mooney (eds), *Contemporary Developments in Games Teaching*, London: Routledge, pp. 147–66.

Mouchet, A. and Bouthier, D. (2008) 'Le coaching des sélections nationales en rugby', in P. Fleurance and S. Pérez (eds), *Interrogations sur le métier d'entraîneur: Interroger les entraîneurs au travail? Revisiter les conceptions qui organisent l'entraînement pour repenser le métier d'entraîneur*, Paris: INSEP, pp. 281–8.

Mouchet, A. and Le Guellec, L. (2012) 'Les communications entraîneurs/joueurs en match de rugby international', in C. Spallanzani, R. Goyette, M. Roy, S. Turcotte, J.F. Desbiens and S. Baudoin (eds), *Mieux former et intervenir dans les activités physiques, sportives et artistiques: Vivre actif et en santé*, Sherbrooke, Canada: PUQ, pp. 109–14.

Mouchet, A., Uhlrich, G. and Bouthier, D. (2005) 'La continuité du jeu en rugby: théorie et méthodologie d'une étude comparative entre nations', *Impulsions*, 4: 81–102.

Mouchet, A., Vermersch, P. and Bouthier, D. (2011) 'Méthodologie d'accès à l'expérience subjective: entretien composite et vidéo', *Savoirs*, 3: 85–105.

Mouchet, A., Harvey, S. and Light, R.L. (2013) 'A study on in-match rugby coaches' communications with players: a holistic approach', *Physical Education and Sport Pedagogy* (ahead of print): 1–18; doi: 10.1080/13573322.2012.665803.

Mucchielli, A. (1996) *Dictionnaire des méthodes qualitatives en sciences humaines et sociales*, Paris: Armand Colin.

Mutch, A. (2003) 'Communities of practice and habitus: a critique', *Organization Studies*, 24(3): 383–401.

Nash, C. and Collins, D. (2006) 'Tacit knowledge in expert coaching: science or art?', *Quest*, 58(4): 465–77.

Nash, C. and Sproule, J. (2009) 'Career development of expert coaches', *International Journal of Sport Science and Coaching*, 4(1): 121–38.

Nash, C. and Sproule, J. (2011) 'Insights into experiences: reflections of an expert and novice coach', *International Journal of Sports Science & Coaching*, 6(1): 149–62.

Nauright, J. and Chandler, T. (eds) (1996) *Making Men: Rugby and Masculine Identity*, London: Frank Cass.

Nelson, L.J. and Cushion, C.J. (2006) 'Reflection in coach education: the case of the national governing body coaching certificate', *The Sport Psychologist*, 20(2): 174–83.

Nelson, L.J., Cushion, C.J. and Potrac, P. (2006) 'Formal, nonformal and informal coach learning: a holistic conceptualisation', *International Journal of Sports Science and Coaching*, 1(3): 247–59.

Nelson, L.J., Cushion, C.J. and Potrac, P. (2013) 'Enhancing the provision of coach education: the recommendations of UK coaching practitioners', *Physical Education and Sport Pedagogy*, 18(2): 204–18; doi: 10.1080/17408989.2011.649725.

Neuendorf, K.A. (2002) *The Content Analysis Guidebook*, London: Sage.

Noffke, S. and Brennan, M. (1991) 'Action research and reflective student teaching at the University of Wisconsin-Madison', in B.R. Tabachnick and K. Zeichner (eds), *Issues and Practices in Inquiry-oriented Teacher Education*, London: Falmer Press, pp. 186–201.

O'Connor, D. and Cotton, W. (2009) *Community Junior Sport Coaching: Final Report*, Sydney, NSW: Department of Sport and Recreation and the Australian Sports Commission.

Ovens, A., Hopper, T. and Butler, J. (2013) 'Reframing, curriculum, pedagogy and research', in A. Ovens, T. Hopper and J. Butler (eds), *Complexity Thinking in Physical Education: Reframing Curriculum, Pedagogy and Research*, London: Routledge, pp. 1–13.

Paques, P., Fruchart, E., Dru, V. and Mullet, E. (2005) 'Cognitive algebra in sport decision-making', *Theory and Decision*, 58(4): 387–406; doi: 10.1007/s11238–005–3890–8.

Parry, J. and Lucidarme, S. (2013) 'The first Youth Olympic Games: innovations, challenges and ethical issues', in S. Harvey and R. Light (eds), *Ethics in Youth Sport: Policy and Pedagogical Applications*, London: Routledge, pp. 40–54.

Passos, P., Araújo, D., Davids, K. and Shuttleworth, R. (2008) 'Manipulating constraints to train decision making in rugby union', *International Journal of Sports Science and Coaching*, 3(1): 125–40; doi: 10.1260/174795408784089432.

Phillips, M.G. (2000) *From Sidelines to Centre Field: A History of Sports Coaching in Australia*, Sydney, NSW: University of New South Wales Press.

Piaget, J. (1974) *La Prise de conscience*, Paris: PUF.

Piggott, D. (2012) 'Coaches' experiences of formal coach education: a critical sociological investigation', *Sport, Education and Society*, 17(4): 535–54; doi: 10.1080/13573322.2011.608949.

Poczwardowski, A., Barott, J.E. and Jowett, S. (2006) 'Diversifying approaches to research on athlete-coach relationships', *Psychology of Sport and Exercise*, 7(2): 125–42; doi: 10.1016/j.psychsport.2005.08.002.

Pope, C.C. (2005) 'Once more with feeling: affect and playing with the TGfU model', *Physical Education and Sport Pedagogy*, 10(3): 271–86; doi: 10.1080/17408980500340885.

Potrac, P. and Jones, R.L. (1999) 'The invisible ingredient in coaching knowledge: a case for recognising and researching the social component', *Sociology of Sport Online*, 2(1). Online at http://physed.otago.ac.nz/sosol/v2i1/v2i1a5.htm (accessed 2 March 2014).

Potrac, P., Brewer, C., Jones, R., Armour, K. and Hoff, J. (2000) 'Toward an holistic understanding of the coaching process', *Quest*, 52(2): 186–99.

Potrac, P., Gilbert, W. and Denison, J. (eds) (2013) *The Routledge Handbook of Sports Coaching*, London: Routledge.

Prawat, R.S. (1999) 'Dewey, Peirce, and the learning paradox', *American Educational Research Journal*, 36(1): 47–76.

Putnam, R. (2000) *Bowling Alone: The Collapse and Revival of American Community*, New York: Simon and Schuster.

Quay, J. and Stolz, S. (2014) 'Game as context in physical education: a Deweyan philosophical perspective', in R. Light, J. Quay, S. Harvey and A. Mooney (eds), *Contemporary Developments in Games Teaching*, London: Routledge, pp. 15–28.

Quennerstedt, M. (2013) 'Practical epistemologies in physical education practice', *Sport, Education and Society*, 18(3): 311–33; doi: 10.1080/13573322.2011.582245.

Reay, D. (1995) '"They employ cleaners to do that": habitus in the primary classroom', *British Journal of Sociology in Education*, 16: 353–71.

Reay, D. (2004) '"It's all becoming a habitus": beyond the habitual use of habitus in educational research', *British Journal of Sociology of Education*, 25(4): 431–44.

Renshaw, I., Chow, J.Y., Davids, K. and Hammond, J. (2010) 'A constraints-led perspective to understanding skill acquisition and game play: a basis for integration of motor learning theory and physical education praxis?', *Physical Education and Sport Pedagogy*, 15(2): 117–37; doi: 10.1080/17408980902791586.

Renshaw, I., Oldham, A.R. and Bawden, M. (2012) 'Nonlinear pedagogy underpins intrinsic motivation in sports coaching', *The Open Sports Sciences Journal*, 5: 88–99.

Reynolds, M. (1997) 'Learning styles: a critique', *Management Learning*, 28(2): 115–33.

Roberts, S.J. (2011) 'Teaching Games for Understanding: the difficulties and challenges experienced by participation cricket coaches', *Physical Education and Sport Pedagogy*, 16(1): 33–48; doi: 10.1080/17408980903273824.

Rodgers, W., Reade, I. and Hall, C. (2007) 'Factors that influence coaches' use of sound coaching practices', *International Journal of Sports Science and Coaching*, 2(2): 155–70; doi: 10.1260/174795407781394284.

Romand, P. and Pantaléon, N. (2007) 'A qualitative study of rugby coaches' opinions about the display of moral character', *Sport Psychologist*, 21(1): 58–77.

Rossi, T. (2000) 'Socially critical pedagogy and the "production of skilled performers": further considerations of teaching and learning in physical education', *Journal of Physical Education New Zealand*, 33(3): 43–52.

Rossi, T., Fry, J.M., McNeill, M. and Tan, C.W.K. (2007) 'The games concept approach (GCA) as a mandated practice: views of Singaporean teachers', *Sport, Education and Society*, 12(1): 93–111; doi: 10.1080/13573320601081591.

Rovegno, I. and Dolly, J.P. (2006) 'Constructivist perspectives on learning', in D. Kirk, D. Macdonald and M. O'Sullivan (eds), *The Handbook of Physical Education*, London: Sage, pp. 242–61.

Roy, M., Perreault, G., Desbiens, J.F., Turcotte, S., Spallanzani, C. and Harnois, H. (2007) 'Étude de la communication en entraînement sportif par l'utilisation d'une démarche multi-méthodologique: exemples avec des entraîneurs en volley-ball et basket-ball [A study on in-match rugby coaches' communications with players: an holistic approach]', *eJRIEPS*, 11: 120–40.

Rubin, H.J. and Rubin, I.S. (2005) *Qualitative Interviewing: The Art of Hearing Data* (2nd edn), Thousand Oaks, CA: Sage.

Rushall, B.S. and Wiznuk, K. (1985) 'Athletes' assessment of the coach: the coach evaluation questionnaire', *Canadian Journal of Applied Sport Sciences*, 10(3): 157–61.

Ryan, G. (2008) *The Changing Face of Rugby: The Union Game and Professionalism since 1995*, Newcastle upon Tyne: Cambridge Scholars.

SANZAR News Service (2013) 'Wallabies promise to play a more expansive game', 14 August. Online at www.sanzarrugby.com/therugbychampionship/news/wallabies-promise-to-play-a-more-expansive-game/ (accessed 21 January 2014).

Saury, J. and Durand, M. (1998) 'Practical knowledge in expert coaches: on-site study of coaching in sailing', *Research Quarterly for Exercise and Sport*, 69(3): 254–66.

Schempp, P. (1998) 'The dynamics of human diversity in sport pedagogy scholarship', *Sociology of Sport Online*, 1(1). Online at http://physed.otago.ac.nz/sosol/v1i1/v1i1a8.htm (accessed 9 July 2011).

Schmidt, R. (1991) *Motor Learning and Performance: From Principles to Practice*, Champaign, IL: Human Kinetics.

Schön, D.A. (1983) *The Reflective Practitioner: How Professionals Think in Action*, New York: Basic Books.

Seligman, M.E. and Csikszentmihalyi, M. (2000) 'Positive Psychology: an introduction', *The American Psychologist*, 55(1): 5–14.

Shulman, L.S. (1986) 'Those who understand: knowledge growth in teaching', *Educational Researcher*, 15(2): 4–14.

Silverman, D. (2006) *Interpreting Qualitative Data: Methods for Analyzing Talk, Text and Interaction*, Thousand Oaks, CA: Sage.

Singleton, R.A. and Straits, B.C. (1999) *Approaches to Social Research* (3rd edn), Oxford: Oxford University Press.

Sirna, K., Tinning, R. and Rossi, T. (2010) 'Social processes of health and physical education teachers' identity formation: reproducing and changing culture', *British Journal of Sociology of Education*, 31(1): 71–84; doi: 10.1080/01425690903385501.

Skinner, J., Stewart, B. and Edwards, A. (2003) 'The postmodernisation of rugby union in Australia', *Football Studies*, 6(1): 51–69.

Slade, D. (2010) *Transforming Play: Teaching Tactics and Game Sense*, Champaign, IL: Human Kinetics.

Small Blacks Model (2013) 'New Zealand rugby'. Online at www.nzrugby.co.nz/small_blacks/under_7s (accessed 5 December 2013).

Smith, M. and Cushion, C.J. (2006) 'An investigation of the in-game behaviours of professional, top-level youth soccer coaches', *Journal of Sports Sciences*, 24(4): 355–66; doi: 10.1080/02640410500131944.

Smith, W. (2006) 'One man's code: why Broncos always come first for Bennett', *The Australian*, pp. 31–2.

Solomon, G. (1999) 'Predictors of coach effectiveness in competitive sport: the role of actual and expected performance', *International Sports Journal*, 3(2): 25–36.

Sparkes, A.C., Schempp, P.G. and Templin, T.J. (1993) 'Exploring dimensions of marginality: reflecting on the life histories of physical education teachers', *Journal of Teaching in Physical Education*, 12(4): 386–98.

Stanley, L.S. (1995) 'Multicultural questions, action research answers', *Quest*, 47(1): 19–33.

Stephenson, B. and Jowett, S. (2009) 'Factors that influence the development of English youth soccer coaches', *International Journal of Coaching Science*, 3(1): 3–16.

Stirling, A.E. (2009) 'Definition and constituents of maltreatment in sport: establishing a conceptual framework for research practitioners', *British Journal of Sports Medicine*, 43(14): 1091–9; doi: 10.1136/bjsm.2008.051433.

Stirling, A.E. and Kerr, G.A. (2008) 'Elite female swimmers' experiences of emotional abuse across time', *Journal of Emotional Abuse*, 7(4): 89–113; doi: 10.1300/J135v07n04_05.

Stoddart, B. (1986) *Saturday Afternoon Fever: Sport in the Australian Culture*, Sydney, NSW: Allen & Unwin.

Strean, W. (1995) 'Youth sport contexts: coaches' perceptions and implications for intervention', *Journal of Applied Sport Psychology*, 7(1): 23–37; doi: 10.1080/10413209508406298.

Street, A.F. (2004) 'Action research', in V. Minichiello, G. Sullivan, K. Greenwood and R. Axford (eds), *Handbook of Research Methods for Nursing and Health Science* (2nd edn), Frenchs Forest, NSW: Prentice Hall Health, pp. 278–94.

Su, Y. (2011) 'Lifelong learning as being: the Heideggerian perspective', *Adult Education Quarterly*, 61(1): 57–72.

Suchman, L. (1987) *Plans and Situated Action*, Cambridge: Cambridge University Press.

Suzuki, N. (2013) 'Maegaki [Introduction]', in N. Suzuki, A. Umezara, S. Satochi and D. Matsumoto (eds), *Manabi no shiten Kara tsukuru shougakkou no taiiku jugyou* [Creating Student-centred Physical Education Lessons for Primary School], Tokyo: Kyoiku-Shuppan.

Swartz, D. (1997) *Culture and Power: The Sociology of Pierre Bourdieu*, Chicago, IL: University of Chicago Press.

Taylor, B. and Garratt, D. (2010) 'The professionalisation of sports coaching: relations of power, resistance and compliance', *Sport, Education and Society*, 15(1): 121–39.

Theodoulides, A. (2003) '"I would never personally tell anyone to break the rules, but you can bend them": teaching moral values through team games', *European Journal of Physical Education*, 8(2): 141–59; doi: 10.1080/1740898030080204.

Thorpe, R. and Bunker, D. (2008) 'Teaching Games for Understanding: do current developments reflect original theory?', *The 4th International Teaching Games for Understanding seminar*, Vancouver, 14–17 May.

Thorpe, R., Bunker, D. and Almond, L. (1986) *Rethinking Games Teaching*, Loughborough: University of Technology.

Tight, M. (2003) *Researching Higher Education*, Maidenhead: Open University Press.

Tinning, R. (1982) 'Improving coaches' instructional effectiveness', *Sports Coach*, 5(4): 37–41.

Tinning, R. (1996) 'Mentoring in the Australian physical education teacher education context: lessons from cooking turkeys and tandoori chicken', in M. Mawer (ed.), *Mentoring in Physical Education: Issues and Insights*, London: Falmer Press, pp. 197–216.

Trombley, S. and Bullock, A. (eds) (2000) *The New Fontana Dictionary of Modern Thought*, Glasgow: HarperCollins.

Trudel, P. (1997) 'L'influence des périodes de jeu et de l'écart au score sur les comportements des entraîneurs lors de matchs au hockey sur glace [Influence of game periods and score on coaches' behaviour during ice hockey matches]', *STAPS*, 43(18): 71–4.

Trudel, P. and Gilbert, W.D. (2006) 'Coaching and coach education', in D. Kirk, D. MacDonald and M. O'Sullivan (eds), *The Handbook of Physical Education*, Thousand Oaks, CA: Sage, pp. 516–39.

Trudel, P., Côté, J. and Bernard, D. (1996) 'Systematic observation of youth ice hockey coaches during games', *Journal of Sport Behavior*, 19(1): 50–65.

Trudel, P., Gilbert, W.D. and Werthner, P. (2010) 'Coaching and coach education', in J. Lyle and C. Cushion (eds), *Sports Coaching: Professionalisation and Practice*, Edinburgh: Elsevier, pp. 135–52.

Trudel, P., Culver, D. and Werthner, P. (2013) 'Looking at coach development from the coach-learner's perspective', in P. Potrac, W. Gilbert and J. Denison (eds), *The Routledge Handbook of Sports Coaching*, London: Routledge, pp. 375–87.

Turner, A.P. (2005) 'Teaching and learning games at the secondary level', in J. Butler and L. Griffin (eds), *Teaching Games for Understanding: Theory, Research, and Practice*, Champaign, IL: Human Kinetics, pp. 71–89.

Turner, A.P. (2014) 'Learning games concepts by design', in R. Light, J. Quay, S. Harvey and A. Mooney (eds), *Contemporary Developments in Games Teaching*, London: Routledge, pp. 193–206.

Vallée, C.N. and Bloom, G.A. (2005) 'Building a successful university program: key and common elements of expert coaches', *Journal of Applied Sport Psychology*, 17(3): 179–96; doi: 10.1080/10413200591010021.

van der Mars, H. (1989) 'Observer reliability: issues and procedures', in P.W. Darst, D.B. Zakrajsek and V.H. Mancini (eds), *Analyzing Physical Education and Sport Instruction* (2nd edn), Champaign, IL: Human Kinetics, pp. 53–80.

Varela, F.J., Thompson, E. and Rosch, E. (1991) *The Embodied Mind: Cognitive Science and Human Experience*, Cambridge, MA: MIT Press.

Vermersch, P. (2000) 'Conscience directe et conscience réfléchie', *Intellectica*, 2(31): 269–311.

Vermersch, P. (2008) *L'Entretien d'explicitation*, Paris: ESF.

Vygotsky, L.S. (1978) *Mind in Society: The Development of Higher Mental Process*, Cambridge, MA: Harvard University Press.

Wallian, N. and Chang, C. (2007) 'Language, thinking and action: towards a semio-constructivist approach in physical education', *Physical Education and Sport Pedagogy*, 12(3): 289–311; doi: 10.1080/17408980701610219.

Watkins, C. and Mortimore, P. (1999) 'Pedagogy: what do we know?', in P. Mortimore (ed.), *Understanding Pedagogy and its Impact on Learning*, London: Paul Chapman/Sage, pp. 1–19.

Webb, J., Shirato, T. and Danaher, G. (2002) *Understanding Bourdieu*, Sydney, NSW: Allen & Unwin.

Wenger, E. (1998) *Communities of Practice: Learning, Meaning, and Identity*, Cambridge: Cambridge University Press.

Wicker, A.W. (2002) 'Ecological psychology: historical contexts, current conceptions, prospective directions', in R.B. Bechtel and A. Churchman (eds), *Handbook of Environmental Psychology* (2nd edn), New York: John Wiley and Sons, pp. 114–26.

Wilkinson, S. (2004) 'Focus group reseach', in D. Silverman (ed.), *Qualitative Research: Theory, Method and Practice* (2nd edn), London: Sage, pp. 168–84.

Williams, A.M. and Hodges, N.J. (2005) 'Practice, instruction and skill acquisition in soccer: challenging tradition', *Journal of Sports Sciences*, 23(6): 637–50; doi: 10.1080/026404 10400021328.

Williams, S.J. and Kendall, L. (2007) 'Perceptions of elite coaches and sports scientists of the research needs for elite coaching practice', *Journal of Sports Sciences*, 25(14): 1577–86; doi: 10.1080/02640410701245550.

Wilson, R. (2011) 'Research methodology for youth sport', in S. Georgakis and K.M. Russell (eds), *Youth Sport in Australia*, Sydney, NSW: University of Sydney Press, pp. 265–85.

Windschitl, M. (2002) 'Framing constructivism in practice as the negotiation of dilemmas: an analysis of the conceptual, pedagogical, cultural, and political challenges facing teachers', *Review of Educational Research*, 72: 131–75.

Woodman, L. (1993) 'Coaching: a science, an art, an emerging profession', *Sport Science Review*, 2(2): 1–13.

Wright, J. and Forrest, G. (2007) 'A social semiotic analysis of knowledge construction and games centred approaches to teaching', *Physical Education and Sport Pedagogy*, 12(3): 273–87; doi: 10.1080/17408980701610201.

Wright, T., Trudel, P. and Culver, D. (2007) 'Learning how to coach: the different learning situations reported by youth ice hockey coaches', *Physical Education and Sport Pedagogy*, 12(2): 127–44; doi: 10.1080/17408980701282019.

Yin, R.K. (2003) *Case Study Research: Design and Methods*, Thousand Oaks, CA: Sage.

INDEX

Note: bold type refers to extended discussion or term highlighted in text; f refers to figure; n refers to footnote; t refers to table